CYBERCRIME

CYBERCRIME

THE INVESTIGATION, PROSECUTION AND DEFENSE OF A COMPUTER-RELATED CRIME

Second Edition

EDITED BY

RALPH D. CLIFFORD
ASSOCIATE DEAN AND PROFESSOR OF LAW
SOUTHERN NEW ENGLAND
SCHOOL OF LAW

CAROLINA ACADEMIC PRESS
Durham, North Carolina

Library of Congress Cataloging-in-Publication Data

Cybercrime : the investigation, prosecution and defense of a computer-related crime / by Ralph D. Clifford ... [et al.]. -- 2nd ed.
    p. cm.
    ISBN 1-59460-150-X (alk. paper)
    1. Computer crimes--United States. 2. Computer--Law and legislation--United States. 3. Transnational crime. I. Clifford, Ralph D., 1954- II. Title.

    KF390.5.C6C924 2006
    345.73'0268--dc22

2005036294

CAROLINA ACADEMIC PRESS

700 Kent Street
Durham, North Carolina 27701
Telephone (919) 489-7486
Fax (919) 493-5668
www.cap-press.com

Printed in the United States of America

CONTENTS

CYBERCRIME

Chapter One

Introduction

Ralph D. Clifford[*]

When the first edition of this book was published, it began with a discussion of the lack of a legal definition of "cybercrime."[1] Then, as is still true today, the term was used by policy makers,[2] the news media[3] and academicians,[4] but it had not been employed within cases or statutes. Now, as

---

[*] Associate Dean and Professor of Law, Southern New England School of Law. Member of the bars of Massachusetts, New York and Connecticut.

1. Ralph D. Clifford, Cybercrime: The Investigation, Prosecution and Defense of a Computer-Related Crime 1–2 (2001).

2. *See, e.g., Internet Denial of Service Attacks and the Federal Response: Hearing Before the Subcomm. on Crime of the House Comm. on the Judiciary and the Subcomm. on Criminal Oversight of the Senate Comm. on the Judiciary,* 106th Cong., 2d Sess. (Feb. 29, 2000) (statement of Eric Holder, Deputy Attorney General of the United States), http://www.cybercrime.gov/dag0229.htm; *Cybercrime: Hearing Before the Subcomm. for the Dept. of Commerce, Justice, State, the Judiciary, and Related Agencies of the Senate Comm. on Appropriations,* 106th Cong., 2d Sess. (Feb 16, 2000) (statement of Louis J. Freeh, Director of the F.B.I.), http://www.fbi.gov/pressrm/congress/congress00/cyber 021600.htm.

3. *See, e.g.* Alison Gerber, *Police Perplexed in Dealing with Cybercrime,* USA Today, http://www.usatoday.com/life/cyber/tech/cti456.htm (Aug. 29, 2000); *NewsHour: Cybercrime and the Congress* (PBS television broadcast, Feb. 16, 2000) (transcript at http://www.pbs.org/newshour/bb/cyberspace/jan-june00/cybersec_2-16.html).

4. John Schultz, *"The Substance of the Crime Was a State of Mind"—How a Mainstream, Middle Class Jury Came to War with Itself,* 68 U.M.K.C. L. Rev. 637, 669–70 (2000); David L. Gripman, Comment, *The Doors Are Locked but the Thieves and Vandals Are Still Getting In: A Proposal in Tort to Alleviate Corporate America's Cyber-crime Problem,* 16 J. Marshall J. Computer & Info. L. 167 (1997); Walter A. Effross, *High-tech Heroes, Virtual Villains, and Jacked-in Justice: Visions of Law and Lawyers in Cyber-*

this second edition is being prepared, the lack of use of a single term within the positive law has become perfectly understandable, as the increasing breadth and complexity of the area eschews the applicability of one word. After all, there is no single type of conduct which can be classified as a "cybercrime;" instead, there is a multifarious collection of misconduct that is sufficiently challenging to society for it to impose sanctions under the criminal law. The unifying theme that ties these diverse areas together into something that conceptually can be labeled "cybercrime" is the misuse of computer technology.

Understanding cybercrime requires an understanding of the technology that is being used to commit the criminal acts.[5] As importantly, one must understand the history[6] of the development of the technology and computer-related criminal law.

---

punk Science Fiction, 45 Buff. L. Rev. 931 (1997); Susan W. Brenner, *Can There be Truly Virtual Crime?*, http://www.cybercrimes.net/Virtual/Virtual.html (1999).

5. A presentation of computer technology is outside of the scope of this book. Anyone involved in cybercrime investigation, prosecution or defense that lacks a comprehensive understanding of how computers and the Internet work will be at an extreme disadvantage. In these cases, an appropriate expert must be retained. Even where the expertise is possessed, however, care must be taken as the technology changes so rapidly. *See* Matthew Dolan, *Cybercrime Fighters are Past Their Prime—at the Age of 16*, Boston Globe, June 26, 2005, at A27.

6. To be addressing an historic issue associated with cybercrime, or any other computer-related law, seems unusual as the history of the field is measured in a handful of decades rather than millennia. *See* Brian Randell, *History of Digital Computers—Origins, in* Encyclopedia of Computer Science 545, 549 (Anthony Ralston, Edwin D. Reilly & David Hemmendinger, eds., 4th ed., 2000) (ENIAC, the first "general-purpose" digital computer, was officially operational in 1946) [hereinafter Encyclopedia of Computer Science]. The pace of "history" within the computer field is unlike that in other fields, however, as the pace of change of computer technology radically exceeds that which has been found in other disciplines. *Cf.* Haim Mendelson, *Computer Laws in* Encyclopedia of Computer Science at 960, 960–61 ("Moore's Law" has accurately predicted that the processing power of a computer doubles every two years leading to a "computer revolution"). It is quite common, for example, for the products currently being sold to have been rendered obsolete already by the next generation of technology that has just begun to be manufactured.

Thus, although there has only been fifty years of computer history, it has been a remarkably paced fifty years, easily comparable to several hundred years of history in other fields. As Robert X. Cringely expressed it, "[i]f the automobile had followed the same development cycle as the computer, a Rolls-Royce would today cost $100, [and] get one million miles to the gallon...." InfoWorld (1996), *reprinted at* www.quoteland.com/qldb/author/48 (visited Feb. 21, 2001). Of course, Mr. Cringely finished his statement

Although "cybercrime" is the newer term, "computer crime" has been recognized at least since the 1960s,[7] and it entered the legal mainstream in the 1970s.[8] This class of crimes included those that used computer technology to commit a violation; indeed, in many instances, the computer was merely the tool used by the criminal to commit a traditionally recognized crime.[9] But the capabilities of a computer also allowed new forms of potentially criminal behavior that would not have been possible without the use of computer technology.[10]

An example of this computer-enabled impropriety was the appropriation by an employee of a New York bank in the late 1970s of the round-off from bank interest calculations.[11] As a bank's computer calculated the interest earned by each deposit account in the bank, the result often included a fraction of a cent. For example, if an account earns 5% interest on a balance of $100.50, the amount of interest would be $5.015. As banks do not maintain fractional cents in the balance of an account — the ½¢ in the example above — the amount was typically discarded. A programmer working for the bank recognized this, inserted his own code into the interest calculation program to accumulate all of the discarded fractions of cents, and deposited the sum of them into his own account. While this crime of taking less than a penny may not seem like much, as the interest calculation was done daily for millions of accounts, he was able to misappropriate between $5,000 and $10,000 per day. By the end of the year, he had accumulated over $2,000,000 in his account.

Misconduct of this type provided significant challenges to the criminal justice system. Although the programmer's misappropriation was perceived as a theft of the bank's money, criminal laws existing at the time often made prosecution difficult or impossible.[12] This led to an initial round of amend-

---

by noting that his hypothetical Rolls-Royce would "explode once a year, killing everyone inside." *Id.*

7. *See* Donn. B. Parker, *Computer Crime in* Encyclopedia of Computer Science 349, 352 (the first federal computer law prosecution was in 1966).

8. *See* U.S. v. Jones, 553 F.2d 351, 353 (4th Cir.), *cert. denied*, 431 U.S. 968 (1977).

9. *See* Tom Forester & Perry Morrison, Computer Ethics 23–25 (2d Ed. 1994) (discussing the use of computers to commit "old" crimes such as theft and forgery as well as "new" crimes of ATM and EFT fraud).

10. *See Id.* at 29–30 (discussing unauthorized use of another's computer and incremental crime in which the computer is used to commit numerous, but small crimes).

11. The author learned of this caper while he was working as a programmer for Citicorp in New York at the time the caper was discovered.

12. *See, e.g.*, Lund v. Virginia, 232 S.E.2d 745, 748 (Va. 1977) ("At common law, larceny is the taking and carrying away of the goods and chattels of another with intent to

ments to state and federal criminal statutes to insure that the newly invented computer crimes would be considered illegal at law.[13] Consequently, legislatures amended the laws to remove impediments to prosecution, including requirements that the crime involve tangible property.[14] Additionally, the law recognized that computer services and time should not be subject to unpenalized misappropriation.[15]

Just as the state and federal legislatures had begun to successfully address this type of computer crime, however, a new technology began its exponential growth — the Internet. The idea of creating the Internet was developed in 1966 by the ARPA office of the Defense Department.[16] Construction of its components began in 1969 and, by the end of that year, computer

---

deprive the owner of the possession thereof permanently."). *See generally*, Jay Joseph Bloombecker, Computer Crime Laws § 2:2 (1993).

Another common problem was getting investigators and prosecutors to treat misuses of computer technology that were within the scope of a criminal statute as a crime. Often, whether because the misuse was not seen as particularly threatening or because the lack of knowledge about computer technology prevented understanding of the misconduct, neither the police nor the prosecutor would pursue complaints. *See* Michael Gemignani & Esther Roditte, *Legal Aspects of Computing in* Encyclopedia of Computer Science 969, 973 ("Initially prosecutors and the courts were unwilling to treat computer crime seriously.").

13. *See, e.g.* N.J. Rev. Stat. Ann. § 2C:20-1(g) (West 1982); Bloombecker, Computer Crime Laws § 1:1[b].

14. *E.g.*, Massachusetts v. Yourawski, 425 N.E.2d 298, 299 (Mass. 1981) ("the intellectual property which appears on the cassette tapes is not 'property' within the definition of property in G.L. c. 266, § 30(2)"). That section of the statue was amended on May 31, 1983 to include "electronically processed or stored data, either tangible or intangible, data while in transit" within the definition of property. 1983 Mass. Acts ch. 147, § 1 (May 31, 1983).

15. *E.g.*, Lund v. Virginia, 232 S.E.2d 745, 748 (Va. 1977) ("services [can] not be the subject of the statutory crime of false pretense"); *id.* ("the unauthorized use of the computer is not the subject of larceny"). The Virginia legislature responded with three sections within the Virginia Computer Crimes Act, Va. Code Ann. §§ 18.2-152.1–18.2-152.15 (1985): § 18.2-152.3 outlaws computer fraud, § 18.2-153.4 prohibits computer trespass, and § 18.2-152.6 outlaws the theft of computer services.

16. Katie Hafner & Matthew Lyon, Where Wizards Stay up Late 40–41 (Touchstone Ed. 1998) [hereinafter Hafner, Wizards]. Despite the common misconception, the incentive for developing the Internet was not to create a network that could survive nuclear war. *Id.* at 77. Instead, the early proponents of the Internet were seeking "to create a new public communications network [with] greater speed and efficiency than existing systems." *Id.* at 66. The military's interest in the network was to support research projects facing complex computations that would benefit from the use of multiple computers. *See* David H. Brandin & Daniel C. Lynch, *Internet in* Encyclopedia of Computer Science 915, 916.

scientists established that networking computers of different types was practical by developing a network of four nodes.[17] By the early 1970s, many more nodes had been added, a simple e-mail system had been coded to run on the network and the concept of linking multiple networks together — the "Internet" — was conceived.[18] For the decade and a half that followed, the Internet was used mostly by academicians and computer scientists. This changed in the late 1980s when the control of the Internet backbone was transferred from the Defense Department to the National Science Foundation and private carriers,[19] and was radically accelerated in 1990 when the World Wide Web was created.[20] Since the early 1990s, private and commercial parties became the majority of the users of the Internet, replacing the earlier dominance of governmental academic users.[21]

The privatization and commercialization of the Web and Internet unfortunately triggered a new kind of computer crime. Previously, with most computers effectively operating in isolation from one another, there was very little opportunity for outsiders to readily manipulate another's computer in order to gain an illicit profit. Computer crimes of the 1970s and 1980s were predominately crimes committed by insiders. When the norm for computers changed from isolation to interconnection, however, the type of crime similarly changed. In the 1990s, the threats to a computer system were as likely to reside outside of the organization as within it, and now, external threats are perceived to be greater than those from the inside.[22]

---

17. HAFNER, WIZARDS at 103, 151–54.

18. *Id.* at 191 & 223–24.

19. *Id.* at 256.

20. *Id.* at 257–58. The "World Wide Web" is a collection of information that is made available over the Internet in a form that allows fairly easy browsing by individuals without sophisticated computer knowledge. It does this by standardizing the publication of information so that the specific computer used by the individual is irrelevant and by making the process of referring to another page within the collection trivial. Today, the Web is the largest single application executing on the Internet. *See generally*, Hal Berghel, *World Wide Web in* ENCYCLOPEDIA OF COMPUTER SCIENCE 1867.

21. *See* David H. Brandin & Daniel C. Lynch, *Internet in* ENCYCLOPEDIA OF COMPUTER SCIENCE 915, 916–21. The commercial dominance of the Internet has so radically altered its character that the academic community is developing its own private internet, usually termed "Internet II." *See Internet II*, http://www.fnc.gov/Internet_II.html (Oct. 11, 1996).

22. *See Cybercrime: Hearing Before the Subcomm. for the Dept. of Commerce, Justice, State, the Judiciary, and Related Agencies of the Senate Comm. on Appropriations*, 106th Cong., 2d Sess. (Feb 16, 2000) (statement of Louis J. Freeh, Director of the F.B.I.),

Although this externalization of the perpetrator explains some of the changes in the criminal law that took place in the 1990s, a more significant cause was the societal impacts of the Web and Internet. These technologies are widely recognized as being fundamentally transformational.[23] Society, itself, was radically altered because of the increasing use of these inventions. A term coined as science-fiction in 1984 was adopted to describe the existence of this new societal force—"cyberspace."[24] Cyberspace is defined by the virtual environment[25] created by computers in which humans interact. When the cyberspace defined in science-fiction in the 1980s became the cyberspace existing in reality in the 1990s, it is not surprising that a reexamination of the criminal law became necessary. Even if "there's no there, there,"[26] criminals have determined how to commit crimes within cyberspace. When they do so, particularly if the crime could only occur because of how cyberspace operates, the term "cybercrime" has been used to describe this behavior.

These cybercrimes are different from the computer crimes of the seventies and eighties. Cyberspace is not just a newer version of older computer technology. Before cyberspace, computer crimes looked like older crimes—finding the bank's money in a computer vault rather than a physical vault, for example. Within cyberspace, however, the nature of the technology al-

---

http://www.fbi.gov/pressrm/congress/congress00/cyber021600.htm ("In short, even though we have markedly improved our capabilities to fight cyber intrusions, the problem is growing even faster and thus we are falling further behind.").

23. *See* Steve Almasy, *The Internet Transforms Modern Life*, CNN.COM, June 24, 2005, *available at* http://www.cnn.com/2005/TECH/internet/06/23/evolution.main/index.html ("The World Wide Web has transformed the way people live, work and play."); Hal Berghel, *World Wide Web in* ENCYCLOPEDIA OF COMPUTER SCIENCE 1867, 1872–73.

24. The source of the term is from William Gibson's science-fiction novel, NEUROMANCER 4–5 (1984). Gibson's best definition of cyberspace is found in his later novel, MONA LISA OVERDRIVE 48 (Bantam Paperback ed. 1989): "*There's no there, there.* They taught that to children, explaining cyberspace." Even if the first sentence was originally applied to Oakland, California by Gertrude Stein, its accuracy to the virtual neighborhood created by the Internet and Web is more apropos.

25. A "virtual" environment is one that "[a]ppears to be rather than actually being." WEBSTER'S NEW WORLD DICTIONARY OF COMPUTER TERMS 608 (5th ed. 1994). *See generally*, William R. Cockayne, *Virtual Reality in* ENCYCLOPEDIA OF COMPUTER SCIENCE 1835; Peter J. Denning, *Virtual Memory*, 2:2 ACM COMPUTING SURVEYS 153 (1970); Peter J. Denning, *Virtual Memory*, 28:4 ACM COMPUTER SURVEYS 213 (1996).

26. WILLIAM GIBSON, MONA LISA OVERDRIVE 48 (Bantam Paperback ed. 1989).

lows fundamental changes in the nature of the misconduct being committed:

- Because of cyberspace's speed, transactions can occur that never would have been possible before its creation. Without the pervasive electronic communication brought by the existence of cyberspace, many business techniques such as just-in-time inventory processing would be impossible. Similarly, the speed of cyberspace allows a criminal to commit a crime remarkably quickly, often in less than a second.[27]

- Because of cyberspace's trusting nature,[28] fraudulent schemes have become commonplace.[29] Phishing attacks[30] and other strategies based on misappropriating another's online identity have become a principal cybercrime of the 2000s.[31] Addressing Internet actors' responsibility for protecting not only themselves but also other users[32] will re-

---

27. Donn. B. Parker, *Computer Crime in* Encyclopedia of Computer Science 349, 350 ("The timing of some crimes is ... different. Traditionally, the duration of criminal acts is measured in minutes, hours, days, weeks, months, and years. Today, some crimes are being perpetrated in less than 0.003 of a second (3 ms.).").

28. *Cf.* Hafner, Wizards at 227 ("The overall idea behind [TCP/IP] was to shift the reliability from the network to the destination hosts.... 'The only thing that we ask [each node on the Internet] to do is to take this chunk of bits and get it across the network.'" (quoting Vint Cerf who, along with Bob Kahn, invented the technology that allows the Internet to operate).

29. *See* Jonathan Krim, *Ubiquitous Technology, Bad Practices Drive Up Data Theft,* Washington Post, June 22, 2005, at D01, *available at* http://www.washingtonpost.com/wp-dyn/content/article/2005/06/21/ar2005062101615.html?sub=AR.

30. A "phishing" attack occurs when a perpetrator sends a fraudulent message to as many users as possible. This message usually indicates that it is from a bank, insurance company, or other business entity and will normally use the trademarks of the entity to make the message look more authentic. The scheme works by informing the user that his or her account with the company has been breached and requesting that the user visit the company's web site to change the account's password. In fact, the web site is not associated with the company, but is designed to fool the user into thinking that it is. When the site is visited, it requests the user to enter his or her account number and current password and to specify a new password. The criminal records the account number and password and uses them to steal the user's property. *See, e.g.,* Joris Evers, *Phishers Going after Small Fry,* CnetNews.com, *available at* http://news.com/Phishers+going+ after+small+fry/2100-7349_3-5731174.html (last updated June 3, 2005).

31. *See* Krim, *Ubiquitous Technology, supra* note 29.

32. *See, e.g.,* Grant Gross, *Phishing Attacks May Be Coming from Your Computer,* PC World (Oct. 18, 2004), *available at* http://www.pcworld.idg.com.au/index.php/id; 454997528;fp;2;fpid;1; Brian *Krebs, Tougher Cyber-Security Measures Urged; Industry Al-*

quire examination over the next decade to establish who is responsible for enhancing the security of the Web and deciding if failures should result in criminal penalties.[33]

- Because of cyberspace's universality, interactions can occur among groups and individuals which would have been unthinkable in an earlier time. As many totalitarian societies are discovering, the Internet undermines the regime's ability to prevent "outside" ideas from being obtained by its citizens. When some of these ideas are considered to be illegal outside of cyberspace, the ease in which they can be spread within cyberspace triggers difficult legal issues.[34]

- Because of cyberspace's one-to-many nature, it allows individuals to more easily publish opinions that would have been publically ignored earlier. Speakers, whether positive or full of hate now have a broad audience.[35] But, as importantly, cyberspace has a many-to-one capability, also. This has allowed an increasingly common form of criminal attack — the "denial of service attack" where many computers, often at the direction of a single individual, simultaneously generate a flood of Web requests for the target site.[36] When the target site can-

---

liance Pushes for a Higher Profile for Computer Vulnerabilities, WASHINGTON POST, Dec. 8, 2004, at E05.

33. See Cybersecurity Liability Seen Increasing, ZDNET, available at http://zdnet. com.com/2100-1105-5180855.html (Mar. 28, 2004) ("Hackers, viruses and other online threats don't just create headaches for Internet users — they could also create prison sentences for corporate executives....").

34. See, e.g., Crispian Balmer, Yahoo! Restricted, http://abcnews.go.com/sections/ world/DailyNews/yahoo001120.html (visited Feb. 16, 2001) (a French court orders Yahoo! to block access to its sites that auction Nazi memorabilia despite Yahoo! assertion that the sites were in the U.S. and the contents of the sites were protected by the First Amendment); Tony Smith, Napster Partner Urged to Curb Nazi Song Swaps, THE REGISTER, http://www.theregister.co.uk/content/6/15598.html (visited Feb. 16, 2001) (The German government pressures Bertelsmann, as Napster's partner, to prevent Napster from being used to exchange neo-Nazi songs).

See also, http://www.cyber-rights.org/isps/somm-dec.htm (visited Feb. 16, 2001). (Felix Somm, the CompuServe managing director in Germany, was convicted of failing to block access to pornographic materials within Germany from CompuServe's U.S. servers. The material in the U.S. would be constitutionally protected speech. Ultimately, the German courts reversed the conviction holding that there were no technologically feasible means for blocking access.).

35. See previous footnote, supra.

36. See Andy Sullivan, Top ISPs Host Most Infected Computers, Report Says, WASHINGTONPOST.COM, June 14, 2005, available at http://www.washingtonpost.com/wp-dyn/content/article/2005/06/14/ar2005061401233.html.

not handle the crush of requests—as no site can—it either ceases operating or is so overwhelmed with bogus requests that it has no ability to process *bona fide* ones.[37] Cyberterrorism has been enabled. The addition of wireless access is further complicating these problems.[38]

- Most importantly, because of cyberspace's lack of physicality, fundamental legal concepts that have been used throughout history are crumbling. Of these concepts, the one causing the most difficulty within the criminal justice system is the decreased importance of a nation's borders (or, similarly, a state's borders). Although the edges of a country are of great significance in the physical society, in cyberspace, they are practically invisible. Often, it is impossible to determine from where a cyberspace message originated. Equally, it is impossible to prevent a message from traveling throughout cyberspace, regardless of any intervening borders.

As all of these changes were, and are, occurring, the societies involved have been required to reexamine many aspects of their criminal laws. The responses to these challenges that have been enacted into criminal law have served to define "cybercrimes." The purpose of this book is to discuss these cybercrimes as they have been defined, and to address the practicalities of investigating, prosecuting and defending them.

In the next chapter, Professor Susan Brenner, an expert in criminal law, discusses the misconduct that has been defined to be a cybercrime within the United States. She starts her discussion by examining the nature of cyber-misconduct to determine how novel this misconduct is when compared to traditional criminal conduct. Then, she examines the cybercrime laws of the United States at both the federal and state levels, discussing their elements and limitations.

In Chapter III, the practical issues associated with investigating and prosecuting a cybercrime case are addressed. Prosecuting Attorney Ivan Orton discusses all aspects of the preparation and presentation of a cybercrime.

---

37. *See* Ellen Messmer and Denise Pappalardo, *One Year after DoS Attacks, Vulnerabilities Remain*, http://www.cnn.com/2001/TECH/internet/02/08/ddos.anniversary.idg/index.html (Feb. 8, 2001) (pessimistically asserting that "[a] year after distributed denial-of-service attacks blasted the likes of Yahoo!, eBay, CNN.com and eTrade offline, no one has found an easy way to defend against a flood of unwanted IP packets.").

38. *See* Seth Schiesel, *Growth of Wireless Internet Opens New Paths for Thieves*, N.Y. Times, Mar. 19, 2005, at A1.

Based on his experience prosecuting cybercrimes, several of which he uses as hypotheticals to more clearly present the legal issues involved, he addresses investigatory issues such as appropriate training standards, computer forensics, and warrant requirements, as well as trial presentation techniques for a cybercrime prosecution.

Chapter IV, written by Defense Attorneys Joseph Savage, Darlene Moreau, and Dianna Lamb, also addresses these practical issues, but from the perspective of an attorney who is defending someone who has been accused of a cybercrime. Not surprisingly, many of the same issues are covered in the fourth chapter as were discussed in the third, but the defense rather than prosecutorial perspective on the issues creates a significantly different understanding of them.

In the final chapter, Professor and former U.S. Attorney, Miriam F. Miquelon Weismann, discusses the increasing international recognition of cybercrimes and the attempts by various international groups to address the problems caused by cyberspace's lack of clear national borders. Her chapter, especially, attempts to forecast where cybercrime prevention efforts will be directed in the immediate future.

Each chapter's presentation differs greatly in style and emphasis, based on each author's unique perspective on cybercrime. The different accentuation in each chapter reflects the dissimilar perspectives the authors bring to cybercrime prosecutions. To obtain a comprehensive understanding of cybercrimes, all views—the police officer's, prosecutor's, defense attorney's, academician's, or policy maker's—are important, particularly those that are different from the reader's own.[39]

The legal system's responses to cybercrimes have been multifaceted. As a consequence, a book discussing them must be also.

---

39. For example, a police officer should be aware of a defense attorney's likely consideration of cybercrime issues to be able to better investigate the occurrence and to adequately prepare the evidence for trial.

Chapter Two

Defining Cybercrime:
A Review of State and
Federal Law

Susan W. Brenner*

There is disagreement ... as to what exactly constitutes a computer crime. The term "computer crime" covers such a wide range of offenses that unanimity has been an elusive goal. For example, if a commercial burglary takes place and a computer is stolen, does this constitute a computer crime, or is it merely another burglary? Does copying a friend's Microsoft Excel disks constitute a computer crime? What about sending obscene pictures over the Internet? The answers to each of these questions may depend entirely upon the jurisdiction in which one finds oneself.[1]

---

* NCR Distinguished Professor of Law & Technology, University of Dayton School of Law. Member of the bars of Indiana and Illinois.

1. Marc D. Goodman, *Why the Police Don't Care About Computer Crime*, 10 Harv. J. L. & Tech. 465 §I(C) (1997) (footnotes omitted), *available at* http://jolt.law.harvard.edu/articles/pdf/v10/10HarvJLTech465.pdf (last visited Nov. 3, 2004) [hereinafter Goodman, *Why the Police Don't Care*].

I. Introduction

Various terms are used to refer to utilizing computer technology in the commission of crimes: High-technology crime, computer crime, information age crime and cybercrime are the more common terms used for this purpose. This chapter uses the term "cybercrime" simply because it is probably the most commonly used term for the use of computer technology to engage in illegal activity.

Although cybercrime is common term for all computer-related crimes, it is important to differentiate among three distinct but related concepts: cybercrime, cyberterrorism, and information warfare.

- Cybercrime consists of using computer technology to commit crimes. As the next section explains, the crimes can be of the traditional type (e.g., arson, theft, extortion) or they can be "new" crimes such as a Distributed Denial of Service attack.
- Cyberterrorism consists of using computer technology to carry out terrorist acts. While terrorist acts are usually crimes (i.e., murder, assault, destruction of property), we differentiate cyberterrorism from cybercrime because the latter is intended to advance a political or social agenda.[2]
- Information warfare denotes states' use of computer technology in an attempt to achieve military or other strategic objectives.[3]

---

2. *See, e.g., Special Oversight Panel on Terrorism Before the House Comm. on Armed Services* (May 23, 2000) (statement of Dorothy E. Denning), *available at* http://www.cs.georgetown.edu/~denning/infosec/cyberterror.html (last visited Nov. 3, 2004):

> Cyberterrorism is the convergence of terrorism and cyberspace. It is generally understood to mean unlawful attacks and threats of attack against computers, networks, and the information stored therein when done to intimidate or coerce a government or its people in furtherance of political or social objectives. Further, to qualify as cyberterrorism, an attack should result in violence against persons or property, or at least cause enough harm to generate fear. Attacks that lead to death or bodily injury, explosions, plane crashes, water contamination, or severe economic loss would be examples. Serious attacks against critical infrastructures could be acts of cyberterrorism, depending on their impact. Attacks that disrupt nonessential services or that are mainly a costly nuisance would not.

3. *See, e.g.,* Eric Hrovat, *Information Warfare: The Unconventional Art in a Digital World* 2 (2003), *available at* http://www.sans.org/rr/papers/29/787.pdf (last visited Nov. 3, 2004):

> Dr. Ivan Goldberg defines information warfare as, "the offensive and defen-

The remainder of this chapter is presented in four sections: Section II considers whether cybercrimes are "new" crimes that require the adoption of new substantive criminal legislation. Section III examines the federal statutes that address cybercrimes, while section IV examines state cybercrime legislation. Section V provides a brief conclusion that summarizes the state of the substantive law governing cybercrimes.

II. Cybercrimes: New Crimes or Old Wine in New Bottles?

Cybercrimes are often characterized as falling into three categories: crimes in which the computer is the target of the criminal activity; crimes in which the computer is a tool used to commit a crime; and crimes in which the use of the computer is an incidental aspect of the commission of the crime.[4]

When a computer is the target of criminal activity, the perpetrator attacks a computer system by breaking into it or by bombarding it from outside.[5] Cybercrimes that fall into this category and that require breaking into the target system include hacking (gaining unauthorized access to a computer system)[6] or cracking (gaining unauthorized access to a computer system in order to commit another crime such as destroying information con-

---

sive use of information systems to deny, exploit, corrupt, or destroy, an adversary's information, information-based processes, information systems, and computer-based networks while protecting one's own. Such actions are designed to achieve advantages over military or business adversaries."
(citing Institute for the Advanced Study of Information Warfare (June 30, 2001), *available at* http://www.psycom.net/iwar.1.html (last modified Mar. 14, 2004)).

4. *See, e.g.* David Carter, *Computer Crime Categories: How Techno-Criminals Operate*, 64 FBI L. ENFORCEMENT BULL. 21 (Jul. 1995), *available at* http://www.fbi.gov/publications/leb/1989-1995/leb95jul.zip (95jul006.txt file) (last visited Nov. 3, 2004).

5. *See, e.g.,* Goodman, *Why the Police Don't Care, supra* note 1, § I(C).

6. For example, in 1994 two young criminals "hacked" into the computer systems at the U.S. Air Force's Rome Air Development Center in New York. *See, e.g.,* RICHARD POWER, TANGLED WEB 66–75 (2000). In addition to exploring the Rome computer systems, the hackers used that system to hack into computers around the world, including South Korea's Atomic Research Institute. *Id. See also Security in Cyberspace Before the Senate Permanent Subcomm. on Investigations* (June 5, 1996) (Statement of the Minority Staff), *available at* http://www.fas.org/irp/congress/1996_hr/s960605b.htm (last visited Nov. 3, 2004).

tained in that system).[7] Target crimes can also involve attacks launched against a computer system, such as the distributed denial of service attacks ["DDos attack"] that were launched against Yahoo!, eBay and CNN in February of 2000.[8] In a DDos attack, the attacker uses compromised computer systems to flood the target system with messages that effectively shut it

---

7. For example, in the mid-1990's, a gang known as the Phonemasters routinely broke into various computer system belonging to telephone companies, credit-reporting services, Dun & Bradstreet and Lexis-Nexis to steal information which they then sold. *See, e.g.,* RICHARD POWER, TANGLED WEB 102–113. *See also* D. Ian Hopper & Richard Stenger, *Large-scale Phone Invasion Goes Unnoticed by All But FBI,* SIGNALTONOISE.NET LIBRARY (Dec. 14, 1999), *available at* http://www.signaltonoise.net/library/phonemasters.htm (last visited Nov. 3, 2004).

8. On February 7, 2000, the Yahoo! site was the victim of a DDos attack that shut it down for at least three hours; on February 8, 2000, eBay was the victim of a similar attack that incapacitated it for hours, and CNN was the victim of an attack that shut down all but 5% of the traffic to its site. *See, e.g.,* RICHARD POWER, TANGLED WEB 126. *See also* Ann Harrison, *The Denial-of-Service Aftermath,* CNN.COM (Feb. 14, 2000), *available at* http://archives.cnn.com/2000/TECH/computing/02/14/dos.aftermath.idg/index.html (last visited Nov. 3, 2004).

In a DDos attack, the perpetrator hacks into hundreds or even thousands of innocent computers and installs software on them that makes them "zombies," slave computers the perpetrator can use to attack a target computer. *See, e.g.,* Bennett Todd, *Distributed Denial of Service Attacks* (Feb. 18, 2000), *available at* http://www.linuxsecurity.com/resource_files/intrusion_detection/ddos-faq.html (last visited Nov. 3, 2004). When the perpetrator is ready to attack, he or she issues a command that instructs the zombies to attack the victim; as a result of the attack, the victim's system is effectively shut down, since it is overloaded with packets coming in from the zombies. *See id.*

[A] denial of service ... attack is an incident in which a user or organization is deprived of the services of a resource they would normally expect to have. Typically, the loss of service is the inability of a particular network service, such as e-mail, to be available or the temporary loss of all network connectivity and services. In the worst cases ... a Web site accessed by millions of people can occasionally be forced to temporarily cease operation. A denial of service attack can also destroy programming and files in a computer system. Although usually intentional and malicious, a denial of service attack can sometimes happen accidentally. A denial of service attack is a type of security breach to a computer system that does not usually result in the theft of information or other security loss. However, these attacks can cost the target person or company a great deal of time and money.

Denial of Service, SearchSecurity.com, *available at* http://searchsecurity.techtarget.com/gDefinition/0,,sid14_gci213591,00.html (last updated May 16, 2001).

down.[9] One can argue that these are not new crimes, since hacking can be analogized to trespassing and cracking can be analogized to burglary, but the analogies founder on the critical differences between the "real world" and the "virtual world."[10] The crimes that fall into this category are more properly treated as "new" crimes that cannot easily be prosecuted under existing law and therefore require the adoption of statutes that specifically target these activities.[11]

Instead of being the victim, a computer system can be the instrument that is used to commit a crime.[12] Here, the computer's role is analogous to the role telephones play in telephone fraud:[13] Fraud can be committed, *inter alia*, face-to-face or by using a telephone.[14] In the latter alternative, the telephone is simply a tool the perpetrator uses to commit fraud; the use of telephone technology (or computer technology) in no way substantively alters the nature of the offense.[15] "Tool" cybercrimes include online fraud,[16] theft

---

9. *See, e.g., Distributed Denial of Service Attack*, SearchSecurity.com, *available at* http://searchsecurity.techtarget.com/gDefinition/0,294236,sid14_gci557336,00.html (last updated May 21, 2004):

> [A DDos] attack is one in which a multitude of compromised systems attack a single target, thereby causing denial of service for users of the targeted system. The flood of incoming messages to the target system essentially forces it to shut down, thereby denying service to the system to legitimate users.
>
> A hacker ... begins a DDoS attack by exploiting a vulnerability in one computer system and making it the DDoS "master." It is from the master system that the intruder identifies and communicates with other systems that can be compromised. The intruder loads cracking tools available on the Internet on multiple—sometimes thousands of—compromised systems. With a single command, the intruder instructs the controlled machines to launch one of many flood attacks against a specified target. The inundation of packers to the target causes a denial of service.

10. *See* Susan W. Brenner, *Can There Be Truly Virtual Crimes?*, Part III, 4 Cal. Crim. L. Rev. 1, ¶¶ 32–127 (2001), *available at* http://boalt.org/CCLR/v4/v4brenner.htm (last visited Nov. 8, 2004) [hereinafter Brenner, *Can There Be Truly Virtual Crimes?*].

11. *See id.*

12. Goodman, *Why the Police Don't Care, supra* note 1, §I(C). *See also* Federal Searching Guidelines §I(C) ("[T]he computer system may be a tool of the offense. This occurs when the computer system is actively used by a defendant to commit the offense. For example, a counterfeiter might use his computer, scanner, and color printer to scan U.S. currency and then print money.").

13. *See,* Brenner, *Can There Be Truly Virtual Crimes?, supra* note 10, ¶¶ 32–127.

14. *See Id.*

15. *See Id.*

16. *See, e.g.,* National White Collar Crime Center & Federal Bureau of Investigation, *Internet Fraud Complaint Center 2002 Internet Fraud Report 3–6* (2003), *avail-*

of funds or information,[17] embezzlement,[18] stalking,[19] forgery,[20] homicide[21] and the creation and/or dissemination of child pornography.[22] Even though these are not "new" crimes, it may be difficult to prosecute this type of activity under existing laws; a jurisdiction's theft statute, for example, may not encompass a "theft" of intangible property when the culpable act consists of copying the property instead of appropriating it entirely.[23] Jurisdictions may therefore find it advisable either to adopt new legislation that addresses crimes in this category or to amend existing legislation to ensure that it is adequate for that purpose.[24]

---

able at http://www1.ifccfbi.gov/strategy/2002_IFCCReport.pdf (last visited Nov. 8, 2004).

17. In 1994, a Russian hacker named Vladimir Levin broke into the computer system at Citibank and incrementally transferred funds variously estimated at $3.7 million and $10 million to accounts in other banks. *See, e.g.,* Ugo Flohr, *Bank Robbers Go Electronic,* BYTE, Nov. 1995, *available at* http://www.byte.com/art/9511/sec3/art11.htm (last visited Nov. 8, 2004). And as noted earlier, the Phonemasters gang stole and sold information from telephone companies, credit-reporting services, Dun & Bradstreet and Lexis-Nexis. *See, e.g.,* RICHARD POWER, TANGLED WEB 102–113.

18. *See, e.g.,* Press Release, U.S. Department of Justice, Vallejo Woman Charged with Embezzling more than $875,035 (May 27, 2004) ("United States Attorney McGregor W. Scott announced today that Jessica Quitugua Sabathia, 31, of Vallejo, California was charged with ten counts of fraudulently using her computer to embezzle more than $875,035 from North Bay Health Care Group"), *available at* http://www.usdoj.gov/criminal/cybercrime/sabathiaCharged.htm (last visited Nov. 8, 2004).

19. *See, e.g.,* U.S. Department of Justice, *1999 Report on Cyberstalking: A New Challenge for Law Enforcement and Industry* (1999), *available at* http://www.usdoj.gov/criminal/cybercrime/cyberstalking.htm (last visited Nov. 8, 2004).

20. *See, e.g.,* GA. CODE ANN. § 16-9-93(d) (1996) ("Any person who creates, alters, or deletes any data contained in any computer or computer network, who, if such person had created, altered, or deleted a tangible document or instrument would have committed forgery under Article 1 of this chapter, shall be guilty of the crime of computer forgery").

21. *See, e.g.,* Tania Hershman, *Israel's "First Internet Murder,"* WIRED NEWS, Jan. 19, 2001, *available at* http://www.wired.com/news/politics/0,1283,41300,00.html (last visited Nov. 8, 2004).

22. *See, e.g.,* Federal Bureau of Investigation, Online Child Pornography: Innocent Images National Initiative (Mar. 2002) ("Computer telecommunications have become one of the most prevalent techniques used by pedophiles to share illegal photographic images of minors and to lure children into illicit sexual relationships"), *available at* http://www.fbi.gov/hq/cid/cac/innocent.htm (last visited Oct. 28, 2004).

23. *See* Brenner, *Can There Be Truly Virtual Crimes?, supra* note 10. *See, e.g.,* State v. Schwartz, 21 P.3d 1128 (Or. App. 2001).

24. *See, e.g.,* GA. CODE ANN. § 16-9-93 (1991) & § 16-9-93.1 (1996); NEV. REV. STAT. 205.481 (1999); VA. CODE ANN. § 18.2-152.14 (1985); W. VA. CODE § 61-3C-15 (1989).

The final category consists of cybercrimes in which the use of a computer or computer system is incidental to the commission of the crime; here, the computer plays a minor role in the offense.[25] This category encompasses, for example, cases in which someone uses a computer to write a blackmail letter in which a drug dealer stores the financial records of his transactions on a computer.[26] Here, the computer is a source of evidence, nothing more.[27] Since the computer plays a non-essential role in the commission of the offense, new legislation is not needed to prosecute the crimes that fall into this category.

The offenses falling into the first two categories—computer as target and computer as instrument—are sufficiently distinct to require the adoption of specialized legislation directed at these kinds of activities. Such legislation can either create new offenses or simply amend an existing statute—such as a theft statute—to broaden its scope so that it encompasses the use of a computer to commit an already-defined offense. The next two sections review the federal and state legislation that has been adopted to this end.

III. Federal Cybercrime Legislation

By one estimate, there are more than forty federal statutes that can be used to prosecute cybercrime.[28] Many of these statutes, such as the wire fraud statute, antedate the rise of cybercrime and were therefore not designed to reach the issues it presents, but other federal legislation has been adopted that specifically targets the more commonly encountered cybercrimes, such as hacking, cracking, virus dissemination, using computers to commit fraud and using computer equipment to create and disseminate child pornography.[29] Unfortunately, federal law is still lacking in some

---

25. See Goodman, *Why the Police Don't Care, supra* note 1, § I(C) ("A computer is incidental to the crime if the computer itself is not required for the crime, but is used in some way connected with the criminal activity").

26. *See id. See, e.g.,* Cyber Forensics, *Blackmail, available at* http://www.cyber-forensics.ltd.uk/Services-Blackmail%20case.htm (last visited Dec. 17, 2004).

27. *See, e.g.,* U.S. Secret Service, *Best Practices for Seizing Electronic Evidence* (2002), *available at* http://www.secretservice.gov/electronic_evidence.shtml (last visited Nov. 8, 2004).

28. *See* Robert Ditzion, Elizabeth Geddes & Mary Rhodes, *Computer Crimes,* 40 Am. Crim. L. Rev. 285, 299 (2003).

29. At the federal level, the basic approach has been to adopt new, cybercrime-specific statutes instead of amending existing laws so they encompass cybercrimes.

areas — such as online stalking and harassment — and legislation that has been adopted to deal with certain issues has been struck down as over broad.

A. Cybercrimes Where the Computer Is the Target

1. Hacking, Cracking, Fraud, Virus Dissemination and Extortion

Section 1030 of Title 18 of the U.S. Code is the basic federal cybercrime provision.[30] It defines a number of computer-related offenses, e.g., hack-

---

Rather than attempting to deal with computer crime by amending every traditional statute to encompass new technologies, Congress has treated computer-related crimes as distinct federal offenses since the passage of the Counterfeit Access Device and Computer Fraud and Abuse Law in 1984. The 1984 Act was intentionally narrowly tailored to protect classified United States' defense and foreign relations information, financial institution and consumer reporting agency files, and access to computers operated for the government. Subsequently, the volume of such legislation greatly expanded to address many other types of computer-related crimes. As new computer crime issues have arisen and more statistics have become available, the law has attempted to adapt. In the Computer Fraud and Abuse Act of 1986, Congress expanded the scope of the law and attempted to define its terms more clearly. Congress continued to expand the scope of the computer crime law in 1988, 1989, and 1990. In 1994, Congress rewrote part of the Act again, and then passed the National Information Infrastructure Protection Act of 1996 [NIIPA].

Laura J. Nicholson, Tom F. Shebar & Meredith R. Weinberg, *Computer Crimes*, 37 AM. CRIM. L. REV. 207, 212 (2000) (notes omitted). *See also* Counterfeit Access Device and Computer Fraud and Abuse Act, Pub. L. No. 98-473, tit. II, ch. XXI, §2102(a), 98 Stat. 1837, 2190 (1984); Computer Fraud and Abuse Act, Pub. L. No. 99-474, §2, 100 Stat. 1213 (1986); Pub. L. No. 100-690, tit. VII, §7065, 102 Stat. 4404 (1988); Pub. L. No. 101-73, tit. IX, §962(a)(5), 103 Stat. 502 (1989); Pub. L. No. 101-647, tit. XII, §1205(e), tit. XXV, §2597 (j), tit. XXXV, §3533, 104 Stat. 4831, 4910, 4925 (1990); Pub. L. No. 103-322, tit. XXIX, §290001 (b)-(f), 108 Stat. 2097-2099 (1994); Pub. L. No. 104-294, tit. II, §201, 110 Stat. 3488, 3491-94 (1996). The original act and the 1986-96 amendments were all codified as 18 U.S.C. §1030 (2000), which is discussed in Section III(A)(1) of this chapter.

30. See Eric J. Bakewell, Michelle Koldaro & Jennifer M. Tjia, *Computer Crimes*, 38 AM. CRIM. L. REV. 481, 487–488 (2001):

Congress has treated computer-related crimes as distinct federal offenses since the passage of the Counterfeit Access Device and Computer Fraud and Abuse Law in 1984 (the "1984 Act"), rather than trying to fit new crimes into old boxes. The 1984 Act was intentionally narrowly tailored to protect classified U.S. de-ing, cracking, virus dissemination, fraud, password trafficking, and extortion.[31]

Section 1030 reaches conduct directed at a "protected computer."[32] A "protected computer" is one that falls into either of two categories:

1. a computer that is used exclusively by a financial institution or the federal government or that is used, albeit nonexclusively, by a financial institution or the federal government but the conduct constituting the offense affects that use; or

---

fense and foreign relations information, financial institution and consumer reporting agency files, and access to computers operated for the government. Later legislation greatly expanded to address many other types of computer-related crimes. The law has attempted to adapt. Because new computer crime issues had arisen and more statistics had become available, Congress expanded the scope of the law by enacting the Computer Fraud and Abuse Act of 1986 ... and thereby attempted to define the terms more clearly. Congress continued to expand the scope of the computer crime law in 1988, 1989, and 1990. In 1994, Congress rewrote part of the 1984 Act again before passing the NIIPA in 1996. (footnotes omitted); Counterfeit Access Device and Computer Fraud and Abuse Act, Pub. L. No. 98-473, tit. II, ch. XXI, § 2102(a), 98 Stat. 1837, 2190 (1984); Computer Fraud and Abuse Act, Pub. L. No. 99-474, § 2, 100 Stat. 1213 (1986); Pub. L. No. 100-690, tit. VII, § 7065, 102 Stat. 4404 (1988); Pub. L. No. 101-73, tit. IX, § 962(a)(5), 103 Stat. 502 (1989); Pub. L. No. 101-647, tit. XII, § 1205(e), tit. XXV, § 2597 (j), tit. XXXV, § 3533, 104 Stat. 4831, 4910, 4925 (1990); Pub. L. No. 103-322, tit. XXIX, § 290001 (b)-(f), 108 Stat. 2097-99 (1994); Pub. L. No. 104-294, tit. II, § 201, 110 Stat. 3488, 3491-94 (1996). The original act and the 1986–96 amendments were all codified as 18 U.S.C. § 1030 which was, in turn, further amended by the PATRIOT Act of 2001, Pub. L. No. 107-56, 115 Stat. 272 (2001).

31. *See* 18 U.S.C. § 1030(a) (2000). Punishment for violating 18 U.S.C. § 1030(a) is discussed in the text, below.

The PATRIOT Act of 2001 clarified the meaning of "loss" as used in the statute. *See* PATRIOT Act of 2001 § 814(d)(11), Pub. L. No. 107-56, 115 Stat. 272 ("the term 'loss' means any reasonable cost to any victim, including the cost of responding to an offense, conducting a damage assessment, and restoring the data, program, system, or information to its condition prior to the offense, and any revenue lost, cost incurred, or other consequential damages incurred because of interruption of service"). Prior to this amendment, the statute did not define "loss". *See, e.g.,* Computer Crime and Intellectual Property Section, Criminal Division, U.S. Department of Justice, *Field Guidance on New Authorities that Relate to Computer Crime and Electronic Evidence Enacted in the USA PATRIOT Act of 2001* (2001) [hereinafter "CCIPS, *Field Guide*"], *available at* http://www.cybercrime.gov/PatriotAct.htm (last visited Nov. 8, 2004). The definition incorporated into the statute was based on the holding in *U.S. v. Middleton,* 231 F.3d 1207, 1210–11 (9th Cir. 2001). *See id.*

32. *See* 18 U.S.C. § 1030(a) (2000).

2.   a computer that is used in interstate or foreign commerce or com-
     munication.[33]

The concept of basing liability on conduct targeting "protected computers"
was introduced by an amendment enacted in 1996; until then, § 1030 only
reached conduct targeting "federal interest computers," e.g., computers used
by the federal government or computers located in more than one state.[34]
As a result of the 1996 amendment, the statute now reaches conduct directed at any computer connected to the Internet, regardless of whether the
computers involved are located in the same state.[35] It also confers international jurisdiction.[36]

---

33. See id. § 1030(e)(2) ("protected computer" means "a computer (A) exclusively
for the use of a financial institution or the U.S. Government, or, in the case of a computer not exclusively for such use, used by or for a financial institution or the U.S. Government and the conduct constituting the offense affects that use by or for the financial institution or the Government; or (B) which is used in interstate or foreign
commerce or communication *including a computer located outside the U.S. that is used
in a manner that affects interstate or foreign commerce or communication of the U.S.*").
The PATRIOT Act of 2001, Pub. L. No. 107-56, 115 Stat. 272, added the language that
appears in italics. See PATRIOT Act of 2001 § 814(d), Pub. L. No. 107-56, 115 Stat. 272.
   "Computer" is defined as "an electronic, magnetic, optical, electrochemical, or other
high speed data processing device performing logical, arithmetic, or storage functions,
and includes any data storage facility or communications facility directly related to or
operating in conjunction with such device, but such term does not include an automated typewriter or typesetter, a portable hand held calculator, or other similar device."
See 18 U.S.C. § 1030(e)(1) (2000).
   34. See, e.g., Eric J. Bakewell, Michelle Koldaro & Jennifer M. Tjia, *Computer Crimes*, 38
AM. CRIM. L. REV. 481, 488 n.41 (2001) ("'Federal Interest computers' under the 1994 Act
included a computer 'which is one of two or more computers used in committing the offense, not all of which are located in the same state'") (citing 18 U.S.C. § 1030(e)(2) (2000)).
   35. See, e.g., id. at 488 n.42 (2001).
   36. In *Four Seasons Hotels and Resorts B.V. v. Consorcio Barr, S.A.* 267 F. Supp. 2d
1268 (S.D. Fla. 2003), a civil action under 18 U.S.C. § 1030(g), the court found that the
defendant violated 18 U.S.C. § 1030(a) by engaging in conduct directed at the plaintiff's
protected computers "located both within and outside of the U.S." 267 F. Supp. 2d at
1322. See, e.g., U.S. v. Ivanov, 175 F. Supp. 2d 367, 369 (D. Conn. 2001) (defendant
charged with computer fraud based on conduct committed when he was physically located in Russia). In the *Ivanov* case, the district court held that it had jurisdiction over
the Russian defendant, for conduct committed while he was in Russia, "first, because
the intended and actual detrimental effects of Ivanov's actions in Russia occurred within
the U.S., and second, because each of the statutes under which Ivanov was charged with
a substantive offense was intended by Congress to apply extraterritorially." Id. at 370.
The *Ivanov* prosecution was brought before the PATRIOT Act amended the statue to
include an explicit jurisdictional reference to the use of a computer located outside the

Section 1030(a) makes it a federal crime to do any of the following:

1. To (i) knowingly access a computer without authorization or by exceeding authorized access and thereby obtain information that is protected against disclosure which the perpetrator has reason to believe could be used to the disadvantage of the U.S. or to the advantage of any foreign nation and (ii) willfully either deliver that information to a person not entitled to receive it or retain the information and refuse to deliver it to the federal agent entitled to receive it;[37]

2. To intentionally access a computer without authorization or by exceeding authorized access and thereby obtain (i) information contained in a financial record of a financial institution, or of a card issuer or contained in a file of a consumer reporting agency on a consumer,[38] (ii) information from any federal department or agency,[39] or (iii) information from any protected computer if the conduct involved an interstate or foreign communication;[40]

3. To intentionally and without authorization access (i) a computer used exclusively by a federal department or agency or (ii) a computer not used exclusively by a federal department or agency when the conduct affects the computer's use by or for the federal government;[41]

U.S. Even before the amendment, however, the Department of Justice had taken the position that extraterritorial jurisdiction existed. *See, e.g.,* Computer Crime and Intellectual Property Section, Criminal Division, U.S. Dept. of Justice, *The National Information Infrastructure Protection Act of 1996: Legislative Analysis* (2003), *available at* http://www.usdoj.gov/criminal/cybercrime/1030_anal.html (last visited Nov. 8, 2004).

37. 18 U.S.C. § 1030(a)(1) (2000).

38. *See, e.g.,* U.S. v. Tanimowo, No. 99-1029, 1999 WL 1024101, at *1 (2d Cir. 1999) (defendant pled guilty to one count of accessing computer without authorization for the purpose of obtaining confidential consumer credit information in violation of 18 U.S.C. § 1030(a)(2)(A)). *See also* U.S. v. Petersen, 98 F.3d 502, 504 (9th Cir. 1996).

39. *See, e.g.,*U.S. v. Gray, 78 F. Supp. 2d 524, 525 (E.D. Va. 1999) (defendant charged with unlawfully accessing a government computer in violation of 18 U.S.C. § 1030(a)(2) and with unlawfully accessing a government computer and causing damage to it in violation of 18 U.S.C. § 1030(a)(5)). *See also* U.S. v. Rice, No. 91-5786, 1992 WL 90278 (4th Cir.), *cert. denied,* 506 U.S. 898 (1992).

40. 18 U.S.C. § 1030(a)(2) (2000). *See, e.g.,* U.S. v. Ferguson, 102 Fed. Appx. 257 (3d Cir. 2004); U.S. v. Johnson, 58 Fed. Appx. 926 (3d Cir. 2003); U.S. v. Harris, 302 F.3d 72 (2002).

41. 18 U.S.C. § 1030(a)(3) (2000). *See, e.g.,* U.S. v. Rice, No. 91-5786, 1992 WL 90278, at *1 (4th Cir.), *cert. denied,* 506 U.S. 898 (1992).

4. To knowingly and with the intent to defraud access a protected computer without authorization or by exceeding authorized access and thereby further the intended fraud and obtain anything of value unless the object of the fraud and the thing obtained consist only of the use of the computer and the value of that use does not exceed $5,000 in any one-year period;[42]

5. To (i) knowingly cause the transmission or a program, information, code or command and thereby intentionally cause damage to a protected computer;[43] (ii) intentionally access a protected computer

---

42. 18 U.S.C. § 1030(a)(4) (2000). *See, e.g.,* U.S. v. Butler, 16 Fed. Appx. 99, 2001 WL 733424, at *1 (4th Cir. 2001) (defendant pled guilty to computer fraud); U.S. v. Bae, 250 F.3d 774, 775 (D.C. Cir. 2001) (defendant pled guilty to computer fraud based on his using lottery terminal to generate lottery tickets for which he did not pay); U.S. v. Sadolsky, 234 F.3d 938, 939, 2000 WL 1808567 (6th Cir. 2000) (defendant pled guilty to seven counts of using a computer to facilitate the commission of fraud in violation of 18 U.S.C. § 1030(a)(4)); U.S. v. Magnuson, 120 F.3d 263 (4th Cir. 1997) (defendant pled guilty to one count of using a computer to facilitate the commission of fraud in violation of 18 U.S.C. § 1030(a)(4)); U.S. v. Petersen, 98 F.3d 502, 505 (9th Cir. 1996) (same); U.S. v. Ivanov, 175 F. Supp. 2d 367, 371 (D. Conn. 2001) (defendant charged with computer fraud for hacking into computers of corporation, obtaining passwords and using them in an attempt to extort money). *But see* U.S. v. Czubinski, 106 F.3d 1069, 1078–79 (1st Cir. 1997) (defendant could not be convicted of computer fraud under 18 U.S.C. § 1030(a)(4) based on unauthorized accessing of taxpayer records because he did not obtain "anything of value" by doing so and therefore did not further a fraudulent scheme).

43. *See* 18 U.S.C. § 1030(a)(5)(A)(I) (2000). *See, e.g.,* U.S. v. Drew, 27 Fed. Appx. 164 (4th Cir. 2001) (defendant convicted of intentionally causing the transmission of a program without authorization and thereby causing damage to a protected computer); U.S. v. Lloyd, 269 F.3d 228, 231 (3d Cir. 2001) (defendant charged with computer sabotage for planting a computer "time bomb" in the central file server of his employer and detonating the time bomb after he was fired); U.S. v. Middleton, 35 F. Supp. 2d 1189 (N.D. Cal. 1999), *aff'd* 231 F.3d 1207 (9th Cir. 2000) (defendant charged with one count of knowingly causing the transmission of a code or program and thereby intentionally causing a protected computer in violation of 18 U.S.C. § 1030(a)(5)). In the *Middleton* case, Middleton, among other things, deleted "the entire billing system" and "two internal databases" from the computer system of his former employer, an Internet service provider. *See* U.S. v. Middleton, 231 F.3d 1207, 1208–09 (9th Cir. 2000). After being charged with violating 18 U.S.C. § 1030(a)(5), Middleton moved to dismiss the charges on the grounds that the company was not an "individual" under 18 U.S.C. § 1030(e)(8)(A). 231 F.3d at 1209–10. Middleton conceded that the computer he broke into was a "protected computer" under § 1030(e)(2)(B), but he claimed that his conduct did not fall within the scope of 18 U.S.C. § 1030(e)(8)(A), which defines "damage" as "any impairment to the integrity or availability of data ... that causes losses aggregating at least $5,000 in value during any

without authorization and thereby recklessly cause damage;[44] (iii) intentionally access a protected computer without authorization and thereby cause damage;[45] and (iv) by conduct falling into any of the three prior categories, cause or attempt to cause physical injury, the modification or impairment of any medical diagnosis, loss aggregating $5,000 in one year period, threat to public health or safety or damage affecting a computer system used by or for a government entity in furtherance of the administration of justice, national security or national defense;[46]

---

one year period to one or more individuals." Id. Middleton argued that Congress did not intend to include corporations in its definition of "individuals." See id. at 1210. The Ninth Circuit disagreed, noting that

> [a] large number of the computers that are used in interstate or foreign commerce or communication are owned by corporations.... It is highly unlikely, in view of Congress' purpose to stop damage to computers used in interstate and foreign commerce and communication, that Congress intended to criminalize damage to such computers only if the damage is to a natural person. Defendant's interpretation would thwart Congress' intent.

Id. at 1211. The Ninth Circuit also reviewed the statute's legislative history and concluded that "18 U.S.C. § 1030(a)(5) criminalizes computer crime that damages natural persons and corporations alike." Id. at 1212–13.

44. See 18 U.S.C. § 1030(a)(5)(A)(ii) (2000).

45. See id. § 1030(a)(5)(A)(iii).

46. See id. § 1030(a)(5)(B)(i)-(v). See, e.g., U.S. v. Lloyd, 269 F.3d 228, 231 (3d Cir. 2001) (defendant charged with computer sabotage for planting a computer "time bomb" in the central file server of his employer and detonating the time bomb after he was fired); U.S. v. Sablan, 92 F.3d 865 (9th Cir. 1996) (former bank employee who used old password to break into computer where she altered and deleted files charged with computer damage); U.S. v. Gray, 78 F. Supp. 2d 524 (E.D. Va. 1999) (defendant charged with unlawfully accessing a government computer in violation of 18 U.S.C. § 1030(a)(2) and with unlawfully accessing a government computer and causing damage to it in violation of 18 U.S.C. § 1030(a)(5)); U.S. v. Khanna, 1998 WL 67678 (S.D.N.Y. 1998) (former consultant to bank charged with gaining unauthorized access to bank's computers where he deleted files and databases). See also U.S. v. Morris, 928 F.2d 504 (2d Cir. 1991), cert. denied, 502 U.S. 817 (1992) (defendant's releasing computer "worm" punishable under prior version of statute).

The PATRIOT Act of 2001 restructured this portion of the statute. Prior to the restructuring,

> in order to violate subsections (a)(5)(A), an offender had to "intentionally [cause] damage without authorization." Section 1030 defined "damage" as impairment to the integrity or availability of data, a program, a system, or information that (1) caused loss of at least $5,000; (2) modified or impairs medical treatment; (3) caused physical injury; or (4) threatened public health or safety.

6.   To knowingly and with intent to defraud traffic in any password or
     other information used to access a computer if (i) the trafficking
     affects interstate or foreign commerce or (ii) the computer to which
     access can be gained is by or for the federal government;[47]

Computer Crime and Intellectual Property Section, Criminal Division, U.S. Department
of Justice, *Field Guidance on New Authorities that Relate to Computer Crime and Electronic Evidence Enacted in the USA PATRIOT Act of 2001*, § 814(B) (2001), *available at*
http://www.usdoj.gov/criminal/cybercrime/PatriotAct.htm (last visited December 27,
2004). The question repeatedly arose, however, whether an offender must *intend* the
$5,000 loss or other special harm, or whether a violation occurs if the person only in-
tends to damage the computer, *that in fact* ends up causing the $5,000 loss or harming
the individuals. It appears that Congress never intended that the language contained in
the definition of 'damage' would create additional elements of proof of the actor's mental state. Moreover, in most cases, it would be almost impossible to prove this additional
intent. CCIPS, *Field Guide, supra* note 31. The PATRIOT Act restructured this section:
    to make clear that an individual need only intend to damage the computer or
    the information on it, and not a specific dollar amount of loss or other spe-
    cial harm. The amendments move these jurisdictional requirements to
    1030(a)(5)(B), explicitly making them elements of the offense.... Under this
    clarified structure, in order for the government to prove a violation of
    1030(a)(5), it must show that the actor caused damage to a protected com-
    puter (with one of the listed mental states), and that the actor's conduct
    caused either loss exceeding $5,000, impairment of medical records, harm to
    a person, or threat to public safety.
Id. See PATRIOT Act of 2001 § 814(a), Pub. L. No. 107-56, 115 Stat. 272. As part of this
restructuring, the PATRIOT Act also moved the definition of "damage" to § 1030(e)(8).
See id. The PATRIOT Act also made it clear that the government can aggregate the loss
an individual causes to different protected computers to meet the jurisdictional threshold of $5,000 in loss. *See, e.g.,* CCIPS, *Field Guide.*
    The PATRIOT Act further modified this section of the statute by adding language
that encompasses conduct intended to damage "a computer system used by or for a government entity in furtherance of the administration of justice, national defense, or national security." PATRIOT Act of 2001 § 814(a), Pub. L. No. 107-56, 115 Stat. 272. The
latter was intended to remedy a significant deficiency in the prior statute, e.g., that jurisdiction did not exist to prosecute damage to a government computer unless the damage resulted in provable loss of $5,000. *See* PATRIOT Act of 2001 § 814(a), Pub. L. No.
107-56, 115 Stat. 272. *See also* CCIPS, *Field Guide* (under the restructured section, "the
government may now aggregate "loss resulting from a related course of conduct affecting one or more other protected computers" that occurs within a one year period in
proving the $5,000 jurisdictional threshold for damaging a protected computer. 18
U.S.C. § 1030(a)(5)(B)(I)").
    47. 18 U.S.C. § 1030(a)(6) (2000). *See generally* Steve Jackson Games, Inc. v. U.S. Se-
cret Service, 816 F. Supp. 432, 439 (W.D. Tex. 1993), *aff'd*, 36 F.3d 457 (5th Cir. 1994).

7. To transmit in interstate or foreign commerce any threat to cause damage to a protected computer with the intent to extort money or any thing of value.[48]

Section 1030(b) makes it a federal crime to attempt to commit any of the above offenses, and section 371 of Title 18 of the U.S. Code can be used to charge conspiracy to violate 18 U.S. Code § 1030.[49]

Section 1030(c) sets out the punishment for these offenses. The basic penalties for violating § 1030(a) are a fine, imprisonment or both; the statute carefully parses the periods of imprisonment that can be imposed for each offense.[50]

The penalties for violating 18 U.S. Code § 1030(a)(1) are:

1. a fine, imprisonment for up to ten years or both if the offender has not previously been convicted of an offense or an attempt to commit an offense under § 1030 or

---

48. 18 U.S.C. § 1030(a)(7) (2000). The PATRIOT Act of 2001 struck the phrase "firm, association, educational institution, financial institution, government entity, or other legal entity" from this provision. *See* PATRIOT Act of 2001 § 814(b), Pub. L. No. 107-56, 115 Stat. 272. *See, e.g.,* U.S. v. Ivanov, 175 F. Supp. 2d 367, 370 (D. Conn. 2001) (defendant charged with transmitting, in interstate and foreign commerce, threat to cause damage to protected computers).

49. Section 371 makes it an offense for "two or more persons" to conspire either to commit an offense against the U.S. or to defraud the U.S. "or any agency thereof in any manner or for any purpose." 18 U.S.C. § 371 (2000). *See, e.g.,* U.S. v. Ioane, 25 Fed. Appx. 675 (9th Cir. 2001) (defendant pled guilty to conspiracy and to violating 18 U.S.C. § 1030(a)); U.S. v. Petersen, 98 F.3d 502, 503 (9th Cir. 1996) (defendant charged with conspiring to violate18 U.S.C. § 1030(a)(4)); U.S. v. Fernandez, 1993 WL 88197 (S.D.N.Y. 1993) (defendant charged with conspiring to violate 18 U.S.C. § 1030(a)(5) (2000)). *See also* U.S. v. Ivanov, 175 F. Supp. 2d 367, 373 (D. Conn. 2001); U.S. v. Farraj, 142 F. Supp. 2d 484, 485 (S.D.N.Y. 2001).

50. The PATRIOT Act of 2001 § 814, Pub. L. No. 107-56, 115 Stat. 272, increased certain of the penalties:

> Section 814 increases the penalty for intentionally damaging a protected computer from imprisonment for not more than 5 years to imprisonment for not more than 10 years. It also raises the penalty for either intentionally or recklessly damaging a protected computer after having previously been convicted of computer abuse from imprisonment for not more than 10 years to imprisonment for not more than 20 years.

Congressional Research Service, *Terrorism: Section by Section Analysis of the USA PATRIOT Act* 52, *available at* http://fpc.state.gov/documents/organization/7952.pdf (last updated Dec. 10, 2001).

2. a fine, imprisonment for up to twenty years or both if the offender
    has previously been convicted of such an offense or an attempt to
    commit such an offense.[51]

One who violates § 1030(a)(2), (a)(3), (a)(5)(A)(iii) or (a)(6) can be imprisoned for not more than one year if the offender has not been convicted
of a prior offense under § 1030 or an attempt to commit such an offense.[52]
If an offender convicted of an offense under § 1030(a)(2), § 1030(a)(3),
§ 1030(a)(6) or an attempt to commit such an offense has a previous conviction for violating § 1030 or for attempting to do so, the maximum period of imprisonment rises to not more than ten years.[53] The period of imprisonment imposed for violating or attempting to violate § 1030(a)(2) is
increased to up to five years if the offense was committed for commercial
advantage or financial gain, if it was committed to further a criminal or tor-
tuous act or if the value of the information obtained exceeds $5,000.[54]

The period of imprisonment for one who violates § 1030(a)(4) or
§ 1030(a)(7) but does not have a prior conviction for violating § 1030(a) or
attempting to do so is not more than five years.[55] The period of imprisonment for one who violates §§ 1030(a)(4), 1030(a)(5)(A)(iii) or 1030(a)(7)
and who has been convicted of a prior offense or attempt under § 1030(a)
is not more than ten years.[56] One violates § 1030(a)(5)(A)(i) but has no prior
convictions under § 1030 faces imprisonment for up to 10 years, and someone who violates § 1030(a)(5)(A)(ii) but has no priors faces imprisonment
for up to five years.[57] Finally, one who violates either § 1030(a)(5)(A)(I) or
§ 1030(a)(5)(A)(ii) faces imprisonment for up to twenty years if he or she
had a prior conviction under § 1030.[58]

In addition to the internal changes in § 1030, the PATRIOT Act of 2001[59]
also added linkages to other federal criminal provisions. For one thing, the
PATRIOT Act incorporated the § 1030 offenses into 18 U.S.C. § 2332b's de-

---

51. 18 U.S.C. § 1030(c)(1) (2000).
52. *Id.* § 1030(c)(2).
53. *Id.*
54. *Id.*
55. *Id.* § 1030(c)(3).
56. *Id.*
57. *Id.* § 1030(c)(4).
58. *Id.*
59. Pub. L. No. 107-56, 115 Stat. 272.

finition of a "federal crime of terrorism".[60] It also incorporated the federal crimes of terrorism defined in 18 U.S.C. § 2332b into the definition of racketeering activity contained in 18 U.S.C. § 1961(1).[61] This means that the § 1030 offenses can be RICO predicates, as long as they were committed in pursuit of terrorism under 18 U.S.C. § 2332b.

2. Unauthorized Access to Stored Electronic Communications

Section 2701(a) of Title 18 of the U.S. Code makes it an offense either to:

1. intentionally access without authorization a facility through which an electronic communication is provided, or
2. intentionally exceed an authorization to access such a facility and thereby obtain, alter or prevent authorized access to a wire or electronic communication while it is in electronic storage.[62]

Section 2701(c) creates an exception to the liability established under § 2701(a) for access which is authorized by

1. the person or entity providing a wire or electronic communication service;
2. a user of that service; or
3. by 18 U.S.C. §§ 2703, 2704 or 2518.[63]

---

60. See 18 U.S.C. § 2332b(g)(5)(B) (2000). See also PATRIOT Act of 2001 § 808, Pub. L. No. 107-56, 115 Stat. 272. For the federal terrorism offenses, see 18 U.S.C. § 2332b(a) (2000).

61. See PATRIOT Act of 2001 § 813, Pub. L. No. 107-56, 115 Stat. 272 (18 U.S.C. § 1961(1) is amended to add "any act that is indictable under any provision listed in section 2332b(g)(5)(B)"). See also 18 U.S.C. § 2332b(g)(5)(B) (2000).

62. See, e.g., Sherman & Co. v. Salton Maxim Housewares, Inc., 94 F. Supp. 2d 817, 821 (E.D. Mich. 2000) ("Because section 2701 ... prohibits only unauthorized access and not the misappropriation or disclosure of information, there is no violation of section 2701 for a person with authorized access to the database no matter how malicious or larcenous his intended use of that access. Section 2701 outlaws illegal entry, not larceny"). See also U.S. v. Councilman, 373 F.3d 197 (1st Cir.), reh'g en banc granted, 2004 WL 2230823 (1st Cir. 2004).

63. See 18 U.S.C. § 2701(c) (2000).

Section 225(b) ["The Cyber Security Enhancement Act"] of the Homeland Security Act of 2002[64] modified the penalty provisions of § 2701. Under § 2701(b) as amended by the Act, if the offense is committed "for purposes of commercial advantage, malicious destruction or damage, or private commercial gain, or in furtherance of any criminal or tortious act in violation of the Constitution or laws of the United States or any State", the offender is subject to

1. a fine, imprisonment for not more than five years or both for a first offense and
2. a fine, imprisonment for not more than ten years or both for a subsequent offense.[65]

Section 2701(b) also provides that in "any other case," the penalties are

1. a fine, imprisonment for not more than one year or both for a first offense and
2. a fine, imprisonment for not more than five years or both for a subsequent offense.[66]

B. Cybercrimes Involving Improper Communications

1. Sending Obscene, Abusive or Harassing Communications

The Internet and other forms of online communication have been a boon to stalkers, as they make it easy for one bent on stalking someone to pursue his or her victim with a fair assurance of anonymity.[67] This anonymity can not only be unnerving to the victim, it also makes it difficult for law enforcement to identify and apprehend the perpetrator.[68] There is as yet no federal statute that is specifically directed at cyberstalkers,[69] but there are statutes that can be used to prosecute the sending of obscene, abusive or harassing communications.

Section 223(a) of Title 47 of the U.S. Code makes it an offense to use a telecommunications device in interstate or foreign communications to:

---

64. Pub. L. 107-296, 116 Stat. 2158 (2002).

65. 18 U.S.C.A. § 2701(b) (Supp. 2004).

66. See Id.

67. *See, e.g.,* U.S. Department of Justice, *1999 Report on Cyberstalking: A New Challenge for Law Enforcement and Industry, at* http://www.usdoj.gov/criminal/cybercrime/cyberstalking.htm [hereinafter *1999 Report on Cyberstalking*].

68. *See id.*

69. *See id.*

1. make, create solicit and initiate the transmission of "any comment, request, suggestion, proposal, image, or other communication which is obscene, or child pornography, with intent to annoy, abuse, threaten, or harass another person;"[70]
2. make, create solicit and initiate the transmission of "any comment, request, suggestion, proposal, image, or other communication which is obscene or child pornography, knowing that the recipient of the communication is under 18 years of age, regardless of whether the maker of such communication placed the call or initiated the communication;"[71]
3. make a telephone call or utilize a telecommunications device, "whether or not conversation or communication ensues, without disclosing his identity and with intent to annoy, abuse, threaten, or harass any person at the called number;"[72]
4. make or cause "the telephone of another repeatedly or continuously to ring, with intent to harass any person at the called number;"[73]
5. make repeated telephone calls or repeatedly initiate communication "with a telecommunications device, during which conversation or communication ensues, solely to harass any person at the called number or who receives the communication;"[74] or
6. knowingly permit any telecommunications facility under his or her control to be used to commit any of the previously-listed activities.[75]

The penalties for these offenses include fines, imprisonment for up to two years, or both.[76]

Section 223(b) of Title 47 of the U.S. Code makes it a federal crime for any person:

1. knowingly to use a telephone to make an obscene or indecent communication for commercial purposes or to allow a telephone facility under his or her control to be used for this purpose, or

---

70. 47 U.S.C.A. § 223(a)(1)(A) (Supp. 2004).
71. *Id.* § 223(a)(1)(B).
72. *Id.* § 223(a)(1)(C).
73. *Id.* § 223(a)(1)(D).
74. *Id.* § 223(a)(1)(E).
75. *Id.* § 223(a)(2).
76. *Id.* § 223(a).

2. knowingly to use a telephone to make an indecent communication for commercial purposes which is available to anyone under the age or eighteen or to allow a telephone facility under his or her control to be used for this purpose.[77]

The penalties for these offenses include fines, imprisonment or both.[78]

As section III(C)(2) of this chapter explains, the constitutionality of the provisions of 47 U.S.C. § 223 which target sending material to minors have been the subject of repeated constitutional challenges.

2. Online Stalking, Harassment and Threats

Section 875 of Title 18 of the U.S. Code makes it a federal crime to transmit any of the following in interstate or foreign commerce:

1. a communication containing a demand for a ransom for the release of any kidnaped person;
2. a communication with the intent to extort any money,
3. a communication threatening to injure a person; and
4. a communication that threatens damage to property.[79]

Section 875 has been used to prosecute individuals who send threatening communications via the Internet. In *U.S. v. Kammersell*,[80] for example, the Tenth Circuit held that the defendant's sending a threatening communication from his computer to the recipient's computer could be prosecuted under the statute even though the defendant and the recipient were located in the same state. The court found that the jurisdictional element of the statute was satisfied because the message was transmitted over interstate telephone lines and traveled through a server located outside the state.[81]

---

77. *Id.* § 223(b).

78. The basic penalty for using a telephone to make an obscene communication for commercial purposes is a fine and/or imprisonment for up to two years; the basic penalty for using a telephone to transmit an indecent communication to a minor is a fine and/or imprisonment for up to six months. *See id.* § 223(b)(1)-(2). The statute also permits the imposition of enhanced penalties for intentional violations. *See id.* § 223(b)(4)-(5).

79. 18 U.S.C. § 875 (2000).

80. 196 F.3d 1137 (10th Cir. 1999), *cert. denied*, 530 U.S. 1231 (2000).

81. *See id.* at 1138–39. *See also* U.S. v. Bonas, 344 F.3d 945 (9th Cir. 2003); U.S. v. Rose, 315 F.3d 956 (8th Cir. 2003). *See generally* U.S. v. Johnson, 221 F.3d 83 (2d Cir. 2000) (defendant's conviction upheld because evidence established that he transmitted a "true threat" in interstate or foreign commerce).

But § 875 cannot be applied in the absence of a "threat," which means it cannot be used against much of the conduct which falls into the category of stalking. The statute's limitations, especially with regard to online conduct, are illustrated by *U.S. v. Alkhabaz*.[82] In *Alkhabaz*, the Sixth Circuit upheld the district court's dismissal of charges that the defendant violated 18 U.S.C. § 875(c) because it found that he did not transmit a "credible threat" to his alleged victim.[83] The defendant, a student at the University of Michigan, had used e-mail to correspond with a friend, much of his part of the correspondence consisting of vivid descriptions of fantasized sexual violence against a woman whose name was the same as that of one of his classmates.[84] When the correspondence came to light, he was prosecuted under § 875 for sending "threats" via interstate commerce.[85] The district court dismissed the charge because it found that the e-mail correspondence did not constitute "true threats" and was, therefore, protected by the First Amendment.[86] The Sixth Circuit affirmed the dismissal because it agreed that the e-mail correspondence did not rise to the level of a "threat."[87]

---

82. 104 F.3d 1492 (6th Cir. 1997).
83. *See id.* at 1495–96.
84. *See id.* at 1498 (Krupansky, J., dissenting):
   By November 1994, Baker's sadistic stories attracted the attention of an individual who called himself "Arthur Gonda," a Usenet service subscriber residing in Ontario, Canada, who apparently shared similarly misdirected proclivities. Baker and Gonda subsequently exchanged at least 41 private computerized electronic mail … communications between November 29, 1994 and January 25, 1995. Concurrently, Baker continued to distribute violent sordid tales on the electronic bulletin board. On January 9, 1995, Baker brazenly disseminated publicly, via the electronic bulletin board, a depraved torture-and-snuff story in which the victim shared the name of a female classmate of Baker's referred to below as "Jane Doe".… This imprudent act triggered notification of the University of Michigan authorities by an alarmed citizen on January 18, 1995. On the following day, Baker admitted to a University of Michigan investigator that he had authored the story and published it on the Internet.
85. *See id.* at 1493.
86. *See id.*
87. *See id.* at 1497:
   Accordingly, to achieve the intent of Congress, we hold that, to constitute "a communication containing a threat" under Section 875(c), a communication must be such that a reasonable person (1) would take the statement as a serious expression of an intention to inflict bodily harm (the *mens rea*), and (2) would perceive such expression as being communicated to effect some change or achieve some goal through intimidation (the *actus reus*).…

There is, however, another federal statute that can be used against stalkers: 18 U.S.C. § 2261A makes it a federal crime to do either of two things:

1. to travel in interstate or foreign commerce within the jurisdiction of the United States with the intent to kill, injure, harass or intimidate another and thereby place that person in reasonable fear of death or serious bodily injury to themselves or to a family member; or

2. to use the mail or any facility of interstate or foreign commerce to engage in a course of conduct that places a person in reasonable fear of death or serious bodily injury to themselves or to a family member.[88]

Like 18 U.S.C. § 875, this statute is structured to encompass only conduct that places one in reasonable fear of death or bodily injury.

3. Spam

At the end of 2003, Congress adopted the "Controlling the Assault of Non-Solicited Pornography and Marketing Act" of 2003[89] which is popularly known as the CAN-SPAM Act and which went into effect on January 1, 2004.[90] While Congress identified the abuses associated with spam, it did

---

Applying our interpretation of the statute to the facts before us, we conclude that the communications between Baker and Gonda do not constitute "communications containing a threat" under Section 875(c). Even if a reasonable person would take the communications between Baker and Gonda as serious expressions of an intention to inflict bodily harm, no reasonable person would perceive such communications as being conveyed to effect some change or achieve some goal through intimidation. Quite the opposite, Baker and Gonda apparently sent e-mail messages to each other in an attempt to foster a friendship based on shared sexual fantasies.

88. See 18 U.S.C. § 2261A (2000).

89. Pub. L. No. 108-187, 117 Stat. 2699 (2003) (to be codified at 15 U.S.C. §§ 7701–13).

90. The legislation was predicated on certain factual findings:

1. Electronic mail has become an extremely important and popular means of communication, relied on by millions of Americans on a daily basis for personal and commercial purposes. Its low cost and global reach make it extremely convenient and efficient, and offer unique opportunities for the development and growth of frictionless commerce.

2. The convenience and efficiency of electronic mail are threatened by the extremely rapid growth in the volume of unsolicited commercial electronic mail. Unsolicited commercial electronic mail is currently estimated to account for over half of all electronic mail traffic, up from an estimated 7

not outlaw spam, as such. Businesses and marketers can now send unsolicited e-mail to anyone with an e-mail address as long as they have iden-

---

percent in 2001, and the volume continues to rise. Most of these messages are fraudulent or deceptive in one or more respects.

3. The receipt of unsolicited commercial electronic mail may result in costs to recipients who cannot refuse to accept such mail and who incur costs for the storage of such mail, or for the time spent accessing, reviewing, and discarding such mail, or for both.

4. The receipt of a large number of unwanted messages also decreases the convenience of electronic mail and creates a risk that wanted electronic mail messages, both commercial and noncommercial, will be lost, overlooked, or discarded amidst the larger volume of unwanted messages, thus reducing the reliability and usefulness of electronic mail to the recipient.

5. Some commercial electronic mail contains material that many recipients may consider vulgar or pornographic in nature.

6. The growth in unsolicited commercial electronic mail imposes significant monetary costs on providers of Internet access services, businesses, and educational and nonprofit institutions that carry and receive such mail, as there is a finite volume of mail that such providers, businesses, and institutions can handle without further investment in infrastructure.

7. Many senders of unsolicited commercial electronic mail purposefully disguise the source of such mail.

8. Many senders of unsolicited commercial electronic mail purposefully include misleading information in the messages' subject lines in order to induce the recipients to view the messages.

9. While some senders of commercial electronic mail messages provide simple and reliable ways for recipients to reject (or "opt-out" of) receipt of commercial electronic mail from such senders in the future, other senders provide no such "opt-out" mechanism, or refuse to honor the requests of recipients not to receive electronic mail from such senders in the future, or both.

10. Many senders of bulk unsolicited commercial electronic mail use computer programs to gather large numbers of electronic mail addresses on an automated basis from Internet websites or online services where users must post their addresses in order to make full use of the website or service.

11. Many States have enacted legislation intended to regulate or reduce unsolicited commercial electronic mail, but these statutes impose different standards and requirements. As a result, they do not appear to have been successful in addressing the problems associated with unsolicited commercial electronic mail, in part because, since an electronic mail address does not specify a geographic location, it can be extremely difficult for law-abiding businesses to know with which of these disparate statutes they are required to comply.

15 U.S.C.A. § 7701 (Supp. 2004).

tified themselves clearly, do not use fraudulent headers and honor consumer requests to cease sending them unsolicited commercial e-mail.[91] Under the Act, junk e-mail is treated like junk postal mail, with non-fraudulent e-mail legalized until the recipient chooses to unsubscribe.[92]

Congress responded to the inconsistencies in state spam statutes by imposing certain general requirements on "commercial electronic mail messages."[93] The CAN-SPAM Act defines a "commercial electronic mail message" as "any electronic mail message the primary purpose of which is the commercial advertisement or promotion of a commercial product or service (including content on an Internet website operated for a commercial purpose)."[94] The term does not include "a transactional or relationship message, which is defined as "an electronic mail message the primary purpose of which" is:

> (i) to facilitate, complete, or confirm a commercial transaction that the recipient has previously agreed to enter into with the sender;
> (ii) to provide warranty information, product recall information, or safety or security information with respect to a commercial product or service used or purchased by the recipient;
> (iii) to provide—
>> (I) notification concerning a change in the terms or features of;
>> (II) notification of a change in the recipient's standing or status with respect to; or
>> (III) at regular periodic intervals, account balance information or other type of account statement with respect to a subscription, membership, account, loan, or comparable ongoing commercial relationship involving the ongoing purchase or use by the recipient of products or services offered by the sender;
> (iv) to provide information directly related to an employment relationship or related benefit plan in which the recipient is currently involved, participating, or enrolled; or

---

91. See id. § 7704(a).
92. See Jacquelyn Trussell, *Is the CAN-SPAM Act the Answer to the Growing Problem of Spam?,* 16 Loy. CONSUMER L. REV. 175, 181 (2004).
93. See 15 U.S.C.A. § 7702(2) (Supp. 2004).
94. *Id.*

(v) to deliver goods or services, including product updates or up-grades, that the recipient is entitled to receive under the terms of a transaction that the recipient has previously agreed to enter into with the sender.[95]

Among other things, unsolicited e-mails must be identified as solicitations or advertisements, and those that contain sexually explicit material must include labels indicating the nature of their contents.[96] The failure to include warning labels on spam containing sexually explicit material is an offense punishable by a fine and/or imprisonment for up to five years.[97] The requirement of labeling sexually explicit e-mails does not apply if the recipient has given "prior affirmative consent" to receiving the message.[98]

The CAN-SPAM Act added several provisions to the U.S. Code, including a new section to title 18. The new § 1037(a) makes it a federal crime knowingly to do any of the following:

(1) access a protected computer without authorization and intentionally initiate the transmission of multiple commercial electronic mail messages from or through such computer,
(2) use a protected computer to relay or retransmit multiple commercial electronic mail messages with the intent to deceive or mislead recipients or any Internet access service as to the origin of such messages,
(3) materially falsify header information in multiple commercial electronic mail messages and intentionally initiate the transmission of such messages,
(4) register, using information that materially falsifies the identity of the actual registrant, for five or more electronic mail accounts or online user accounts or two or more domain names, and intentionally initiate the transmission of multiple commercial electronic mail messages from any combination of such accounts or domain names, or
(5) falsely represent oneself to be the registrant or the legitimate successor in interest to the registrant of 5 or more Internet Proto-

---

95. *Id.* § 7702(17).
96. *See id.* § 7704.
97. *See id.* § 7704(d).
98. *See id.* § 7704(d)(2). For the definition of "affirmative consent," *see id.* § 7702(1).

col addresses, and intentionally initiate the transmission of multiple commercial electronic mail messages from such addresses, or conspire to do so.[99]

The term "protected computer" has the same meaning as in 18 U.S. Code § 1030(e)(2)(B), and the term loss has the same meaning as in 18 U.S. Code § 1030(e).[100] As used in sections (a)(3) & (a)(4), the term "materially" denotes header information or registration information that is

> altered or concealed in a manner that would impair the ability of a recipient of the message, an Internet access service processing the message on behalf of a recipient, a person alleging a violation of this section, or a law enforcement agency to identify, locate, or respond to a person who initiated the electronic mail message or to investigate the alleged violation.[101]

"Multiple" means "more than 100 electronic mail messages during a 24-hour period, more than 1,000 electronic mail messages during a 30-day period, or more than 10,000 electronic mail messages during a 1-year period."[102]

The CAN-SPAM Act specifies criminal penalties for acts violating section 1037(a). A violator is subject to a fine and/or imprisonment for up to five years if

1. the offense was committed in furtherance of a felony under federal or state law, or
2. the defendant had previously been convicted under section 1037 or under 1030 for conduct involving the transmission of multiple commercial e-mail messages or for unauthorized access to a computer system.[103]

A violator is subject to a fine and/or imprisonment for up to three years if

1. the offense of conviction was a violation of section 1037(a)(1);

---

99. 18 U.S.C.A. § 1037(a) (Supp. 2004). For the definition of "header information" *see* 15 U.S.C.A. § 7702(8) (Supp. 2004).

100. *See* Pub. L. 108-187 § 3, 117 Stat. 2703 (2003); 18 U.S.C.A. § 1037(d)(1) (Supp. 2004).

101. 18 U.S.C.A. § 1037(d)(2) (Supp. 2004).

102. *Id.* § 1037(d)(3). Other terms used in this provision are defined in section 3 of the CAN-SPAM Act. *See id.* § 1037(d)(4).

103. *See id.* § 1037(b)(1).

2. the offense was a violation of section 1037(a)(4) that involved "20 or more falsified electronic mail or online user account registrations, or 10 or more falsified domain name registrations;"
3. the volume of e-mail messages transmitted in furtherance of the offense "exceeded 2,500 during any 24-hour period, 25,000 during any 30-day period, or 250,000 during any 1-year period;"
4. the offense caused loss to one or more persons aggregating $5,000 or more in value during any 1-year period;
5. as a result of the offense any individual involved in its commission "obtained anything of value aggregating $5,000 or more during any 1-year period; or
6. the offense was undertaken by the defendant in concert with three or more other persons with respect to whom the defendant occupied a position of organizer or leader.[104]

Violators are subject to a fine and/or imprisonment for up to one year for any offense not falling within the categories set out above.[105]

The statute also provides for the forfeiture of

1. any property that constitutes or is traceable to the gross proceeds obtained from the offense of conviction and/or
2. any equipment, software, or other technology used or intended to be used to commit or to facilitate the commission of the offense.[106]

The procedures used to initiate such a criminal forfeiture are those specified in 21 U.S.C. § 853 (2000) and in Fed. R. Crim. Pro. 32.2.[107]

The first prosecution under the CAN-SPAM Act was brought in the Eastern District of Michigan in April of 2004.[108] The four defendants were charged with intentionally and materially falsifying "header information in multiple commercial electronic mail messages" and "intentionally initiat[ing] the transmission of such messages through protected computers" for the purpose of advertising fraudulent diet patches.[109] The affidavit

---

104. *Id.* § 1037(b)(2).
105. *See id.* § 1037(b)(3).
106. *See id.* § 1037(c)(1).
107. *See id.* § 1037(c)(2).
108. *See* United States v. Lin, No. 04-80383, (E.D. Mich. Apr. 23, 2004) (criminal complaint), *available at* http://www.ftc.gov/os/2004/04/040429phhoenixavatarcriminal-cmplt.pdf.
109. *Id.*

accompanying the complaint used to initiate the prosecution outlines the conduct alleged to constitute the offense in detail.[110]

The provisions of the CAN-SPAM Act do not pre-empt the application of any federal criminal provision, including prohibitions on obscenity and the sexual exploitation of children.[111]

C. Cybercrimes Involving Minors

1. Sexual Exploitation of Children

In 1996, Congress, concerned about the increased proliferation of child pornography, adopted the Child Pornography Protection Act ["CPPA"], which was codified as 18 U.S.C. §§ 2251–60 (2000). As one source explained, much of the impetus for the CPPA came from the use of computer technology:

> Advances in computer and computer imaging technology have only exacerbated the problem. With these technological advances, child pornographers can now create child pornography without using "real" children. The computer-generated images pornographers can create are virtually indistinguishable from child pornography using real children. In addition to revolutionizing the production of child pornography, technological changes facilitated its distribution. As of December 1995, nearly one million sexually explicit pictures of children were on the Internet at any given time. Of these pictures, over eight hundred were graphic depictions of "adults or teenagers engaged in sexual activity with children between eight and ten years of age."[112]

---

110. *See id.*

111. *See* 15 U.S.C.A. § 7707(a)(1) (Supp. 2004).

112. Michael J. Eng, Note, *Free Speech Coalition v. Reno: Has the Ninth Circuit Given Child Pornographers a New Tool To Exploit Children?*, 35 U.S.F. L. Rev. 109, 109–10 (2000) (notes omitted) (quoting Jennifer Stewart, Comment, *If This Is The Global Community, We Must Be on the Bad Side of Town: International Policing of Child Pornography on the Internet*, 20 Hous. J. Int'l L. 205, 207 (1997)) [hereinafter Eng, *Free Speech Coalition v. Reno*].

Congress first outlawed child pornography, which has been held to be outside the protections of the First Amendment,[113] in 1977.[114] The 1977 enactment focused on the use of children—"real" minors—in the production of child pornography.[115]

The development of computer technology allowed the creation of "virtual" child pornography, something the drafters of the 1977 legislation had not taken into consideration:

[C]hild pornographers can now create ... [c]omputer-generated child pornography [which] is divided into two categories—virtual and computer-altered child pornography. Virtual child pornography does not depict a real or identifiable child. Through a technique called "morphing," the image of a Playboy Bunny or Penthouse Pet can be scanned into a computer and transformed through animation techniques into a sexually explicit image of a child. Although the morphed image is "virtual," it is practically indistinguishable from an "unretouched" photographic image of a real child in a sexually explicit pose. By contrast, computer-altered child pornography depicts the image of a real or identifiable child. A photograph of an innocent child can be scanned into the computer, and with the "cut and paste" feature, the child's head can be superimposed onto the body of someone who is engaged in sexually explicit activity. Furthermore, with image-altering software and computer hardware, that same photograph of the innocent child can be altered in such a manner as to remove the child's clothing and to arrange the child into "sexual positions involving children, adults and even animals."[116]

---

113. *See* Osborne v. Ohio, 495 U.S. 103 (1990); New York v. Ferber, 458 U.S. 747 (1982). In *Ferber*, the Supreme Court concluded that child pornography can be outlawed because of the compelling interest in protecting children, who are used in its production, and because child pornography is "intrinsically related" to the sexual abuse of children. *See id.* at 758–59. In *Osborne*, it seemed to go further, holding that child pornography can be outlawed, among other things, because it represents a permanent record of a child's sexual abuse and because pedophiles can use it in an attempt to lure other children into sexual activity. *See* 495 U.S. at 111.

114. *See* The Protection of Children Against Sexual Exploitation Act of 1977, Pub. L. 95-225, § 2(a), 92 Stat. 7 (1978) (codified as amended at 18 U.S.C. §§ 2251–53 (2000)).

115. *See, e.g.,* Eng, *Free Speech Coalition v. Reno, supra* note 112, at 111–12.

116. *Id.* (notes omitted).

Further advances in computer technology allow the creation of computer-generated Images (CGI), which do not in any way involve the use of "real" persons.[117]

As noted above, the CPPA was adopted to bring federal legislation outlawing child pornography up to date, to allow it to deal with the enforcement problems that had arisen due to the emergence of computer-generated child pornography.[118] To this end, it introduced a new definition of child pornography: Section 2256(8) of Title 18 defined "child pornography" as "any visual depiction, including any photograph, film, video, picture, or computer or computer-generated image or picture ... of sexually explicit conduct" in which:

1. the production of the visual depiction involved the use of a minor engaging in sexually explicit conduct;
2. the visual depiction is or appears to be of a minor engaging in sexually explicit conduct;
3. the visual depiction was created, adapted or modified to appear that an identifiable minor is engaging in sexually explicit conduct; or
4. the visual depiction is advertised, promoted, presented, described or distributed in a way that gives the impression it contains a visual depiction of a minor engaging in sexually explicit conduct.[119]

The CPPA also created a number of offenses, the first of which was codified as 18 U.S.C. § 2251 (2000). Section 2251 prohibits:

1. the persuasion, enticement, inducement, or transportation of minors with the intent that the minor engage in sexually explicit conduct for the purpose of producing any visual depiction of such conduct if such materials will be transported in interstate or foreign commerce;
2. a parent or anyone in control of a minor from permitting a minor to engage in sexually explicit conduct, for the purpose of producing any visual depiction of such conduct if the parent knows that

---

117. *See, e.g.,* Susan S. Kreston, *Defeating the Virtual Defense in Child Pornography Prosecutions,* 4 J. High. Tech. L. 49 (2004).

118. *See, e.g.,* Eng, *Free Speech Coalition v. Reno, supra* note 112, at 112. Since computer-generated child pornography need not involve the participation of "real" children, it fell outside the compass of the 1977 legislation which made the use of actual minors a requisite for imposing criminal liability. *See id.*

119. *18 U.S.C. § 2256(8) (2000). See* Ashcroft v. Free Speech Coalition, 535 U.S. 234, 241 (2002).

such materials will be transported in interstate or foreign commerce;

3. employing using, persuading and/or enticing a minor to engage in "any sexually explicit conduct" outside the United States "for the purpose of producing any visual depiction of such conduct;" and

4. printing or publishing advertisements for the sexual exploitation of children.

The statute also makes it a federal crime to conspire or attempt to commit any of these crimes.[120] Substantive violations of the statute, along with conspiring and/or attempting to commit a substantive violation, are punishable by a fine, imprisonment for not less than fifteen or more than thirty years, a fine or both a fine and imprisonment.[121] If the offender has a prior conviction, under either state or federal law, for sexually exploiting children, the allowable period of imprisonment rises to not less than twenty-five or more than fifty years; if the offender has two or more prior convictions, again under state or federal law, the allowable period of imprisonment rises to not less than thirty-five years or more than life.[122] If someone causes the death of another person while engaging in conduct that constitutes an offense under the statute, he or she is to be punished by death or imprisonment for "any term of years or for life."[123]

Another section of the CPPA—codified at 18 U.S.C. § 2252 (2000)—prohibits:

1. knowingly transporting in interstate commerce, by any means, including by computer or mail, visual depictions of minors engaged in sexually explicit conduct;[124]

2. knowingly receiving or distributing visual depictions of minors engaged in sexually explicit conduct that have been mailed or shipped in interstate commerce;[125]

3. selling or possessing such depictions with intent to sell them;[126] and

4. possessing books, magazines, periodicals, films and other matter which contain such depictions.[127]

---

120. *See* 18 U.S.C. § 2251(e) (2000).
121. *See id.*
122. *See id.*
123. *See id.*
124. *See id.* § 2252(a)(1).
125. *See id.* § 2252(a)(2).
126. *See id.* § 2252(a)(3).
127. *See id.* § 2252(a)(4).

The statute makes an offense to conspire or attempt to violate any of these prohibitions.[128] Conspiring to commit, attempting to commit or committing the first three substantive offenses is punishable by a fine, imprisonment for not less than five years or more than twenty years or both, unless the person has a prior conviction, under state or federal law, for the sexual exploitation or abuse of children; if the person has such a conviction, the period of allowable imprisonment rises to not less than fifteen years or more than forty years.[129] Conspiring to commit, attempting to commit or committing the fourth offense is punishable by a fine, imprisonment for not more than ten years or both, unless the person has a prior conviction, under state or federal law, for the sexual exploitation or abuse of children; if the person has such a conviction, the period of allowable imprisonment rises to not less than ten years nor more than twenty years.[130]

Section 2252 creates an affirmative defense for the fourth offense — possessing visual depictions of minors engaged in sexually explicit conduct.[131] To establish this defense, an accused must show that he or she possessed less than three matters containing depictions prohibited by the statute and either took reasonable steps to destroy those depictions or reported the matter to a law enforcement agency and gave the agency access to the depictions.[132]

Another provision of the CPPA, codified at 18 U.S.C. § 2252A (2000), makes it an offense to do any of the following:

1. knowingly mail, transport or ship child pornography in interstate or foreign commerce by any means, including by computer;
2. knowingly receive or distribute child pornography or any material that contains child pornography and that has been mailed, transported or shipped in interstate or foreign commerce by any means, including by computer;
3. knowingly reproduce child pornography for distribution through the mails or in interstate or foreign commerce by any means, including by computer;
4. knowingly sell or possess with the intent to sell child pornography;

---

128. *See id.* § 2252(a)(5).
129. *See id.* § 2252(b)(1).
130. *See id.* § 2252(b)(2).
131. *See id.* § 2252(c).
132. *See id.*

5. knowingly possess "any book, magazine, periodical, film, videotape, computer disk, or any other material that contains an image of child pornography"; and
6. knowingly distributes, offers or sends a visual depiction of a minor engaging in sexually explicit conduct to a minor if the depiction was shipped in or otherwise implicated interstate or foreign commerce.[133]

The statute also makes it a crime either to conspire or to attempt to commit any of these offenses.[134]

Section 2252A also creates an affirmative defense to each of the violations it defines. The defense to a charge of committing offenses in the first five categories outlined above requires a defendant to establish:

1. that each of the "actual" person or persons featured in the alleged child pornography was an adult at the time the material was produced or
2. that the material was not produced using any actual minor(s).[135]

The statute imposes certain procedural requirements for invoking this defense.[136] It also creates another affirmative defense to a charge of committing the fifth offense it defines, e.g., knowingly possessing child pornography.[137] To qualify for this defense, a defendant must establish that he or she:

1. possessed less than three images of child pornography and
2. "promptly and in good faith, and without retaining or allowing any person, other than a law enforcement agency, to access" any of those items "took reasonable steps to destroy each such image" or "reported the matter to a law enforcement agency and afforded that agency access to each such image."[138]

One who commits, conspires to commit or attempts to commit the offenses in the first four and sixth categories outlined above is to be fined, imprisoned for not less than five years or more than twenty years or both,

---

133. *Id.* § 2252A(a).
134. *See id.* § 2252A(b).
135. *See id.* § 2252A(c).
136. *See id.*
137. *See id.* § 2252A(d).
138. *Id.*

but if the person has a prior conviction for child pornography or other offenses involving the abuse of children, he or she is to be fined and imprisoned for not less than fifteen years nor more than forty years.[139] One who commits, conspires to commit or attempts to commit the remaining offense defined by 18 U.S.C. §2252A(a), e.g., possessing child pornography, is to be fined, imprisoned for not more than ten years or both, but if the person has a prior conviction for child pornography or other offenses involving the abuse of children, he or she is to be fined and imprisoned for not less than ten years nor more than twenty years.[140]

These provisions criminalizing child pornography are a relatively recent addition to the list of federal crimes: In 1982, the Supreme Court held that pornography portraying minors engaging in sexually explicit activity can be criminalized even though it is not obscene under the standard the Court enunciated in *Miller v. California*, 413 U.S. 15 (1973).[141] The *Ferber* Court held that child pornography can be criminalized without violating the First Amendment because of the harms its production inflicts upon children; the Court emphasized the physical and emotional abuse inflicted upon these children and the fact that the pornography itself inflicts further suffering, as their victimization is viewed and reviewed for years.[142]

In 2001, a coalition of free speech advocates challenged the then-applicable provisions of the federal child pornography statutes; they argued that because no "real" children are harmed in the creation of "virtual" child pornography, it does not fall within the rationale of *Ferber* and is therefore a category of speech that cannot constitutionally be criminalized.[143] Before the Supreme Court, the Department of Justice argued that virtual child pornography can be criminalized because (a) pedophiles use it to seduce children into sexual acts and (b) it stimulates pedophiles into molesting children.[144] The Supreme Court rejected these arguments and held that the prohibition of virtual child pornography violated the First Amendment, so the statutory provisions at issue were unconstitutional and unenforceable.[145]

Congress acted quickly to restore the ban: On April 30, 2003, the President signed the Prosecutorial Remedies and Other Tools to End the Ex-

---

139. *See id.* §2252A(b)(1).
140. *See id.* §2252A(b)(2).
141. *See* New York v. Ferber, 458 U.S. 747, 764 (1982).
142. *See id.*
143. *See* Ashcroft v. Free Speech Coalition, 535 U.S. 234, 239–44 (2002).
144. *See id.* at 249–55.
145. *See id.* at 252–57.

ploitation of Children Today Act of 2003[146] [the "PROTECT Act"], which reinstituted the criminalization of virtual child pornography. The revised statutes make it a crime to possess, manufacture or distribute pornography containing visual depictions of:

1. a real child engaging in sexual acts or
2. "a digital image, computer image, or computer-generated image that is, or is indistinguishable from, that of a minor engaged in sexually explicit conduct."[147]

The Protect Act also created an entirely new offense: Producing, receiving, possessing or manufacturing obscene child pornography.[148] Obscene child pornography is defined as "a visual depiction of any kind, including a drawing, cartoon, sculpture, or painting," that depicts:

1. a minor engaging in sexually explicit conduct and is obscene under the *Miller* standard; or
2. "an image that is, or appears to be, of a minor engaging in graphic bestiality, sadistic or masochistic abuse, or sexual intercourse, including genital-genital, oral-genital, anal-genital, or oral-anal, whether between persons of the same or opposite sex;" *and* lacks serious literary, artistic, political, or scientific value.[149]

Many believe the child pornography provisions of the PROTECT Act are unconstitutional under the *Ashcroft* standard[150] because they are not based on evidence which establishes the need to criminalize pornography the creation of which does not involve the infliction of harm to "real" children.[151]

---

146. Pub. L. No. 108-21, 117 Stat. 650 (2003).

147. 18 U.S.C.A. § 2256(8)(B) (Supp. 2004) (as amended). *See, e.g.,* U.S. v. Taitano, 2004 WL 2126853 *1 (D. N. 2004):

Under the PROTECT Act it has been illegal since April 30, 2003, (1) to show minor children engaged in sexually explicit conduct, or (2) to show digital or computer-generated images of minor children that are indistinguishable from minor children engaged in sexually explicit conduct, or (3) to show a visual depiction that has been created, adapted, or modified to resemble an identifiable minor child engaging in sexually explicit conduct.

148. *See* 18 U.S.C.A. § 1466A (Supp. 2004).

149. *Id.*

150. See infra text accompanying notes 143–145.

151. When the PROTECT Act was introduced, the American Civil Liberties Union argued that it was unconstitutional under *Ashcroft* because it

(1) "[I]mposes criminal liability on people who possess or produce material protected by the First Amendment;" (2) "[C]hills protected speech because it

This was, after all, the basis of the Court's holding in the *Ashcroft* case. Others raise additional concerns, one being that the provisions of the PROTECT Act substantially relieves the government of its burden to prove the federal child pornography offenses beyond a reasonable doubt.[152] The above-quoted provision criminalizing pornography that features digital images which are "indistinguishable from" a minor essentially shifts the burden to the defendant; that is, the government shows that the images are of sufficient quality to be indistinguishable from images of a real child. At this point, the only way the defense can avoid conviction is either:

1. to show that the images are distinguishable from those of a real child (which is likely to become increasingly difficult as technology advances) or
2. to show that the images are actually of a real child.[153]

The latter is likely to be quite beyond the capacity of those who are prosecuted for merely possessing child pornography; and, indeed, another reason why the *Ashcroft* Court struck down the earlier provisions was they had a similar effect. That is, they created a "real child" affirmative defense and, as the Court noted, when "the defendant is not the producer of the work, he may have no way of establishing the identity, or even the existence, of the actors."[154]

2. Sending Offensive Material to Minors

Two provisions of the Communications Decency Act of 1996[155] ["CDA"] attempt to protect minors from "indecent" material being transmitted on-

places the burden on the defendant to prove the material was produced using an adult or was 'virtually' created;" (3) Includes a "pandering" provision which sweeps in non-commercial speech and includes the ambiguous term "purported material;"(4) Restricts the defendant from providing a defense, in that it frees the government from the "burden" of producing the actual minor allegedly involved in the material, and thus "violates the right to confront one's accusers;" and (5) Contains an extraterritorial jurisdiction provision that may be used by other countries to restrict speech in the United States.
Susan Hanley Kosse, *Try, Try Again: Will Congress Ever Get It Right? A Summary Of Internet Pornography Laws Protecting Children And Possible Solutions*, 38 U. RICH. L. REV. 721, 766–67 (2004)

152. See John P. Feldmeier, *Close Enough for Government Work: An Examination of Congressional Efforts to Reduce the Government's Burden of Proof in Child Pornography Cases*, 30 N. KY. L. REV. 205 (2003).

153. *See id.*

154. Ashcroft v. Free Speech Coalition, 535 U.S. 234, 255 (2002).

155. Pub. L. No. 104-104, § 502, 110 Stat. 133 (codified at 47 U.S.C. § 223).

line:[156] Section 223(a)(1)(B)(ii) of Title 47 of the U.S. Code makes it an offense for someone "knowingly" to transmit "obscene or indecent" messages to minors. Section 223(d) of Title 47 of the U.S. Code makes it an offense to use interstate or foreign commerce to send or display offensive material to persons under 18.

In *Reno v. American Civil Liberties Union,*[157] the Supreme Court invalidated portions of these statutes on First Amendment grounds. The Court held that these provisions were facially over broad in violation of the First Amendment.[158] It found that in trying to prevent minors from being exposed to potentially harmful speech, the provisions effectively suppressed speech adults have a constitutional right to receive from and communicate to each other.[159] Finally, the Court determined that there had not been a showing that a less restrictive alternative would not be at least as effective in achieving the purposes of the statute.[160]

In response to the *Reno* decision, Congress passed the Child Online Protection Act[161] ["COPA"], in 1998. COPA imposes criminal penalties of a $50,000 fine and six months in prison for knowingly posting, for "commercial purposes," of online content that is "harmful to minors."[162] COPA defines "[h]armful to minors" as "any communication, picture, image,

---

156. *See* Reno v. American Civil Liberties Union, 521 U.S. 844, 858–59 (1997).
157. 521 U.S. 844 (1997).
158. *See id.* at 869–74.
159. *See id.* at 874:
   Given the vague contours of the coverage of the statute, it unquestionably silences some speakers whose messages would be entitled to constitutional protection. That danger provides further reason for insisting that the statute not be overly broad. The CDA's burden on protected speech cannot be justified if it could be avoided by a more carefully drafted statute.
160. *See id.* at 878–79:
   The breadth of the CDA's coverage is wholly unprecedented.... [T]he scope of the CDA is not limited to commercial speech or commercial entities. Its open-ended prohibitions embrace all nonprofit entities and individuals posting indecent messages or displaying them on their own computers in the presence of minors. The general, undefined terms "indecent" and "patently offensive" cover large amounts of nonpornographic material with serious educational or other value. Moreover, the "community standards" criterion as applied to the Internet means that any communication available to a nationwide audience will be judged by the standards of the community most likely to be offended by the message....
161. Pub. L. 105-277, 112 Stat. 2681 (1998) (codified as 47 U.S.C. § 231).
162. 47 U.S.C. § 231(a)(1) (2000).

graphic image file, article, recording, writing, or other matter of any kind that is obscene" or that

1. the "average person, applying contemporary community standards, would find ... is designed to appeal to ... the prurient interest"
2. "depicts, describes, or represents, in a manner patently offensive with respect to minors, an actual or simulated sexual act or sexual contact, an actual or simulated normal or perverted sexual act, or a lewd exhibition of the genitals or post-pubescent female breast;" and
3. "taken as a whole, lacks serious literary, artistic, political, or scientific value for minors."[163]

"Minors" are defined as "any person under 17 years of age."[164] Under COPA, one acts for "commercial purposes only if such person is engaged in the business of making such communications."[165] "Engaged in the business" of making such communications means that the person "devotes time, attention, or labor to such activities, as a regular course of such person's trade or business, with the objective of earning a profit as a result of such activities."[166] While COPA "labels all speech that falls within these definitions as criminal speech,"[167] it provides an affirmative defense to those who employ specified means to prevent minors from gaining access to the prohibited materials on their websites. One can escape liability by showing that he has restricted minors' access to harmful material

1. by requiring use of a credit card, debit account, adult access code, or adult personal identification number;
2. by accepting a digital certificate that verifies age; or
3. by "any other reasonable measures that are feasible under available technology."[168]

COPA was the object of a challenge that took it through several lower courts and twice to the Supreme Court.[169] In *Ashcroft v. American Civil Liberties Union*,[170] the Supreme Court upheld the Third Circuit's determina-

163. *Id.* § 231(e)(6).
164. *Id.* § 231(e)(7).
165. Id. § 231(e)(2)(A).
166. *Id.* § 231(e)(2)(B).
167. Ashcroft v. American Civil Liberties Union, 124 S. Ct. 2783, 2789 (2004).
168. 47 U.S.C. § 231(c)(1) (2000).
169. *See* Ashcroft, 124 S. Ct. at 2790.
170. 124 S. Ct. 2783 (2004).

tion that enforcement of COPA should be enjoined because it "likely" violated the First Amendment.[171] The Court agreed with those challenging COPA that less restrictive alternatives—such as filtering software—might be even more effective than the statute in protecting children from harmful content.[172] The Court therefore affirmed the Third Circuit's upholding an injunction entered by the district court.[173]

3. Transmitting Information about a Minor

Section 2425 of Title 18 of the U.S. Code makes it a federal crime for someone "using the mail or any facility or means of interstate or foreign commerce, or within the special maritime and territorial jurisdiction of the United States" to "knowingly" initiate the transmission of the name, address, telephone number, social security number, or electronic mail address of one whom he or she knows to be under sixteen years of age "with the intent to entice, encourage, offer, or solicit any person to engage in any sexual activity for which any person can be charged with a criminal offense."[174]

The statute criminalizes attempts to violate its provisions,[175] and 18 U.S.C. § 371 can be used to charge a conspiracy to violate § 2425.[176] A violation of 18 U.S.C. § 2425 is punishable by a fine, imprisonment for not more than five years or both.[177]

D. Cybercrimes Involving Fraud and Other Traditional Misconduct

1. Mail and Wire Fraud

Although they are not cybercrime-specific statutes, both mail fraud and wire fraud can be used to prosecute those who use computers and the Internet to commit fraud.[178]

---

171. *See id.* at 2795.

172. *See id.*

173. *See id.*

174. 18 U.S.C. § 2425 (2000).

175. *See id.*

176. *See, e.g.,* U.S. v. Giordano, 324 F. Supp. 2d 349 (D. Conn. 2003).

177. *See* 18 U.S.C. § 2425 (2000). *See, e.g.,* U.S. v. Taylor, 338 F.3d 1280 (11th Cir. 2003).

178. As section III(A)(1) of this chapter explains, computer-assisted fraud can also be prosecuted under 18 U.S.C. § 1030.

The mail fraud and wire fraud statutes differ only in terms of the predicate that confers federal jurisdiction to prosecute what is, in effect, a simple fraud offense: Section 1341 of Title 18 makes it an offense for anyone who, "having devised or intending to devise any scheme or artifice to defraud, or for obtaining money or property by means of false or fraudulent pretenses" to use the U.S. mails or "any private or commercial interstate carrier" (such as Federal Express) "for the purpose of executing such scheme or artifice or attempting so to do."[179] Section 1343 of the title makes it an offense for anyone who,

> having devised or intending to devise any scheme or artifice to defraud, or for obtaining money or property by means of false or fraudulent pretenses, representations, or promises, transmits or causes to be transmitted by means of wire, radio, or television communication in interstate or foreign commerce, any writings, signs, signals, pictures, or sounds for the purpose of executing such scheme or artifice [to defraud].[180]

Because of the similarity of the language employed in the two statutes, courts have held that they are "*in pari materia* and are, therefore" to be construed in a similar fashion.[181]

Both offenses consist of two elements. The elements of mail fraud are:

1. that the defendant devised or intended to devise a scheme to defraud; and
2. that the mails were used for the purpose of executing the scheme to defraud.[182]

The elements of wire fraud are:

1. that the defendant intentionally participated in a scheme to defraud or for obtaining money or property by means of false or fraudulent pretenses; and
2. that wire transmissions were used for the purpose of executing the scheme to defraud.[183]

---

179. 18 U.S.C. § 1341 (2000).
180. Id. § 1343.
181. *See, e.g.,* U.S. v. Tarnopol, 561 F.2d 466, 475 (3d Cir. 1977).
182. *See, e.g.,* Carter v. U.S., 530 U.S. 255, 261 (2000).
183. *See, e.g.,* U.S. v. Autuori, 212 F.3d 105, 115 (2d Cir. 2000); U.S. v. deVegter, 198 F.3d 1324, 1328 n.4 (11th Cir. 1999), *cert. denied,* 530 U.S. 1264 (2000).

Wire fraud may seem the more obvious choice for prosecuting cyber-crimes and, indeed, has been successfully used for this purpose.[184] In *U.S. v. Schreier*,[185] for example, the Tenth Circuit upheld the defendants' convictions for wire fraud because it found they had acquired property belonging to American Airlines by accessing the airline's computer reservation system and manipulating its frequent flyer program, replacing names of actual passengers who made particular flights with that of a fictitious person whom they enrolled as a member of the frequent flyer program.[186] The defendants thereby caused American Airlines to issue coupons that could be used to obtain tickets for American Airlines flights and, as the court noted, "created liability for the airline and obtained property for themselves."[187]

Wire fraud and mail fraud charges can, however, work in tandem in the cybercrime context. Assume, for example, that a perpetrator is using an online auction to commit fraud by selling products he falsely represents as being antiques.[188] The offender has clearly devised a scheme to defraud those to whom he sells his false antiques. The remaining element to charge mail fraud or wire fraud is, as noted earlier, the execution or attempted execution of the scheme to defraud by using the mails or the wires. This hypothetical perpetrator can be charged with wire fraud based on his use of the Internet to execute the fraud, e.g., to access the online auction site where he advertises his merchandise and arranges sales with the victims of his fraud. And since he is unlikely to be in a position to accept pay-

---

184. *But see* U.S. v. Czubinski, 106 F.3d 1069, 1072–74 (1st Cir. 1997) (court reversed defendant's wire fraud conviction because it found that his unauthorized browsing of confidential taxpayer information did not defraud Internal Revenue Service of its property within the meaning of the wire fraud statute; the court found that the government failed to prove beyond a reasonable doubt that the defendant intended to carry out a scheme to defraud the Internal Revenue Service by depriving it of its property interest in intangible information).

185. 908 F.2d 645, 646 (10th Cir. 1990), *cert. denied*, 498 U.S. 1069 (1991).

186. *See id.* at 646–47.

187. *See id.* at 647–48. The court found it irrelevant that the scheme involved defrauding the airline out of intangible property: "We need not pursue a metaphysical argument regarding whether the 'property' existed as such in the possession of American to conclude that the creation of a liability on the part of a corporation is no less the misappropriation of its property than would be the theft of an asset worth an equal amount". *Id.* at 647 (citing Carpenter v. U.S., 484 U.S. 19, 25 (1989)).

188. Cf. Graeme Weardon, *Judge Raps Ebay over Fraud*, CNET NEWS.COM, *available at* http://news.com.com/2100-1038_3-5481601.html (according to the U.K. Judge, "it seems to be extremely easy to commit fraud on the Internet.").

ment by credit card, the perpetrator will no doubt have the victims send him payment by check, cash or money order; since these payments will travel either via the U.S. mails or a private commercial carrier like Federal Express, and since the sending of payment is an essential part of executing the scheme to defraud, the perpetrator can also be charged with mail fraud.[189]

The general federal conspiracy provision, 18 U.S.C. § 371, can be used to charge conspiracy to commit mail fraud or wire fraud.[190]

As to punishment, 18 U.S.C. § 1341 provides that a basic violation of its provisions is punishable by a fine, imprisonment for not more than twenty years or both. If the violation affects a financial institution, the offender can be fined "not more than $1,000,000," imprisoned for not more than thirty years, or both.[191] The punishment for wire fraud under 18 U.S. Code is identical, i.e., a fine, imprisonment for not more than twenty years, or both for basic violations and a fine of up to $1,000,000, imprisonment for not more than thirty years, or both if the violation affected a financial institution.[192]

2. Fraud in Connection with Access Devices

Section 1029 of Title 18 of the U.S. Code makes it a federal crime to engage in certain activities involving "access devices," which are defined as "any card, plate, code, account number, electronic serial number, mobile identification number, personal identification number, or other telecommunications service, equipment, or instrument identifier, or other means of account access that can be used ... to obtain money, goods, services, or any other thing of value."[193] Section 1029 also prohibits activities involving

---

189. *See, e.g.,* U.S. v. Hartman, 74 Fed. Appx. 159 (3d Cir. 2003); U.S. v. Jackson, 61 Fed. Appx. 851 (4th Cir. 2003).

190. Section 371 makes it an offense for "two or more persons" to conspire either to commit an offense against the United States or to defraud the United States "or any agency thereof in any manner or for any purpose." 18 U.S.C. § 371 (2000). *See, e.g.,* Pereira v. U.S. 347 U.S. 1, 12 (1954) (conspiracy to commit mail fraud); U.S. v. Petersen, 98 F.3d 502, 503 (9th Cir. 1996) (conspiracy to commit wire fraud).

191. *See* 18 U.S.C. § 1341 (2000).

192. *See id.* § 1343.

193. 18 U.S.C. § 1029(e)(1) (2000). *See* U.S. v. Brady, 820 F. Supp. 1346, 1356–57 (D. Utah), *aff'd,* 13 F.3d 334 (10th Cir. 1993) (EPROM—erasable programmable read-only memory—not an access device under the statute).

counterfeit access devices, which it defines as "any access device that is counterfeit, fictitious, altered, or forged, or an identifiable component of an access device or a counterfeit access device."[194]

As to offenses, § 1029 makes it a federal crime to do any of the following:

1. knowingly and with the intent to defraud produce, use or traffic in a counterfeit access device;[195]
2. knowingly and with the intent to defraud traffic in or use one or more access devices during any one-year period and thereby obtain anything of a value aggregating $1,000 or more;[196]
3. knowingly and with the intent to defraud possess fifteen or more devices which are counterfeit or unauthorized access devices;[197]
4. knowingly and with the intent to defraud produce, traffic in, have custody or control of or possess access device-making equipment;[198]
5. knowingly and with the intent to defraud effect transactions with one or more access devices issued to another person or other persons to receive anything of value during any one-year period of a value aggregating $1,000 or more;[199]

---

194. 18 U.S.C. § 1029(e)(2) (2000). *See, e.g.,* U.S. v. Brannan, 898 F.2d 107 (9th Cir. 1990), *cert. denied,* 498 U.S. 833 (1991) (credit cards defendant acquired by submitting false information were counterfeit access devices); U.S. v. Brewer, 835 F.2d 550 (5th Cir. 1987) (long distance telephone service access codes fabricated by defendant were counterfeit access devices).

195. 18 U.S.C. § 1029(a)(1) (2000). *See, e.g.,* U.S. v. Peyton, 353 F.3d 1080 (9th Cir. 2003); U.S. v. Johnson, 132 F.3d 1279, 1282 (9th Cir. 1997).

196. 18 U.S.C. § 1029(a)(2) (2000). *See, e.g.,* U.S. v. Moiseev, 2004 WL 1923602 (9th Cir. 2004); U.S. v. Swint, 223 F.3d 249 (3d Cir. 2000); U.S. v. Casey, 158 F.3d 993, 994 (8th Cir. 1998); U.S. v. Thomas, 1998 WL 514001 (2d Cir. 1998).

197. 18 U.S.C. § 1029(a)(3) (2000). *See, e.g.,* U.S. v. Muhammad, 2004 WL 1949321 (4th Cir. 2004); U.S. v. Sepulveda, 115 F.3d 882, 885 (11th Cir. 1997); U.S. v. Petersen, 98 F.3d 502, 505 (9th Cir. 1996). In one prosecution, Kevin Mitnick, an infamous hacker, was charged with several offenses, including wire fraud, but pled guilty to possession of unauthorized access devices with the intent to defraud, in violation of 18 U.S.C. § 1029(a)(3) (2000). *See* U.S. v. Mitnick, 145 F.3d 1342 (9th Cir.), *cert. denied,* 525 U.S. 917 (1998).

198. 18 U.S.C. § 1029(a)(4) (2000). *See, e.g.,* U.S. v. Dentman, 44 Fed. Appx. 856 (9th Cir. 2002); U.S. v. Liu, 180 F.3d 957, 959 (8th Cir. 1999); U.S. v. Cabrera, 172 F.3d 1287, 1289 (11th Cir. 1999).

199. 18 U.S.C. § 1029(a)(5) (2000). *See, e.g.,* U.S. v. Smith, 367 F.3d 737 (8th Cir. 2004). *Cf.,* U.S. v. Darnell, 2000 WL 728376 (9th Cir. 2000) (restitution order); U.S. v.

6. without the authorization of the issuer of an access device, knowingly and with the intent to defraud solicit someone for the purpose, either, of offering an access device or selling information regarding or an application to obtain an access device;[200]

7. knowingly and with intent to defraud use, produce, traffic in, have custody or control of, or possess a telecommunications instrument that has been modified or altered to obtain unauthorized use of telecommunications services;[201]

8. knowingly and with intent to defraud use, produce, traffic in, have control or custody of, or possess a scanning receiver;[202]

9. knowingly and with the intent to defraud use, produce, traffic in, have custody or control of or possess hardware or software knowing it has been configured to insert or modify telecommunications identifying information associated with or contained in a telecommunications instrument so that the instrument can be used to obtain telecommunications service without authorization;[203] or

10. without the authorization of a credit card owner or its agent, knowingly and with the intent to defraud cause or arrange for another person to present one or more records of transactions made by an access device to the owner or its agent for payment.[204]

Spinner, 180 F.3d 514, 515 (3d Cir. 1999) (indictment dismissed for lack of jurisdiction), *cert. denied*, 530 U.S. 1221 (2000).

200. 18 U.S.C. § 1029(a)(6) (2000). *See, e.g.,* U.S. v. O'Shield, 1998 WL 104625 (7th Cir. 1998).

201. 18 U.S.C. § 1029(a)(7) (2000). *See, e.g.,* U.S. v. Mendez-Carrero, 196 F. Supp. 2d 138 (D.P.R. 2002); U.S. v. Alvelo-Ramos, 957 F. Supp. 18, 18 (D.P.R. 1997).

202. 18 U.S.C. § 1029(a)(8) (2000).

203. Id. § 1029(a)(9). *See, e.g.,* U.S. v. Chow, 2001 WL 1347236 (E.D.N.Y. 2001); U.S. v. Alvelo-Ramos, 957 F. Supp. 18, 18 (D.P.R. 1997). It is not a violation of this sub-section for "an officer, employee, or agent of, or a person engaged in business with, a facilities-based carrier, to engage in conduct (other than trafficking) otherwise prohibited ... for the purpose of protecting the property or legal rights of that carrier, unless such conduct is for the purpose of obtaining telecommunications service provided by another facilities-based carrier without the authorization of such carrier." 18 U.S.C. § 1029(g)(1) (2000). The statute creates an affirmative defense to a charge of violating this sub-section; to qualify for the defense, the person charged with the violation must establish, by a preponderance of the evidence, that "the conduct charged was engaged in for research or development in connection with a lawful purpose." *Id.* § 1029(g)(2).

204. 18 U.S.C. § 1029(a)(10) (2000).

The sanctions for the offenses set out in 18 U.S.C. § 1029(a) are divided into two categories: the basic penalty for the offenses listed in paragraphs (1), (2), (3), (6), (7) and (10), above, is a fine, imprisonment for not more than ten years or both, and for the offenses listed in paragraphs (4), (5), (8) and (9), above it is a fine, imprisonment for not more than fifteen years or both.[205] If the offender has a prior conviction under § 1029, the penalty rises to a fine, imprisonment for not more than twenty years or both.[206] The statute also permits the forfeiture of any property "used or intended to be used to commit the offense.[207]

Section 1029 also makes it a crime for someone to attempt[208] or to conspire to violate its prohibitions.[209] The punishment for an attempt is the same as that for the offense attempted; the punishment for conspiracy is a fine not greater than that allowed for the offense which was the object of the conspiracy or imprisonment for a period that is not longer than one-half the period of imprisonment allowed for the substantive offense, or both a fine and imprisonment.[210]

The USA PATRIOT Act added a new subsection to 18 U.S.C. § 1029.[211] The new subsection (h) confers extraterritorial jurisdiction: Anyone who, acting outside the jurisdiction of the United States, engages in any act that would constitute an offense under §§ 1029(a) or 1029(b) if committed within the jurisdiction of the United States is subject to the penalties specified in the statute if two conditions are met:

1. the offense involves an access device issued, owned, managed or controlled by a financial institution or other entity within the jurisdiction of the United States; and
2. the person transports, delivers, stores or holds an article used in the commission of the offense within the jurisdiction of the United States.[212]

---

205. *Id.* § 1029(c).
206. *Id.*
207. *Id.*
208. *Id.* § 1029(b)(1). *See, e.g.,* U.S. v. Casey, 158 F.3d 993, 994 (8th Cir. 1998).
209. 18 U.S.C. § 1029(b)(2) (2000) (penalty imposable upon anyone who "is a party to a conspiracy to commit an offense under subsection (a) ... if any of the parties engages in conduct in furtherance of such offense"). *See, e.g.,* U.S. v. Okoko, 365 F.3d 962 (11th Cir. 2004); U.S. v. Sepulveda, 115 F.3d 882, 885 (11th Cir. 1997).
210. *See* 18 U.S.C. § 1029(b) (2000).
211. *See* USA PATRIOT Act, Pub. L. 107-56, tit. III, § 377, 115 Stat. 342 (2001).
212. *See* 18 U.S.C.A. § 1029(h) (Supp. 2004).

3. Transporting Stolen Property

Section 2314 of Title 18 of the U.S. Code makes it an offense to transport stolen goods worth $5,000 or more in interstate or foreign commerce. As Section II(F)(1) of this chapter explains, the Supreme Court has held that § 2314 cannot be used to prosecute those who infringe copyrights, on the theory that they are "transporting" stolen property in interstate or foreign commerce.[213] It can, though, be used to prosecute anyone who physically transports stolen property—including stolen computer hardware—in interstate or foreign commerce, as long as the property is worth $5,000 or more and the other requirements are met.[214]

The statute can be used to prosecute the interstate transportation of intangible property, such as computer data. In *U.S. v. Farraj*,[215] for example, the district court held that a paralegal who e-mailed an excerpt from his firm's trial plan for tobacco litigation could be held liable for violating 18 U.S.C. § 2314.[216] A court reached the same conclusion in *U.S. v. Kwan*[217] which involved the prosecution of an employee who took computer files and disks from his employer and physically carried them across state lines.

E. Identity Theft

Section 1028 of Title 18 of the U.S. Code criminalizes various acts constituting fraud in connection with identification documents. Specifically, it makes if a federal crime to commit any of the following under the circumstances outlined in § 1028(c):

---

213. *See* Dowling v. U.S., 473 U.S. 207 (1985).

214. *See, e.g.,* U.S. v. Pollani, 146 F.3d 269, 270 (5th Cir. 1998) (defendant prosecuted under § 2314 for aiding and abetting the transportation of stolen computer parts). *But see* U.S. v. Tasy, 203 F.3d 1060, 1062 (8th Cir. 2000) (lack of evidence that defendants transported stolen computers in interstate commerce or were motivating factor in their movement interstate precluded prosecution under the statute). Courts have held that the statute cannot be used to prosecute the "transportation" of software because its intangible nature means it is not encompassed by the statute's prohibition on transporting "goods" or "wares." *See, e.g.,* U.S. v. Brown, 925 F.2d 1301, 1308 (10th Cir. 1991); U.S. v. Wang, 898 F. Supp. 758, 760 (D. Colo. 1995).

215. 142 F. Supp. 2d 484 (S.D.N.Y. 2001).

216. *See id.* at 490 ("the Court is persuaded that ... the transfer of electronic documents via the internet across state lines does fall within the purview of § 2314.").

217. 2003 WL 21180401 (S.D.N.Y. 2003).

1. knowingly and without lawful authority produce an identification document, authentication feature, or a false identification document;
2. knowingly transfer an identification document, authentication feature, or a false identification document knowing that such document or feature was stolen or produced without lawful authority;
3. knowingly possess with intent to use unlawfully or transfer unlawfully five or more identification documents (other than those issued lawfully for the use of the possessor), authentication features, or false identification documents;
4. knowingly possess an identification document (other than one issued lawfully for the use of the possessor), authentication feature, or a false identification document, with the intent such document or feature be used to defraud the United States;
5. knowingly produce, transfer, or possess a document-making implement or authentication feature with the intent such document-making implement or authentication feature will be used in the production of a false identification document or another document-making implement or authentication feature which will be so used;
6. knowingly possess an identification document or authentication feature that is or appears to be an identification document or authentication feature of the United States which is stolen or produced without lawful authority knowing that such document or feature was stolen or produced without such authority;
7. knowingly transfer, possess, or use, without lawful authority, a means of identification of another person with the intent to commit, or to aid or abet, or in connection with, any unlawful activity that constitutes a violation of Federal law, or that constitutes a felony under any applicable State or local law; or
8. knowingly traffic in false authentication features for use in false identification documents, document-making implements, or means of identification.[218]

The circumstances outlined in § 1028(c) are that the identification is or appears to be issued under the authority of the United States; the offense in-

---

218. *Id.* § 1028(a).

volves defrauding the United States; or either the prohibited conduct affects interstate or foreign commerce or the document or the implement used to make such a document is sent through the mail.[219]

The statute prescribes penalties ranging from five to fifteen years imprisonment, along with the possibility of a fine and forfeiture.[220] It also criminalizes attempts and conspiracies to commit the offenses outlined above.[221]

As used in § 1028, "authentication feature" means "any hologram, watermark, certification, symbol, code, image, sequence of numbers or letters, or other feature that either individually or in combination with another feature is used by the issuing authority on an identification document" to determine if the document is counterfeit, altered, or otherwise falsified.[222] The term "document-making implement" means any implement, device or computer software that is "specifically configured or primarily used for making an identification document, a false identification document, or another document-making implement."[223] The statute defines "identification document" as

> a document made or issued by or under the authority of the United States Government, a State, political subdivision of a State, a foreign government, political subdivision of a foreign government, an international governmental or an international quasi-governmental organization which, when completed with information concerning a particular individual, is of a type intended or commonly accepted for the purpose of identification of individuals.[224]

It defines a "false identification document" as a document "of a type intended or commonly accepted for the purposes of identification" that

1. is not issued by or under the authority of a governmental entity or was issued under the authority of a governmental entity but was subsequently altered; and
2. appears to be issued by or under the authority of the United States Government, a State, a political subdivision of a State, a foreign

---

219. *Id.* § 1028(c).
220. *See id.* §§ 1028(b) & (h).
221. *See Id.* § 1028(f).
222. *Id.* § 1028(d)(1).
223. *Id.* § 1028(d)(2).
224. *Id.* § 1028(d)(3).

government, a political subdivision of a foreign government, or an international governmental or quasi-governmental organization.[225]

"False authentication feature" is defined as an authentication feature that either

1. is genuine in origin, but, without has been altered without the authorization of the issuing authority;
2. is genuine, but has been distributed, or is intended for distribution, without the authorization of the issuing authority; or
3. appears to be genuine, but is not.[226]

"Issuing authority" is defined as any governmental entity that is authorized to issue identification documents, means of identification, or authentication features.[227] It includes the United States Government, a State, a political subdivision of a State, a foreign government, a political subdivision of a foreign government, or an international government or quasi-governmental organization.[228] "Means of identification" is "any name or number that may be used, alone or in conjunction with any other information, to identify a specific individual."[229] It includes any of the following:

1. name, social security number, date of birth, official State or government issued driver's license or identification number, alien registration number, government passport number, employer or taxpayer identification number;
2. biometric data;
3. unique electronic identification number, address, or routing code; or
4. telecommunication identifying information or access device as defined in 18 U.S.C. § 1920(e).[230]

"Personal identification card" means an identification document issued by a State or local government solely for the purpose of identification.[231]

---

225. *Id.* § 1028(d)(4).
226. *Id.* § 1028(d)(5).
227. See id. § 1028(d)(6).
228. *See Id.*
229. *Id.* § 1028(d)(7).
230. *See Id.*
231. *See Id.*

In July of 2004, Congress added another identity theft provision to the U.S. Code which criminalizes "aggravated identity theft."[232] It creates aggravated penalties for misusing another's identification document to commit specified federal felonies or a federal crime of terrorism under 18 U.S.C. § 2332b(g)(5)(B).[233]

F. Intellectual Property Crimes

The protection of intellectual property under federal law encompasses four discrete areas: copyrights; trademarks; trade secrets and patents.[234] Patent infringement does not carry criminal penalties, and so is outside the scope of this chapter.[235] The remaining areas will each be discussed in turn.

1. Copyright Infringement

Copyright infringement in the form of software piracy is a cybercrime,[236] a very expensive cybercrime.[237] Federal copyright law, which is codified in title 17 of the U.S. Code, protects "rights of authorship" in various kinds of intellectual property, including computer software.[238] To be protected under

---

232. 18 U.S.C.A. § 1028A (Supp. 2004).

233. *Id.* § 1028A(a).

234. *See, e.g.,* Computer Crime and Intellectual Property Section, Criminal Division, U.S. Department of Justice, *Prosecuting Intellectual Property Crimes Manual* § I(A) (2001), *available at* http://www.cybercrime.gov/ipmanual/01ipma.htm (last visited Nov. 8, 2004) [hereinafter *Prosecuting I.P. Crimes Manual*]

235. *See id.* at § I(C).

236. *See* 17 U.S.C. § 506 (2000); *Prosecuting I.P. Crimes Manual* at § I(C).

237. *See, e.g.,* Business Software Alliance & IDC, *First Annual BSA and IDC Global Software Piracy Study* 1 (2004), *available at* http://www.bsa.org/globalstudy/loader. cfm?url=/commonspot/security/getfile.cfm&pageid=16947&hitboxdone=yes (last visited Nov. 8, 2004):

> Last year, the world spent more than $50 billion (US dollars) for commercial packaged software that runs on personal computers (PCs). Yet, software worth almost $80 billion was actually installed. For every two dollars' worth of software purchased legitimately, one dollar's worth was obtained illegally. The piracy rate—the number of pirated software units divided by the total number of units put into use—was 36 percent in 2003.

238. *See, e.g., Prosecuting I.P. Crimes Manual, supra* note 234, § I(A). Computer software was explicitly granted copyright protection by the Computer Software Copyright Act of 1980, Pub. L. No. 96-517, § 10, 94 Stat. 3028 (1980) (codified at 17 U.S.C. §§ 101, 117 (2000)), but has been included within the scope of copyright since the 1976 Copyright Act was adopted. Tandy Corp. v. Personal Micro Computers, Inc., 524 F. Supp. 171, 173 (N.D. Cal. 1981).

federal copyright law, intellectual property must be "original" and must be "fixed in any tangible medium of expression."[239] For a work to be "original," it must have "originated" with—that is, have been created by—the author claiming the copyright. Originality does not require novelty, but to be original an item must contain a minimum quantity of creative expression[240] and cannot simply be a copy of another, pre-existing item.[241] For a work to be "fixed" in a "tangible medium of expression," it must be embodied in a form which is "sufficiently permanent or stable to permit it to be perceived, reproduced, or otherwise communicated for a period of more than transitory duration."[242] Finally, the author's registration of the copyright is a prerequisite for a criminal action for copyright infringement.[243] The registration need not, however, have preceded the act of infringement—it is sufficient if the registration precedes the filing of the criminal action.[244]

---

239. *See* 17 U.S.C. §§ 101 & 102(a) (2000). *See also Prosecuting I.P. Crimes Manual, supra* note 234, § II(A) ("Copyright law protects the original *expression* of an idea or concept in tangible form (be it a novel, a song, a carpet design, or computer source code), but does not extend to protection of the idea or concept itself").

240. See Feist Pub., Inc. v. Rural Tele. Serv. Co., 499 U.S. 340, 345 (1991); Ralph D. Clifford, *Random Numbers, Chaos Theory and Cogitation: A Search for the Minimal Creativity Standard in Copyright Law*, 82 Denv. U. L. Rev 259, 268–70 (2005).

241. *See, e.g.,* J. Dianne Brinson, *Proof of Economic Power in A Sherman Act Tying Arrangement Case: Should Economic Power Be Presumed When The Tying Product Is Patented Or Copyrighted?*, 48 La. L. Rev. 29, 63 (1987) (notes omitted):

    While only "original" works qualify for copyright, the copyright "originality" requirement does not demand product novelty, in the patent sense. The copyright "originality" requirement is satisfied if the work "originated" with the author, meaning that the author did not copy someone else's work. An author who independently created a work identical to an existing work not only would not be an infringer, he would be entitled to copyright protection on his own work.

242. 17 U.S.C. § 101 (2000). *See, e.g.,* Kodadek v. MTV Networks, Inc., 1996 WL 807435 (C.D. Cal. 1996), *aff'd,* 152 F.3d 1209 (9th Cir. 1998).

243. *See* 17 U.S.C. § 411(a) (2000). *See, e.g.,* Leicester v. Warner Bros., 232 F.3d 1212 (9th Cir. 2000). *See also Prosecuting I.P. Crimes Manual, supra* note 234, § III(A).

244. *See* 17 U.S.C. § 411(a) (2000). *See, e.g.,* Hagendorf v. Brown, 699 F.2d 478, 480 (9th Cir. 1983); Marshall & Swift v. BS & A Software, 871 F. Supp. 952, 957-58 (W.D. Mich. 1994). *See also Prosecuting I.P. Crimes Manual, supra* note 234, § III(B)(1) ("Criminal prosecutions should be sought only after the infringed works have been registered, although technical irregularities in the registration process will not invalidate an otherwise proper registration").

The most stringent penalties for copyright infringement are contained in 17 U.S.C. § 506(a) (2000), which encompasses software piracy.[245] Section 506(a) makes it a federal crime for someone willfully to infringe a copyright *either* for purposes of commercial advantage or private financial gain[246] *or* by reproducing or distributing, during any 180-day period, one or more copies of one or more copyrighted works having a total retail value in excess of $1,000.[247] The basic elements of felony copyright infringement, therefore, are:

1. that a copyright existed;
2. that the defendant infringed the copyright by the reproduction or distribution of the copyrighted work;
3. that the defendant acted willfully; and
4. that the defendant reproduced or distributed at least ten copies of one or more copyrighted works with a total value of more than $2,500 within a 180-day period.[248]

---

245. *See, e.g., Prosecuting I.P. Crimes Manual, supra* note 234, § III(B).

246. The Commentary to the Sentencing Guideline for this offense defines "commercial advantage or private financial gain" as "the receipt, or expectation of receipt, of anything of value, including other protected works." *See* U.S. SENTENCING GUIDELINES MANUAL § 2B5.3, cmt. (2003) [hereinafter U.S.S.G.].

Prior to the 1997 amendments to § 506, proof that the defendant acted for commercial advantage or private financial gain

[w]as required to prove any federal copyright crime.... These amendments reflect Congressional recognition that the Internet provides a growing means for large-scale electronic piracy that has a substantial market impact, even where the infringer does not have a profit motive. *See* H.R. Rep. No. 105-339, at 4 (1997). Software copying and distribution on the Internet are inexpensive and easy, thus reducing infringers' economic need for a financial return when making and distributing copies. Willful infringers may be driven by a variety of non-profit motives, including a rejection of the copyright laws, anti-corporate sentiments, or a desire to gain respect in the Internet community. These willful large-scale infringers may be driven by a financial motivation that may be difficult to articulate or prove to a jury.

Prosecuting I.P. Crimes Manual, supra note 234, § III(B)(5). *See also* No Electronic Theft (NET) Act, Pub. L. No. 105-147, 111 Stat. 2678 (1997).

247. *See* 17 U.S.C. § 506(a) (2000). *See also id.* § 501(a) (infringement of copyright consists of violating the exclusive rights of the copyright owner as provided by 17 U.S.C. §§ 106–22).

248. *See* 18 U.S.C. § 2319(b) (2000). *See also* Doris Estelle Long, *E-Business Solutions to P2P Piracy: A Practical Guide*, 779 PLI PATENTS, COPYRIGHTS, TRADEMARKS AND LITERARY PROPERTY COURSE HANDBOOK SERIES 727, 745 (2004) [hereinafter Long, *E-Business Solutions*]; *Prosecuting I.P. Crimes Manual, supra* note 234, § III(B).

To obtain a misdemeanor conviction, the government must prove:

1. that a copyright existed;
2. that the defendant infringed the copyright by reproducing and/or distributing the copyrighted work;
3. that the defendant acted willfully; and
4. that the defendant either reproduced or distributed the copyrighted material for the purposes of commercial advantage or private financial gain or that he distributed or copied one or more copyrighted works with a total retail value of more than $1,000 within a 180-day period.[249]

If the government can show that the defendant acted for purposes of commercial advantage or private financial gain, this acts as a penalty enhancer.[250] The Department of Justice's manual on prosecuting intellectual property crimes also notes that a case involving commercial motivation is likely to be more appealing to a jury.[251]

With regard to punishment, §506(a) incorporates the provisions of 18 U.S.C. §2319 (2000).[252] Section 2319(a) states that those who violate §506(a) are to be punished in accordance with the provisions of 18 U.S.C. §2319(b) and §2319(c), these penalties to be "in addition to any other provisions of title 17 or any other law."

18 U.S.C. §2319(b) specifies the punishment for felony violations of 17 U.S.C. §506(a)(1), which involves infringement for purposes of commercial advantage or private financial gain. If the crime involved the reproduction or distribution of at least ten copies of one or more copyrighted works that had a total retail value of more than $2,500, the offender can be imprisoned for up to five years, fined in accordance with the applicable statute or both.[253] If the offense did not involve the reproduction or distribution of this threshold amount of goods, the offender can be imprisoned

249. *See* 18 U.S.C. §2319(c)(3) (2000). *See also* Long, *E-Business Solutions, supra* note 248.

250. *See Prosecuting I.P. Crimes Manual, supra* note 234, §III(B)(5) (if this element is proven, "the statutory maximum prison sentence can rise to 5 years, rather than 3 years").

251. *See id.* §III(B)(5).

252. *See* 17 U.S.C. §506(a) (2000) ("Any person who infringes a copyright willfully … shall be punished as provided under section 2319 of title 18, United States Code").

253. *See* 18 U.S.C. §2319(b)(1) (2000).

for up to one year, fined in accordance with the applicable statute or both.[254] If the offense is a second or subsequent offense involving the reproduction or distribution of the threshold amount of goods, the offender can be imprisoned for up to ten years, fined in accordance with the applicable statute or both.[255]

18 U.S.C. § 2319(c) specifies the punishment for felony violations of 17 U.S.C. § 506(a)(2), which involves the reproduction or distribution of one or more copies or one or more copyrighted works having a total retail value in excess of $1,000. If the offense involved the reproduction or distribution of ten or more copies of one or more copyrighted works that have a total retail value of $2,500 or more, the offender can be imprisoned for up to three years, fined in accordance with the applicable statute or both.[256] If the offense involves the reproduction or distribution of one or more copies of one or more copyrighted works that have a total retail value of more than $1,000, the offender can be sentenced to up to one year in prison, fined in accordance with the applicable statute or both.[257] If the offense is a second or subsequent offense, the offender can be imprisoned for up to six years, fined in accordance with the applicable statute or both.[258]

In calculating an offender's sentence, the court will base its calculations on the legitimate retail value of the infringed items.[259] The "retail value" of "an infringed item or an infringing item is the retail price of that item in the market in which it is sold."[260]

There are two basic substantive defenses to a charge of criminal copyright infringement:

1.　the "first sale" doctrine;[261] and

---

254. *See id.* § 2319(b)(3).
255. *See id.* § 2319(b)(2).
256. *See id.* § 2319(c)(1).
257. *See id.* § 2319(c)(3).
258. *See id.* § 2319(c)(2).
259. *See* U.S.S.G., *supra* note 246, § 2B5.3, appl. n. 2(A) (2003) ("The infringement amount is the retail value of the infringed item, multiplied by the number of infringing items"). *See, e.g.,* U.S. v. Slater, 348 F.3d 666, 669–670 (7th Cir. 2003); U.S. v. Rothberg, 2002 WL 171963 (N.D. Ill. 2002).
260. *See* U.S.S.G., *supra* note 246, § 2B5.3, appl. n. 2(C) (2003).
261. *See Prosecuting I.P. Crimes Manual, supra* note 234, § III(C)(2):
　　The "first sale" doctrine limits the copyright owner's "exclusive rights" to authorize or distribute copies of a copyrighted work to the public.... It provides that a sale of a "lawfully made" copy terminates the copyright holder's authority to interfere with or control subsequent sales or distributions of that

2. the claim that the defendant did not act "willfully."

The first sale doctrine lets someone who legally buys a copyrighted work freely distribute the copy she bought.[262] But the first sale doctrine only lets a purchaser distribute the copy she actually bought; it does not let her make copies of the purchased item and distribute those copies.[263] Since most computer software is distributed through licensing agreements, the first sale doctrine typically does not apply when someone is charged with software piracy.[264]

---

particular copy.... In short, through the first sale doctrine, the first purchaser and any subsequent purchaser of that specific copy of a copyrighted work receive the right to sell, display or dispose of their copy. If copyright owner A sells a copy of a work to B, B may sell that particular copy without violating the law. B does not, however, receive the right to reproduce and distribute additional copies made from that work. Thus, if B makes any unauthorized copies of that work, he or she violates the law.
See, e.g., U.S. v. Bernstene, 1982 WL 1284 *4–5 (C.D. Cal. 1982), *aff'd,* 715 F.2d 459 (9th Cir. 1983), *cert. denied,* 465 U.S. 1022 (1984).

262. *See* 17 U.S.C. § 109(a) (2000). *See, e.g.,* U.S. v. Cohen, 946 F.2d 430, 434–35 (6th Cir. 1991). *See also See* U.S.S.G., *supra* note 246, § 2B5.3, appl. n.2(C) (2003). The first sale doctrine is only available as a defense to a charge of copyright infringement by distribution; it does not apply to a charge of infringement by reproduction. *See Prosecuting I.P. Crimes Manual, supra* note 234 § III(C)(2).

263. *See* 17 U.S.C. § 109(a) (2000). *See, e.g.,* U.S. v. Moore, 604 F.2d 1228, 1232 (9th Cir. 1979). *See also Prosecuting I.P. Crimes Manual, supra* note 234, § III(C)(2).

264. *See, e.g., Prosecuting I.P. Crimes Manual, supra* note 234, § III(C)(2):
Most computer software is distributed through the use of licensing agreements. Under this distribution system, the copyright holder remains the "owner" of all distributed copies. For this reason, alleged infringers should not be able to establish that any copies of these works have been the subject of a first sale. Thus, if A, the copyright owner, simply loans a copy of a work to B, B obtains no ownership interest in the work and is unable to assert first sale as a defense to an infringement action. This is an important limitation, as the distribution systems for some artistic works, most notably motion pictures and computer software, rely on licensing agreements, leases, or other devices to transfer possession of copies of a copyrighted work. Under these distribution systems, the copyright holder remains the "owner" of all distributed copies.
See also Eric Goldman, *Warez Trading and Criminal Copyright Infringement,* 51 J. Copyright Soc'y U.S.A. 395, 400 (2004) (notes omitted):
The First Sale doctrine, which allows redistribution of a legitimately-acquired physical copy of a copyrighted work, is a frequently-raised defense in physical-space criminal copyright cases. However, it offers little help to warez traders because the doctrine only applies to physical copies (not electronic

As to willfulness, the No Electronic Theft Act[265] amended 17 U.S.C.
§ 506(a) so it explicitly states that "evidence of reproduction or distribution
of a copyrighted work, by itself, shall not be sufficient to establish willful
infringement."[266] Unfortunately, the amendment provided no further guidance as to what "willful infringement" means.[267] Courts disagree as to
whether the defendant must have willfully intended to copy the copyrighted
material or willfully intended to infringe the owner's copyright in that material.[268] The failure to define "willfulness" in this context reflects the differing views members of Congress held on the issue.[269] Most courts have

---

ones) and only negates distribution (not reproduction) liability.
Extra care must be taken, however, if the license is in the form of a shrink-wrap license
as the validity of these licenses is controversial. *Compare* Step-Saver Data Sys., Inc. v.
Wyse Tech., 939 F.2d 91 (3d Cir. 1991) (finding shrink-wrap license invalid), *with*
ProCD, Inc. v. Zeidenberg, 86 F.3d 1447 (7th Cir. 1996) (finding shrink-wrap license
valid).

265. Pub. L. No. 105-147, 111 Stat. 2678 (1997).
266. 17 U.S.C. § 506(a)(2) (2000).
267. *See, e.g., Prosecuting I.P. Crimes Manual, supra* note 234, § III(B)(3):
   The statute was amended to require more than general intent and to ensure
   that, for instance, "an educator who in good faith believes that he or she is engaging in a fair use of copyrighted material could not be prosecuted under
   the bill." 143 Cong. Rec. S12689 (daily ed. Nov. 13, 1997). Despite this help-
   ful clarification, the legislation provides no definition of "willful infringement," reaffirming the Supreme Court's observation that "willful ... is a word
   of many meanings, its construction often being influenced by its context."
   Spies v. United States, 317 U.S. 492, 497 (1943).
268. *See, e.g., Prosecuting I.P. Crimes Manual, supra* note 234, § III(A)(1)(c).
269. *See id.* (quoting 143 Cong. Rec. H9884, H9886 (daily ed. Nov. 4, 1997)):
   On the one hand, Senator Hatch, the Chairman of the Senate Judiciary Committee, suggested that "'Willful' ought to mean the intent to violate a known
   legal duty." 143 Cong. Rec. S12689 (1997) (daily ed. Nov. 13, 1997) (citing
   Cheek v. United States, 498 U.S. 192 (1991)). In the House, on the other hand,
   Representatives Goodlatte and Coble, who introduced and sponsored the bill,
   emphasized that:
      The Government should not be required to prove that the defendant was
      familiar with the criminal copyright statute or violated it intentionally.
      Particularly in cases of clear infringement, the willfulness standard
      should be satisfied if there is adequate proof that the defendant acted
      with reckless disregard of the rights of the copyright holder. In such cir-
      cumstances, a proclaimed ignorance of the law should not allow the in-
      fringer to escape conviction.

interpreted willfulness as requiring specific intent to violate the copyright laws.[270]

Along with the first sale doctrine and willfulness, two other issues can be raised defensively. One is the statute of limitations: The government has five years after the offense occurs in which to bring a prosecution for criminal copyright infringement.[271] The other issue is fair use, an equitable doctrine codified in 17 U.S.C. § 107.[272]

[T]he fair use doctrine excepts the otherwise infringing use of a work where it is used for purposes such as criticism, comment, news reporting, teaching (including multiple copies for classroom

---

270. See Mary Jane Saunders, *Criminal Copyright Infringement and the Copyright Felony Act*, 71 DENV. U. L. REV. 671, 687–88 (1994) (notes omitted):

For a conviction on charges of criminal copyright infringement, the government must prove a specific criminal intent to infringe. Without the requisite criminal intent or mens rea, no criminal violation has occurred, even if the number of unauthorized copies or phonorecords reproduced or distributed is significant....

Not every criminal statute requires evidence of specific intent to violate the law. Indeed, criminal law presumes generally that every person knows the law, and that ignorance of the law or a mistake of law is no defense to criminal prosecution. A requirement of specific intent to violate the law is most often reserved for relatively intricate areas of law, such as criminal tax evasion.

The government does not have to show that a defendant has detailed knowledge of the statute prohibiting the conduct in question to prove that the defendant exhibited specific intent to violate the law. If the government did have to make such a showing, defense lawyers could argue that their clients should be acquitted simply because they were unfamiliar with the intricacies of a substantive area of law such as copyright.

The better view is that specific intent to violate the law is established by proof that the defendant intended to act as he did and that the defendant's actions were knowing or voluntary, not accidental. This approach is consistent with well settled case authority regarding the meaning of willfulness in a wide variety of contexts.

See also Geraldine Szott Moohr, *The Crime of Copyright Infringement: An Inquiry Based on Morality, Harm, and Criminal Theory*, 83 B.U. L. REV. 731, 739 n.29 (2003) ("Most courts have adopted a rigorous definition of willfulness"); U.S. v. Moran, 757 F. Supp. 1046, 1050–51 (D. Neb. 1991).

271. See, e.g., *Prosecuting I.P. Crimes Manual, supra* note 234, § III(C)(1). See also 17 U.S.C. § 507 (2000).

272. See, e.g., *Prosecuting I.P. Crimes Manual, supra* note 234, § III(C)(3).

use), scholarship, or research. Serious questions of fair use often arise in civil copyright infringement cases. The statute provides four factors that should, at a minimum, be considered when determining whether a use is a fair use: (1) the purpose and character of a use, including whether such use is of a noncommercial nature; (2) the nature of the work; (3) the amount and substantiality of the portion used in relation to the copyrighted work as a whole; and (4) the effect of the use upon the potential market for the copyrighted work.[273]

The fair use doctrine is unlikely to be available as a defense in a prosecution under 17 U.S.C. § 506(a)(1) because the government is required to prove that the defendant acted for purposes of commercial advantage or private financial gain.[274] The fair use doctrine may, however, be invoked defensively in prosecutions under 17 U.S.C. § 506(a)(2), "which criminalizes large-scale infringement even where the infringer does not act for purposes of commercial advantage or private financial gain."[275] Since prosecutions under § 506(a)(2) often involve the infringement of commercially popular works, the last two factors set out above can be used to overcome a fair use defense.[276]

In addition to 17 U.S.C. § 506(a), other sections of title 17 and sections of title 18 of the U.S. Code can be used to prosecute criminal copyright infringement.[277] The remaining title 17 offenses are defined by 17 U.S.C. §§ 506(c)[278] and 506(d),[279] which address the protection of copyright no-

---

273. *Id.* § III(C)(1). *See also* 17 U.S.C. § 507 (2000).

274. *See generally* U.S. v. Slater, 348 F.3d 666, 669 (7th Cir. 2003). *But cf.* Cambell v. Acuff-Rose Music, Inc., 510 U.S. 569 (1994) (finding commercial use fair).

275. *See, e.g., Prosecuting I.P. Crimes Manual, supra* note 234, § III(C)(3).

276. *See, e.g., id.* § III(C)(3) ("In such cases, the works are generally copied in their entirety, and the wide availability of the free, pirated copies ... can have a drastic effect on the potential market for legitimate works").

277. *See, e.g., id.* § III(A).

278. *See* 17 U.S.C. § 506(c) (2000) ("Any person who, with fraudulent intent, places on any article a notice of copyright or words of the same purport that such person knows to be false, or who, with fraudulent intent, publicly distributes or imports for public distribution any article bearing such notice or words that such person knows to be false, shall be fined not more than $2,500").

279. *See id.* § 506(d) ("Any person who, with fraudulent intent, removes or alters any notice of copyright appearing on a copy of a copyrighted work shall be fined not more than $2,500").

tices, and by 17 U.S.C. § 506(e), which makes it an offense to include false representations in an application for copyright.[280]

The title 18 offenses that can apply to copyright infringement include mail and wire fraud,[281] smuggling,[282] trafficking in counterfeit labels[283] and trafficking in sound recordings of live musical performances.[284] Years ago, prosecutors sometimes charged those who infringed copyrights with the interstate transportation of stolen property in violation of 18 U.S.C. § 2314 (2000); the Supreme Court eliminated this alternative when it held, in

---

280. *See id.* § 506(e) ("Any person who knowingly makes a false representation of a material fact in the application for copyright registration provided for by section 409, or in any written statement filed in connection with the application, shall be fined not more than $2,500").

281. *See* 18 U.S.C. § 1341 (2000) (mail fraud) and § 1343 (wire fraud). The mail and wire fraud statutes are discussed in more detail earlier in this chapter.

282. Under 17 U.S.C. §§ 501(a) and 602 (2000), the "[c]ommercial importation of unauthorized copies of copyrighted works constitutes copyright infringement." U.S. DEPARTMENT OF JUSTICE, FEDERAL PROSECUTION OF INTELLECTUAL PROPERTY RIGHTS § III(D)(4) (1997), *available at* http://www.usdoj.gov/criminal/cybercrime/intell_prop_rts/SectIII.htm (last visited Nov. 10, 2004). The Department of Justice advises prosecutors to consider charging those who engage in such activity with smuggling under 18 U.S.C. § 545. *See Id.* Section 545 makes it an offense, punishable by a fine, imprisonment of up to five years or both, to do the following: (1) knowingly and willfully, with the intent to defraud the United States, smuggle, clandestinely introduce, or attempt to smuggle or clandestinely introduce into the United States merchandise which should have been invoiced; or (2) fraudulently or knowingly import or bring into the United States any merchandise contrary to law. *See, e.g.,* U.S. v. Gallo, 599 F. Supp. 241, 245 (W.D.N.Y. 1984) (smuggling statute could be used against infringers of copyright).

283. *See* 18 U.S.C. § 2318(a) (2000) ("Whoever ... knowingly traffics in a counterfeit label affixed or designed to be affixed to ... a copy of a computer program or documentation or packaging for a computer program ... and whoever ... knowingly traffics in counterfeit documentation or packaging for a computer program, shall be fined under this title or imprisoned for not more than five years, or both"). *See, e.g.,* U.S. v. Chay, 281 F.3d 682, 682 (7th Cir. 2002); U.S. v. Sow, 2003 WL 1597085 (S.D.N.Y. 2003); U.S. v. Bao, 189 F.3d 860, 862 (9th Cir. 1999).

284. *See* 18 U.S.C. § 2319A (2000). *See, e.g.,* U.S. v. Moghadam, 175 F.3d 1269, 1271 (11th Cir. 1999), *cert. denied,* 529 U.S. 1036 (2000). Section 2319A is often known as the "anti-bootlegging statute." In *U.S. v. Martignon,* 2004 WL 2149105 (S.D.N.Y. 2004), the district court held that the statute is unconstitutional under the Copyright Clause of the U.S. Constitution. *See id.* at *11. Among other things, the court held that the "anti-bootlegging statute's failure to impose a durational limitation on its regulation is 'fundamentally inconsistent' with the Copyright Clause's requirement that copyright-like regulations only persist for 'Limited Times.'" *Id.* at *10.

Dowling v. U.S.[285] that the stolen property statute does not apply to acts of copyright infringement.[286] The *Dowling* Court found that § 2314 cannot be used for this purpose because the statute punishes those who physically seize and transport property belonging to another, thereby depriving the owner of the possession and use of his or her property; as the Court explained, the infringer of a copyright neither assumes physical control over the copyright nor wholly deprives the owner of its use.[287] The statute has, however, been used to prosecute those who steal computer hardware and/or software and transport them in interstate or foreign commerce.[288] It has also been used to prosecute those who use electronic means to transport stolen data in interstate or foreign commerce.[289]

Section 371 of title 18 of the U.S. Code, which is the basic federal conspiracy provision, is used to prosecute conspiracy to commit criminal copyright infringement.[290]

In 1998, Congress adopted the Digital Millennium Copyright Act,[291] ["DMCA"] which added two new sections to title 17 of the U.S. Code: Section 1201 makes it unlawful to circumvent measures used to protect copyrighted works,[292] while section 1202 makes it unlawful to tamper with copy-

---

285. 473 U.S. 207 (1985).

286. *See id.* at 216–29.

287. *See id.*

288. *See, e.g.,* U.S. v. Lloyd, 269 F.3d 228, 231 (3d Cir. 2001).

289. *See, e.g.,* U.S. v. Farraj, 142 F. Supp. 2d 484, 486–89 (S.D.N.Y. 2001) (electronic mail transfer of excerpt of trial plan for tobacco class action fell within purview of § 2314). *See also* U.S. v. Kwan, 2003 WL 21180401 (S.D.N.Y. 2003) (statute encompassed conduct of defendant who took confidential documents, computer files and computer diskettes from his former employer's office and transported them to another state).

290. *See, e.g.,* U.S. v. Slater, 348 F.3d 666, 666 (7th Cir. 2003); U.S. v. Hernandez, 952 F.2d 1110 (9th Cir.), *cert. denied,* 506 U.S. 920 (1992); U.S. v. Minor, 846 F.2d 1184, 1185 (9th Cir. 1988).

291. Pub. L. No. 105-304, 112 Stat. 2860 (1998).

292. *See* 17 U.S.C. § 1201(a)(1)(A) (2000) ("No person shall circumvent a technological measure that effectively controls access to a work protected under this title"). *See also id.* § 1201(b)(1)(A) ("No person shall manufacture, import, offer to the public, provide, or otherwise traffic in any technology, product, service, device, component, or part thereof, that ... is primarily designed or produced for the purpose of circumventing protection afforded by a technological measure that effectively protects a right of a copyright owner under this title ... in a work or a portion thereof"). Under § 1201(a)(1), to "circumvent a technological measure" means "to descramble a scrambled work, to decrypt an encrypted work, or otherwise to avoid, bypass, remove, deactivate, or impair a technological measure, without the author-

right management information.[293] Another new section added by the

ity of the copyright owner," and a technological measure "'effectively controls access to a work" if the measure, in the ordinary course of its operation, requires the application of information, or a process or a treatment, with the authority of the copyright owner, to gain access to the work." *Id.* § 1201(a)(3)(A)-(B). *See, e.g., U.S. v. Elcom Ltd.,* 203 F. Supp. 1111 (N.D. Cal. 2002). *See also Universal City Studios, Inc. v. Reimerdes,* 111 F. Supp. 2d 294, 319–20 (S.D.N.Y. 2000), *aff'd sub nom. Universal City Studios, Inc. v. Corley,* 273 F.3d 429 (2d Cir. 2001); *RealNetworks, Inc. v. Streambox, Inc.,* 2000 WL 127311 (W.D. Wash. 2000). Under 17 U.S.C. § 1201(b)(1)(A), to "circumvent protection afforded by a technological measure" means "avoiding, bypassing, removing, deactivating, or otherwise impairing a technological measure," and a technological measure "'effectively protects a right of a copyright owner under this title' if the measure, in the ordinary course of its operation, prevents, restricts, or otherwise limits the exercise of a right of a copyright owner under this title." 17 U.S.C. § 1201(b)(2)(A)-(B) (2000).

293. *See* 17 U.S.C. § 1202(a) (2000) ("No person shall knowingly and with the intent to induce, enable, facilitate, or conceal infringement … provide copyright management information that is false, or … distribute or import for distribution copyright management information that is false"). *See also id.* § 1202(b) (no one shall, "without the authority of the copyright owner or the law (1) intentionally remove or alter any copyright management information, (2) distribute or import for distribution copyright management information knowing the copyright management information has been removed or altered without authority of the copyright owner or the law, or (3) distribute, import for distribution, or publicly perform works, copies of works, or phonorecords, knowing that copyright management information has been removed or altered without authority of the copyright owner or the law, knowing … that it will induce, enable, facilitate, or conceal an infringement of any right under this title"). Section 1202(c) defines "copyright management information" as

> any of the following information conveyed in connection with copies or phonorecords of a work or performances or displays of a work, including in digital form, except that such term does not include any personally identifying information about a user of a work or of a copy, phonorecord, performance, or display of a work:
>
> (1) The title and other information identifying the work, including the information set forth on a notice of copyright.
>
> (2) The name of, and other identifying information about, the author of a work.
>
> (3) The name of, and other identifying information about, the copyright owner of the work, including the information set forth in a notice of copyright.
>
> (4) With the exception of public performances of works by radio and television broadcast stations, the name of, and other identifying information about, a performer whose performance is fixed in a work other than an audiovisual work.

DMCA, 17 U.S.C. § 1204, creates criminal penalties for violating either sections 1201 or 1202 of the DMCA.[294]

In 2001, the Department of Justice brought the first prosecution under the DMCA against Elcom Ltd., a Russian accused of trafficking in technology designed and marked for use in circumventing technology that protected the rights of a copyright owner.[295] Elcom Ltd. moved to dismiss the charges against it, claiming § 1201(b):

1. was unconstitutionally vague as applied to its conduct and therefore violated the Due Process Clause of the Fifth Amendment;

2. violated the First Amendment "because it constitutes a content-based restriction on speech that is not sufficiently tailored to serve a compelling government interest, because it impermissibly infringes upon the First Amendment rights of third parties to engage in fair use, and because it is too vague in describing what speech it prohibits, thereby impermissibly chilling free expression;" and

3. was unconstitutional because Congress exceeded its constitutional power in enacting the DMCA.[296]

The district court rejected all three arguments.[297]

---

(5) With the exception of public performances of works by radio and television broadcast stations, in the case of an audiovisual work, the name of, and other identifying information about, a writer, performer, or director who is credited in the audiovisual work.

(6) Terms and conditions for use of the work.

(7) Identifying numbers or symbols referring to such information or links to such information.

(8) Such other information as the Register of Copyrights may prescribe by regulation, except that the Register of Copyrights may not require the provision of any information concerning the user of a copyrighted work.

See, e.g., Kelly v. Arriba Soft Corp., 77 F. Supp. 2d 1116, 1121–22 (C.D. Cal. 1999).

294. See 17 U.S.C. § 1204(a) (2000) ("Any person who violates section 1201 or 1202 willfully and for purposes of commercial advantage or private financial gain ... shall be fined not more than $500,000 or imprisoned for not more than 5 years, or both, for the first offense; and ... shall be fined not more than $1,000,000 or imprisoned for not more than 10 years, or both, for any subsequent offense").

295. See Press Release, U.S. Department of Justice, First Indictment under Digital Millennium Copyright Act Returned Against Russian National, Company, in San Jose, California (Aug. 28, 2001), available at http://www.usdoj.gov/criminal/cybercrime/Sklyarovindictment.htm (last visited Nov. 8, 2004).

296. U.S. v. Elcom Ltd., 203 F. Supp. 2d 1111, 1122 (N.D. Cal. 2002).

297. See id. at 1122–42.

As to the first argument, Elcom Ltd claimed that "'[s]ection 1201(b) is doomed to inherent vagueness because not all tools are banned, and the language of the statute renders it impossible to determine which tools it in fact bans.'"[298] The district court rejected this argument because it found that the "inescapable conclusion" to be drawn from the statutory language and the legislative history is that Congress

> sought to ban all circumvention tools because most of the time those tools would be used to infringe a copyright. Thus, while it is not unlawful to circumvent for the purpose of engaging in fair use, it is unlawful to traffic in tools that allow fair use circumvention....
>
> Accordingly, there is no ambiguity in what tools are allowed and what tools are prohibited because the statute bans trafficking in or the marketing of *all* circumvention devices.... The law, as written, allows a person to conform his or her conduct to a comprehensible standard and is thus not unconstitutionally vague.[299]

As to the second argument, the district court found that the First Amendment was implicated by the prosecution because the DMCA "bans trafficking in the [defendant's computer program], software which at some level contains expression, thus implicating the First Amendment;" and software "is expression that is protected by the copyright laws and is therefore 'speech' at some level, speech that is protected at some level by the First Amendment."[300] The court found that the DMCA is a content-neutral regulation and therefore analyzed its impact on the First Amendment under the intermediate scrutiny appropriate for such regulations.[301] It held that the DMCA does not violate the First Amendment because it "does not burden substantially more speech than is necessary to achieve the government's asserted goals of promoting electronic commerce, protecting copyrights, and preventing electronic piracy."[302] The court also rejected Elcom Ltd.'s argument that the DMCA unconstitutionally infringes upon the First Amendment rights of third parties to engage in fair use, holding that to the extent it "impacts a lawful purchaser's 'right' to make a back-up copy, or to space-shift that copy to another computer, the limited impairment of that one right does not significantly ... impair ... the First Amendment rights of

---

298. *Id.* at 1123 (quoting Elcom Ltd.'s Due Process Motion to Dismiss at 15).
299. *Id.* at 1126.
300. *Id.*
301. *See id.* at 1127–29.
302. *Id.* at 1133.

users so as to render the DMCA unconstitutionally over broad."[303] The court also rejected Elcom Ltd.'s argument that the DMCA impermissibly chills free expression because it does not clearly indicate what speech it prohibits. It explained that because the DMCA "is not a content-based restriction on speech and its restrictions do not 'provoke uncertainty among speakers' about what speech is permitted and what speech is prohibited", it is "not unconstitutionally vague in violation of the First Amendment."[304]

Elcom Ltd.'s final argument was that the DMCA is unconstitutional because Congress exceeded its authority in enacting the statute.[305] The court began its analysis of this argument by explaining that Congress' authority to legislate in this area derives from two Constitutional sources: the Intellectual Property Clause and the Commerce Clause.[306] The court determined that the issue defined by the arguments made by Elcom Ltd. and by the government was "whether the DMCA was within Congress' Commerce Power ... and if so, whether Congress was nevertheless prohibited from enacting the DMCA because of other restraints on Congress' power imposed by the Intellectual Property Clause."[307] As to the first issue, it found that Congress "plainly has the power to enact the DMCA under the Commerce Clause."[308] As to the second issue, the court applied a two-part analysis derived from the Eleventh Circuit's decision in *United States v. Moghadam*.[309] The first part of the analysis focused on whether the DMCA "is 'not fundamentally inconsistent' with the purpose of the Intellectual Property Clause."[310] It found that the DMCA's anti-device provisions are not fundamentally inconsistent with the Intellectual Property Clause because

> [p]rotecting the exclusive rights granted to copyright owners ... by preventing trafficking in tools that would enable widespread piracy and unlawful infringement is consistent with the purpose of the

---

303. *Id.* at 1135.
304. *Id.* at 1137 (quoting Reno v. American Civil Liberties Union, 521 U.S. 844, 871–72 (1997)).
305. *See id.*
306. *See id. See also* U.S. Const. art. I, § 8, cl. 8 (Intellectual Property Clause) & art, I, § 8, cl. 3.
307. 203 F. Supp. 2d at 1138.
308. *Id.*
309. *Id.* at 1139–40 (citing *United States v. Moghadam*, 175 F.3d 1269, 1276–77 (11th Cir. 1999)).
310. *Id.* at 1140 (quoting 175 F.3d at 1280–81).

Intellectual Property Clause's grant to Congress of the power to 'promote the useful arts and sciences' by granting exclusive rights to authors in their writings [and] Congress did not ban the use of circumvention tools out of a concern that enacting such a ban would unduly restrict the fair use doctrine and expressly sought to preserve fair use.[311]

The second part of the analysis required the court to determine whether the DMCA "is nevertheless 'irreconcilably inconsistent' with a limitation contained within the Intellectual Property Clause."[312] The court found that the DMCA is not because

1. it does not eliminate fair use;
2. it does not grant rights to anyone in any public domain work; and
3. it does not allow a copyright holder to effectively prevent a work "from ever entering the public domain, despite the expiration of the copyright."[313]

Having lost on its motion to dismiss the charges, Elcom Ltd. went to trial in December of 2002 and was acquitted on all counts.[314] According to the jury foreman, "the jurors agreed ElcomSoft's product was illegal but acquitted the company because they believed the company didn't mean to violate the law."[315] If nothing else, the acquittal demonstrates the need for the prosecution to prove that a defendant acted willfully, in accordance with the standard noted earlier.[316]

The Department of Justice finally secured its first conviction under the DMCA in September of 2003.[317] Thomas Whitehead was convicted "of one

---

311. *Id.* at 1140–41 (quoting U.S. CONST. art. I, § 8, cl. 8).

312. *Id.* at 1141.

313. *Id.*

314. *See, e.g.,* Jon Healey, *Russian Firm Cleared in Digital-Piracy Trial,* L.A. TIMES, Dec. 18, 2002, at C1, *available at* 2002 WL 103225287.

315. Lisa M. Bowman, *ElcomSoft Verdict: Not Guilty,* CNET NEWS.COM, Dec. 17, 2002, *available at* http://news.com.com/2100-1023-978176.html (last visited Nov. 8, 2004):

"We didn't understand why a million-dollar company would put on their Web page an illegal thing that would (ruin) their whole business if they were caught," [the foreman] said in an interview after the verdict. [He] added that the panel found the DMCA itself confusing, making it easy for jurors to believe that executives from Russia might not fully understand it.

316. See infra text accompanying notes 265–270.

317. *See* Press Release, U.S. Department of Justice, Federal Jury Convicts Smart-Card Hacker for Violating Digital Millennium Copyright Act (Sept. 22, 2003), *avail-*

count of conspiracy, two counts of selling devices designed to unlawfully decrypt satellite television programming and three counts of violating the DMCA."[318]

> Whitehead was convicted for purchasing software code necessary to reprogram DirecTV access cards. Whitehead paid a co-conspirator $250 a month to continually update the software to circumvent the latest DirecTV security measures. Whitehead then used the software to create and sell illegally modified DirecTV access cards ... to a nationwide client base. This conduct violated the DMCA which prohibits trafficking in technology primarily designed to circumvent a technological measure effectively controlling access to a copyrighted work.[319]

One source of copyright infringement in the computer context is "warez" sites, e.g., "anonymous, often short-lived file-transfer protocol ["FTP"] sites that exist solely to disseminate unlicenced copies of software and/or passwords for pirate software."[320] The existence of these sites generated discussion as to whether the Internet Service Providers ["ISPs"] used to host them should be held liable for acts of copyright infringement perpetrated via the sites.[321] In 1998, Congress adopted the Online Copyright Infringement Liability Limitation Act[322] which shields ISPs from liability for monetary, injunctive or equitable relief for copyright infringement as long as certain conditions are met. An ISP under the statute[323] is not liable for infringement resulting from its "transmitting, routing, or providing connections for, material" through a system or network it controls or operates "or by reason of the intermediate and transient storage of that material in the course of such transmitting, routing, or providing connections" if:

---

able at http://www.cybercrime.gov/whiteheadConviction.htm (last visited Nov. 8, 2004).

318. *Id.*

319. *Id.*

320. Ronnie Heather Brandes, Bonnie L. Kane & Kelly A. Librera, *Intellectual Property Crimes*, 37 AM. CRIM. L. REV. 657, 687 (2000) [hereinafter Brandes, *I.P. Crimes*].

321. *See, e.g., id.* at 688.

322. Pub. L. No. 105-304, 112 Stat. 2877 (1998) (Codified at 17 U.S.C. § 512 (2000)).

323. "[S]ervice provider" is defined as "an entity offering the transmission, routing, or providing of connections for digital online communications, between or among points specified by a user, of material of the user's choosing, without modification to the content of the material as sent or received." 17 U.S.C. § 512(k)(1) (2000).

(1) the transmission of the material was initiated by or at the direction of a person other than the service provider;

(2) the transmission, routing, provision of connections, or storage is carried out through an automatic technical process without selection of the material by the service provider;

(3) the service provider does not select the recipients of the material except as an automatic response to the request of another person;

(4) no copy of the material made by the service provider in the course of such intermediate or transient storage is maintained on the system or network in a manner ordinarily accessible to anyone other than anticipated recipients, and no such copy is maintained on the system or network in a manner ordinarily accessible to such anticipated recipients for a longer period than is reasonably necessary for the transmission, routing, or provision of connections; and

(5) the material is transmitted through the system or network without modification of its content.[324]

An ISP is not liable for copyright infringement by virtue of storing information on a system it controls or operates if it:

1. does not have actual knowledge that the stored material or an activity involving the stored material is infringing or, absent actual knowledge, is not aware of "facts or circumstances from which infringing activity is apparent" or "upon obtaining such knowledge or awareness, acts expeditiously to remove, or disable access to, the material;"

2. does not receive "a financial benefit directly attributable to the infringing activity" if the service provider has the right and ability to control such activity; and

3. upon being notified of possible infringement "responds expeditiously to remove, or disable access to, the material that is claimed to be infringing or to be the subject of infringing activity."[325]

---

324. *Id.* § 512(a).

325. *Id.* § 512(c)(1). This limitation of liability applies only if the ISP has designated an agent to receive notice of claimed infringement. *See id.* § 512(c)(2). In *In re Aimster Copyright Litigation*, 334 F.3d 643, 655 (7th Cir. 2003), *cert. denied*, 124 S. Ct. 1069 (2004), the Seventh Circuit held that Aimster, which operated an online file-sharing service, did not come within the statute's safe harbor provisions because

In *Hendrickson v. eBay, Inc.,*[326] the district court applied the statute to hold that the statute's immunity provisions protected both eBay, Inc., and its employees from liability for allegedly infringing material offered for sale on the auction site.

2. Trademark Infringement

The primary protection for trademarks is provided by the Lanham Act.[327] The Act defines a "trademark" as including

> any word, name, symbol, or device, or any combination thereof—
> (1) used by a person, or
> (2) which a person has a bona fide intention to use in commerce and applies to register on the principal register established by this chapter,
> to identify and distinguish his or her goods, including a unique product, from those manufactured or sold by others and to indicate the source of the goods, even if that source is unknown.[328]

The Lanham Act only allows the recovery of civil damages for acts of trademark infringement.[329] Criminal penalties for trademark violations are imposed by the Trademark Counterfeiting Act.[330] To prove a violation of 18 U.S.C. § 2320(a) (2000), the government must establish that:

---

[f]ar from doing anything to discourage repeat infringers of the plaintiffs' copyrights, Aimster invited them to do so, showed them how they could do so with ease using its system, and by teaching its users how to encrypt their unlawful distribution of copyrighted materials disabled itself from doing anything to prevent infringement.

326. 165 F. Supp. 2d 1082 (C.D. Cal. 2001).

327. Act of July 5, 1946, ch. 540, 60 Stat. 427 (codified at 15 U.S.C. §§ 1051–1141n (2000)).

328. 15 U.S.C. § 1127 (2000). The procedures and requirements for registering trademarks are set out in *id.* §§ 1051–64.

329. *See id.* § 1114.

330. 18 U.S.C. § 2320(a) (2000) ("Whoever intentionally traffics or attempts to traffic in goods or services and knowingly uses a counterfeit mark on or in connection with such goods or services shall, if an individual, be fined not more than $2,000,000 or imprisoned not more than 10 years, or both, and, if a person other than an individual, be fined not more than $5,000,000. In the case of an offense by a person under this section that occurs after that person is convicted of another offense under this section, the person convicted, if an individual, shall be fined not more than $5,000,000 or imprisoned not more than 20 years, or both, and if other than an individual, shall be fined not more than $15,000,000"). *See, e.g.,* U.S. v. Sultan, 115 F.3d 321, 325 (5th Cir. 1997). *Cf.*

1. the defendant trafficked or attempted to traffic in goods or services;
2. the trafficking or the attempt to traffic was intentional;
3. the defendant used a counterfeit mark on or in connection with such goods or services; and
4. the defendant knew that the mark so used was counterfeit.[331]

"Traffic" means to "transport, transfer, or otherwise dispose of, to another, as consideration for anything of value, or make or obtain control of with intent so to transport, transfer or dispose of."[332] A "counterfeit mark" is either

(A) a spurious mark—
(I) that is used in connection with trafficking in goods or services;
(ii) that is identical with, or substantially indistinguishable from, a mark registered for those goods or services on the principal register in the United States Patent and Trademark Office and in use, whether or not the defendant knew such mark was so registered; and
(iii) the use of which is likely to cause confusion, to cause mistake, or to deceive; or

(B) a spurious designation that is identical with, or substantially indistinguishable from, a designation as to which the remedies of the Lanham Act are made available by reason of section 220506 of title 36.[333]

The term does not include "any mark or designation used in connection with goods or services of which the manufacturer or producer was, at the time of the manufacture or production in question authorized to use the mark or designation for the type of goods or services so manufactured or produced, by the holder of the right to use such mark or designation."[334]

U.S. v. Habegger, 370 F.3d 441, 444 (4th Cir. 2004) (evidence insufficient to establish criminal violation).

331. *See, e.g.,* U.S. v. Habegger, 370 F.3d 441, 444 (4th Cir. 2004).
332. *See id.*
333. 18 U.S.C. § 2320(e)(1) (2000).
334. *Id.*

3. Trade Secret Infringement

The Economic Espionage Act of 1996[335] made the theft of trade secrets a federal crime.[336] The Act created two crimes: "economic espionage,"[337] which requires that the theft benefit a foreign government, and a generic offense, "theft of trade secrets."[338] The Act defines "trade secret" as

> all forms and types of financial, business, scientific, technical, economic, or engineering information, including patterns, plans, compilations, program devices, formulas, designs, prototypes, methods, techniques, processes, procedures, programs, or codes, whether tangible or intangible, and whether or how stored, compiled, or memorialized physically, electronically, graphically, photographically, or in writing if—
> (A) the owner thereof has taken reasonable measures to keep such information secret; and

---

335. Pub. L. No. 104-294, 110 Stat. 3488 (1996).

336. *Prosecuting I.P. Crimes Manual, supra* note 234, § VIII(A):

> Until 1996 there was no federal statute that explicitly criminalized the theft of commercial trade secrets.... Federal courts, however, under limited circumstances, did uphold convictions for the interstate transportation of stolen trade secrets or proprietary economic information under 18 U.S.C. § 231, or for the disclosure of information in violation of a confidential or fiduciary relationship under 18 U.S.C. § 1341 or 1343.
>
> Because federal prosecutors sometimes had trouble "shoe-horning" the theft of trade secrets into the above statutes and because of the increased recognition of the increasingly important role that intellectual property plays in the well-being of the American economy, Congress enacted the Economic Espionage Act of 1996, effective October 11, 1996. *See* Pub. L. No. 104-294, 110 Stat. 3488 (1996). In general, it criminalizes the theft of trade secrets.

337. *See* 18 U.S.C. § 1831(a). Subsection (b) provides that if an organization commits the offense defined by § 1831(a), it "shall be fined not more than $10,000,000." *Id.* § 1831(b). "Foreign instrumentality" is defined as "any agency, bureau, ministry, component, institution, association, or any legal, commercial, or business organization, corporation, firm, or entity that is substantially owned, controlled, sponsored, commanded, managed, or dominated by a foreign government", and "foreign agent" is defined as "any officer, employee, proxy, servant, delegate, or representative of a foreign government". *Id.* § 1839(1)-(2).

338. *See Id.* § 1832(a). *See, e.g.,* U.S. v. Martin, 228 F.3d 1, 10–11 (1st Cir. 2000). Subsection (b) provides that if an organization commits the offense defined by § 1832(a), it "shall be fined not more than $5,000,000." 18 U.S.C. § 1832(b) (2000).

(B) the information derives independent economic value, actual or potential, from not being generally known to, and not being readily ascertainable through proper means by, the public....[339]

The Economic Espionage Act gives the federal government the authority to prosecute based on conduct occurring outside the United States if

1. the offender is a "natural person who is a citizen or permanent resident alien of the United States" or an organization "organized under the laws of the United States" or a political subdivision thereof, or
2. "an act in furtherance of the offense was committed in the United States."[340]

The Economic Espionage Act has been used to prosecute the theft of computer data.[341] It has also been used to prosecute attempts and conspiracies to appropriate trade secrets.[342] Attempt and conspiracy charges are convenient for prosecutors because, according to at least two circuits, in a prosecution for an inchoate offense the government is not required to give the defense unrestricted access to information concerning the trade secrets that were the object of the alleged attempt and/or conspiracy.[343]

IV. State Cybercrime Legislation

The sections below survey how state laws address the more significant cybercrime offenses. The citations to state statutes below are illustrative, not exhaustive.

---

339. 18 U.S.C. § 1839(3) (2000). "Owner" is defined as "the person or entity in whom or in which rightful legal or equitable title to, or license in, the trade secret is reposed." *Id.* § 1839(4).

340. 18 U.S.C. § 1837 (2000).

341. *See, e.g.,* U.S. v. Lange, 312 F.3d 263 (7th Cir. 2002).

342. *See, e.g.,* U.S. v. Yang, 281 F.3d 534 (6th Cir. 2002).

343. *See* U.S. v. Hsu, 155 F.3d 189, 203–04 (3d Cir. 1998) (prosecution need not prove that an actual trade secret was used in an attempt or a conspiracy to misappropriate trade secrets in violation of Economic Espionage Act — prosecution can satisfy its burden by proving beyond a reasonable doubt that defendant sought to acquire information which he or she believed to be a trade secret, regardless of whether information actually qualified as such"). *See also* U.S. v. Yang, 281 F.3d 534 (6th Cir. 2002).

A. Cybercrimes Where the Computer Is the Target

1. Hacking and Cracking

Every state prohibits hacking (gaining unauthorized access to a computer) and cracking (gaining unauthorized access to a computer for the purpose of committing theft, vandalism or other crimes). While there are exceptions, states tend to use a two-tiered approach to criminalizing basic unauthorized access (simple hacking) and unauthorized access that results in the commission of some further criminal activity such as copying or destroying data (aggravated hacking).[344] Generally, the states that use this approach define simple hacking and aggravated hacking as distinct crimes and tend to make simple hacking a misdemeanor and aggravated hacking a felony.[345]

Some use a single statute to criminalize both activities.[346] Others have separate provisions.[347] Hawaii has one of the more complicated statutory structures; its Penal Code creates three distinct intrusion crimes and two different damage crimes.[348]

The substance of the simple hacking prohibitions tends to be consistent but there is a fair degree of variation in how they characterize the crimes.

---

344. *See, e.g.,* Del. Code Ann. tit. 11, §§ 932 & 933 (1995) (unauthorized access and computer theft). *See also* Alaska Stat. §§ 11.46.484 & 11.46.740 (Michie 2000) (criminal mischief and criminal use of a computer).

345. *See, e.g.,* Md. Code Ann., Crim. Law § 7-302 (1996); Vt. Stat. Ann. tit. 13, § 4102 (Supp. 2004) (simple hacking a misdemeanor); *id.* § 4104 (aggravated hacking a felony). *Cf.* Iowa Code Ann. § 716.6B (West Supp. 2004) (unauthorized access is a simple misdemeanor, while access that results in damage is either a serious or an aggravated misdemeanor, depending on the nature of the loss).

346. *See, e.g.,* Cal. Penal Code § 502(c) (West Supp. 2004); Conn. Gen. Stat. § 53a-251 (2003); Idaho Code § 18-2202 (Michie 1997); Kan. Stat. Ann. § 21-3755(b) (Supp. 2004); Md. Code Ann., Crim. Law § 7-302(b) (1996); Mich. Comp. Laws Ann. § 752.794 (West Supp. 2004); N.H. Rev. Stat. Ann. § 638:17 (Supp. 2004); Wisc. Stat. Ann. § 943.70 (West Supp. 2004). *See also* S.C. Code Ann. §§ 16-16-10(j) & 16-16-20 (Law. Co-op. Supp. 2004) ("computer hacking" encompasses both simple and aggravated hacking).

347. *See, e.g.,* Vt. Stat. Ann. tit. 13, § 4102 (Supp. 2004) (simple hacking); *id.* § 4104 (access to alter, damage or interfere with computer, computer system, software or data).

348. *See* Haw. Rev. Stat. §§ 708-895.5, 708-895.6 & 708.895.7 (Supp. 2004) (unauthorized computer access in the first degree, second degree and third degree); *id.* §§ 708-892 & 708.892.5 (first and second degree computer damage involving unauthorized computer access).

Some characterize simple hacking as "unauthorized access."[349] Others cast it as "computer trespass."[350] Still other states define it as "unauthorized use" or "computer tampering."[351]

The substance of the prohibitions targeting aggravated hacking also tend to be consistent, but these statutes vary more in structure than do the simple hacking provisions. They all prohibit unauthorized access that results in the copying, alteration and/or deletion of data or damage to a computer system.[352] A number also outlaw the use of a computer to engage in other criminal acts.[353] New York has a "cyber-burglary" statute that makes it a crime to break into a computer or computer system intending "to commit or attempt to commit or further the commission of any felony."[354]

A number of states criminalize the dissemination of viruses, worms and other types of malware.[355] Many of these prohibitions target the dissemination of a "computer contaminant."[356] "Computer contaminant" is defined as encompassing viruses, worms and other harmful programs. California, for example, defines it as

> any set of computer instructions that are designed to modify, damage, destroy, record, or transmit information within a computer, computer system, or computer network without the intent or per-

---

349. E.g., Cal. Penal Code § 502 (West Supp. 2004); Md. Code Ann., Crim. Law § 7-302 (1996); Vt. Stat. Ann. tit. 13, § 4102 (Supp. 2004).

350. E.g., Ark. Code Ann. § 5-41-104 (Michie 1997); N.Y. Penal Law § 156.10 (McKinney 1998).

351. E.g., Cal. Penal Code § 502 (West Supp. 2004) (unauthorized use); Ariz. Rev. Stat. Ann. § 13-2316 (West 2000) (computer tampering).

352. See, e.g., Ga. Code Ann. § 16-9-93 (1999); N.C. Gen. Stat. § 14-458 (Supp. 2004).

353. See, e.g., Ark. Code Ann. § 5-41-103 (Michie 1997); Del. Code Ann. tit. 11, § 2738 (2004); Idaho Code § 18-2202 (Michie 1997).

354. N.Y. Penal Law § 156.10 (McKinney 1998).

355. See, e.g., 720 Ill. Comp. Stat. 5/16D-3 (Supp. 2004); Me. Rev. Stat. Ann. tit. 17, § 433(1)(c) (West Supp. 2004); Mich. Comp. Laws Ann. § 752.795 (West 2004); Minn. Stat. Ann. § 609.88(1)(c) (West Supp. 2004); Neb. Rev. Stat. § 28-1345 (1995); N.C. Gen. Stat. § 14-455 (Supp. 2004).

356. See, e.g., Ariz. Rev. Stat. Ann. § 13-2316(A)(3) (West 2000); Ark. Code Ann. § 5-41-202(A)(5) (Michie Supp. 2004); Cal. Penal Code § 502(c)(8) (West Supp. 2004); Fla. Stat. Ann. § 815.06(1)(e) (West Supp. 2004); Nev. Rev. Stat. 205.4765(5) (Supp. 2004); N.H. Rev. Stat. Ann. § 638:17 (Supp. 2004); N.J. Stat. Ann. § 2C:20-23 (West Supp. 2004); N.D. Cent. Code § 12.1-06.1-08 (Supp. 2004); S.C. Code Ann. § 16-16-20 (Law. Co-op. Supp. 2004); Tenn. Code Ann. § 39-14-602(b)(3) (Supp. 2004); W. Va. Code § 61-3C-7 (2000).

mission of the owner of the information. They include, but are not limited to, a group of computer instructions commonly called viruses or worms, that are self-replicating or self-propagating and are designed to contaminate other computer programs or computer data, consume computer resources, modify, destroy, record, or transmit data, or in some other fashion usurp the normal operation of the computer, computer system, or computer network.[357]

Some states outlaw attempts to disseminate malware.[358]

2. Denial of Service Attacks

Some states outlaw denial of service attacks.[359] South Carolina includes denial of service attacks in its prohibition on disseminating malware; the statute defines "computer contaminant" as encompassing denial of service attacks.[360] A few states explicitly outlaw attempted denial of service attacks.[361]

B. Cybercrimes Involving Improper Communications

1. Cyberstalking

A number of states outlaw online stalking or harassment. Some statutes require that the offender transmit a "credible threat" to injure the victim, the victim's family or "any other person."[362] Other stalking statutes are broader, making it a crime to use a computer to "engage in a course of conduct" that would cause a "reasonable person" to "suffer intimidation or se-

---

357. Cal. Penal Code § 502(b)(1) (West Supp. 2004).

358. See, e.g., Ark. Code Ann. § 5-41-202 (Michie Supp. 2004); 720 Ill. Comp. Stat. § 16D-3(a)(4) (Supp. 2004); Nev. Rev. Stat. § 205.4765(5) (Supp. 2004); W. Va. Code § 61-3C-7 (2000).

359. See, e.g., 18 Pa. Cons. Stat. Ann. § 7612(a) (West Supp. 2004) (One "commits an offense if he intentionally or knowingly engages in a scheme or artifice, including ... a denial of service attack upon any computer, computer system ... or any part thereof that is designed to ... deny the access of information ... by users of that ... system"). See also Cal. Penal Code § 502 (West Supp. 2004); Conn. Gen. Stat. § 53a-251 (2003); Del. Code Ann. tit. 11, § 934 (2004); N.H. Rev. Stat. Ann. § 638:17 (Supp. 2004); N.C. Gen. Stat. § 14-456 (Supp. 2004); W. Va. Code § 61-3C-8 (2000); Wyo. Stat. Ann. § 6-3-504 (Michie 1999).

360. S.C. Code Ann. § 16-16-10(k)(3) (Law. Co-op. Supp. 2004).

361. See, e.g., Conn. Gen. Stat. § 53-451 (2003); R.I. Gen. Laws § 11-52-1 (2002); Va. Code Ann. § 18.2-152.2 (Michie Supp. 2004).

362. See, e.g., Colo. Rev. Stat. Ann. § 18-9-111(1)(e) (West Supp. 2004); Ga. Code Ann. § 16-5-90(a)(1) (1999).

rious inconvenience, annoyance or alarm," as well as fearing death or injury to themselves or to members of their family.[363]

2. State Spam Laws

In 2003, Congress adopted the CAN-SPAM Act of 2003.[364] Among other things, the CAN-SPAM Act has certain pre-emptive effects with regard to state spam legislation. It supersedes any state statute "that expressly regulates the use of electronic mail to send commercial messages, except to the extent that" it "prohibits falsity or deception in any portion of a commercial electronic mail message or information attached thereto."[365] The CAN-SPAM Act is not to be construed as pre-empting

1. state laws "that are not specific to electronic mail, including State trespass, contract, or tort law;" or
2. other state laws to the extent that they "relate to acts of fraud or computer crime."[366]

Consequently, states can still prosecute spammers for fraud, false advertising, trespass or other crimes. Virginia's anti-spam statute is an example of a state provision that can still be used against spammers. It makes it an offense to:

(1) use[] a computer ... with the intent to falsify or forge electronic mail transmission information or other routing information ... in connection with the transmission of unsolicited bulk electronic mail ... ; or
(2) knowingly sell[], give[], or otherwise distribute[] or possess[] with the intent to sell, give or distribute software that (i) is primarily designed or produced for the purpose of facilitating or enabling the falsification of electronic mail transmission information or other routing information; (ii) has only limited commercially significant purpose or use other than to facilitate or enable the falsification of electronic mail transmission information or other routing information; or (iii) is marketed by that person acting alone or with another for use in facilitating or enabling the falsifi-

---

363. Ariz. Rev. Stat. Ann. § 13-2316(5) (West 2000); Mass. Gen. Laws 265 § 43A(a)(1) (2000); Okla. Stat. tit. 21, § 1953 (Supp. 2004).

364. Pub. L. No. 108-187, 117 Stat. 2699 (2003). *See* Section III(B)(3), *infra*, for a discussion of the provisions of this act.

365. 15 U.S.C.A. § 7707(b)(1) (Supp. 2004).

366. *Id.* § 7707(b)(2).

cation of electronic mail transmission information or other routing information....[367]

A violation is a misdemeanor unless

1. the volume of spam transmitted "exceeded 10,000 attempted recipients in any 24-hour period, 100,000 attempted recipients in any 30-day time period, or one million attempted recipients in any one-year time period;"
2. the revenue generated by a spam transmission exceeded $1,000 or the total revenue generated by all spam transmitted exceeded $50,000; or
3. the person employed a minor to assist in the transmission of spam that fell into either of these categories.[368]

At the end of May, 2004, Maryland adopted a similar provision.[369]

C. Cybercrimes Involving Minors

States consistently make it a crime to use a computer to solicit a minor for sex.[370] Some of these statutes specifically state that the offense is com-

---

367. VA. CODE ANN. § 18.2-152.3:1(A) (Michie Supp. 2004).

368. VA. CODE ANN. § 18.2-152.3:1(B) (Michie Supp. 2004). A few states have comparable statutes. See, e.g., ARK. CODE ANN. § 5-41-205 (Michie Supp. 2004); CONN. GEN. STAT. §§ 53-451(b)(7) & 53-451(c) (2003); DEL. CODE ANN. tit. 11, §§ 937(2) & 937(3) (2004); 720 ILL. COMP. STAT. §§ 5/16D-3(a)(5) & 5/16D-3(a-5) (Supp. 2004); LA. REV. STAT. ANN. § 14:73.6(B) (West Supp. 2004); NEV. REV. STAT. 205.492(1)-(3) (Supp. 2004); 18 PA. CONS. STAT. ANN. § 7661 (West Supp. 2004); TENN. CODE ANN. § 39-14-603(a) (Supp. 2004).

369. See Maryland Spam Deterrence Act, 2004 Md. Senate Bill 604 (to be codified as MD. CODE ANN., CRIM. LAW § 3-805.1).

370. See, e.g., ALA. CODE § 13A-6-110 (Supp. 2004); DEL. CODE ANN. tit. 11, § 1112A (2004); GA. CODE ANN. § 16-12-100.2 (Supp. 2004); 720 ILL. COMP. STAT. 5/11-6 (Supp. 2004); IND. CODE ANN. § 35-42-4-6 (West 2004); IOWA CODE ANN. § 728.12 (West Supp. 2004); Me. Rev. Stat. Ann. tit. 17A, § 259 (West 2004); MICH. COMP. LAWS ANN. § 750.145a (West 2004); MINN. STAT. ANN. § 609.352 (West 2003); N.H. REV. STAT. ANN. § 649-B:4 (Supp. 2004); N.C. GEN. STAT. § 14-202.3 (1999); OKLA. STAT. tit. 21, § 1040.13a (Supp. 2004); S.D. CODIFIED LAWS § 22-22-24.5 (Michie Supp. 2004); TEX. PENAL CODE ANN. § 15.031 (Vernon Supp. 2004); UTAH CODE ANN. § 76-4-401 (Supp. 2004); W. VA. CODE § 61-3C-14b (Supp. 2004).

mitted if the perpetrator believed the person whom he was soliciting for sex was a minor, even though that was not true.[371]

States are also consistent in outlawing the use of computers to create, possess and/or distribute child pornography.[372] In the wake of the Supreme Court's decision in *Ashcroft v. Free Speech Coalition*,[373] some states have revised their child pornography statutes and courts in other states have construed their statutes as not encompassing the possession or distribution of "virtual" child pornography.[374]

D. Cybercrimes Involving Fraud and Other Traditional Misconduct

1. Computer Forgery

Some states make computer forgery a distinct offense.[375] A typical computer forgery statute provides as follows: "Any person who creates, alters, or deletes any data contained in any computer or computer network, who, if such person had created, altered, or deleted a tangible document or instrument would have committed forgery ... shall be guilty of the crime of computer forgery."[376] New Jersey makes it a crime to possess "forgery devices," which include computers, computer equipment and computer software "specifically designed or adapted to such use."[377]

371. *See, e.g.,* 720 Ill. Comp. Stat. 5/11-6 (Supp. 2004); Ind. Code Ann. § 35-42-4-6 (West 2004); Me. Rev. Stat. Ann. tit. 17A, § 259 (West Supp. 2004); Mich. Comp. Laws Ann. § 750.145a (West 2004); Okla. Stat. tit. 21, § 1040.13a (Supp. 2004); S.D. Codified Laws § 22-22-24.5 (Michie Supp. 2004); Tex. Penal Code Ann. § 15.031 (Vernon Supp. 2004).

372. *See, e.g.,* Alaska Stat. § 11.61.125 (Michie Supp. 2004); Ark. Code Ann. § 5-27-603 (Michie Supp. 2004); Del. Code Ann. tit. 11, § 1109 (2004); Ind. Code Ann. § 35-42-4-4 (West 2004); R.I. Gen. Laws § 11-9-1.3 (2002); Tex. Penal Code § 43.26 (Vernon Supp. 2004).

373. 535 U.S. 234 (2002).

374. *See, e.g.,* State v. May, 829 A.2d 1106 (N.J. Super. 2003). *But see* People v. Alexander, 791 N.E.2d 506 (Ill. 2003) (Illinois statute banned virtual child pornography and therefore violated First Amendment).

375. Ga. Code Ann. § 16-9-93(d) (1999); Nev. Rev. Stat. 205.481 (Supp. 2004); Va. Code Ann. § 18.2-152.14 (Michie 1996); W. Va. Code § 61-3C-15 (2000).

376. Ga. Code Ann. § 16-9-93(d) (1999).

377. N.J. Stat. Ann. § 2C:21-1(c) (West Supp. 2004).

2. Computer Fraud and Theft

A substantial number of states outlaw using computers to commit fraud.[378] Some make "computer fraud" a separate crime.[379] Many include using a computer to commit fraud in their basic aggravated hacking statute.[380] Rather than making computer fraud a separate crime, a few states increase the penalties for aggravated hacking if the crime was committed for the purpose of devising or executing a scheme to defraud.[381]

Some states also incorporate embezzlement crimes into their computer fraud statutes.[382]

A number of states outlaw "computer theft."[383] It can encompass any of several different crimes, including information theft, software theft, computer hardware theft and theft of computer services.[384] It can also encompass the theft of computer hardware.[385] Finally, computer theft can consist of using a computer to steal other types of property.[386]

---

378. *See, e.g.,* Ariz. Rev. Stat. Ann. § 13-2316(1) (West Supp. 2004); Cal. Penal Code § 502(c)(1)(A) (West Supp. 2004); Haw. Rev. Stat. § 708-891 (Supp. 2004); Ky. Rev. Stat. Ann. § 434.845 (Banks-Baldwin Supp. 2004); La. Rev. Stat. Ann. § 14:73.5 (West 1997); N.J. Stat. Ann. § 2C:20-25(c) (West Supp. 2004); Or. Rev. Stat. § 164.377(2)(a) (Supp. 2004); Va. Code Ann. § 18.2-152.3 (Michie Supp. 2004).

379. *See, e.g.,* Ark. Code Ann. § 5-41-103 (Michie 1999); Haw. Rev. Stat. § 708-891 (Supp. 2004).

380. *See, e.g.,* Ariz. Rev. Stat. Ann. § 13-2316(A)(1) (West 2000); Ky. Rev. Stat. Ann. § 434.845 (Banks-Baldwin Supp. 2004).

381. *See, e.g.,* Ala. Code § 13A-8-102(d)(2) (Supp. 2004); Fla. Stat. Ann. § 815.04(4) (West Supp. 2004); Mo. Ann. Stat. § 569.095(2) (West Supp. 2004).

382. *See, e.g.,* N.M. Stat. Ann. § 30-45-3 (Michie 1994); Va. Code Ann. § 18.2-152.3 (Michie Supp. 2004).

383. *See, e.g.,* Colo. Rev. Stat. § 18-5.5-102(1)(d) (2000); Ga. Code Ann. § 16-9-93(a) (1999); Idaho Code § 18-2202(1) (Michie 1997); Iowa Code § 714.1(8) (Supp. 2004); Minn. Stat. Ann. § 609.89 (West Elec. Supp. 2004); N.J. Stat. Ann. § 2C:20-25 (West Supp. 2004); 18 Pa. Cons. Stat. Ann. § 7613 (West Supp. 2004); R.I. Gen. Laws § 11-52-4 (2002); Vt. Stat. Ann. tit. 13, § 4105(a) (Supp. 2004); Va. Code Ann. § 18.2-152.6 (Michie Supp. 2004).

384. *See, e.g.,* Cal. Penal Code § 502(c)(2) (West Supp. 2004); Iowa Code § 714.1(8) (Supp. 2004); N.J. Stat. Ann. § 2C:20-25(b) (West Supp. 2004); Va. Code Ann. § 18.2-152.6 (Michie Supp. 2004).

385. *See, e.g.,* R.I. Gen. Laws § 11-52-4 (2002).

386. *See, e.g.,* La. Rev. Stat. Ann. § 14:73.2 (West 1997); Mich. Comp. Laws Ann. § 752.795 (West 2004); Utah Code Ann. § 76-6-703 (1999).

3. Computer Extortion

A few states specifically outlaw the use of computers to commit extortion. One approach they take is to include computer extortion within the definition of computer fraud.[387] Another approach is to incorporate computer extortion into the state's general extortion statute.[388] Yet another approach is to have a computer extortion offense that incorporates the state's computer hacking and cracking statute.[389]

E. Identity Theft

A number of states have "identity theft" or "identity fraud" statutes that typically make it a crime "knowingly and with intent to defraud for economic benefit" to obtain, possess, transfer, use or attempt "to obtain, possess, transfer or use, one or more identification documents or personal identification number" of someone else.[390] Some states also make it a crime to traffic in stolen identities.[391]

F. Cyberterrorism

Only a few states have specifically outlawed cyberterrorism. Arkansas, for example, defines terrorism as committing an "act of terrorism" with "the intent to intimidate or coerce a civilian population, influence the policy of a unit of government by using intimidation or coercion, affect the conduct

---

387. *See, e.g.,* ARK. CODE ANN. § 5-41-103 (Michie 1999) (computer fraud defined as accessing a computer for the purpose of devising or executing a "scheme or artifice to defraud or extort"). *See also* CAL. PENAL CODE § 502 (West Supp. 2004); OKLA. STAT. tit. 21, § 1953 (Supp. 2004).

388. *See, e.g.,* HAW. REV. STAT. § 707-764 (Supp. 2004) (extortion to threaten to cause damage to computer, computer system or computer network).

389. *See, e.g.,* N.C. GEN. STAT. § 14-457 (1999) (computer extortion consists of threatening to damage a computer in violation of N.C. GEN. STAT. § 14-455 (Supp. 2004)).

390. ALA. CODE § 13A-8-192(a) (Supp. 2004). *See also* CAL. PENAL CODE § 530.5 (West Supp. 2004); CONN. GEN. STAT. § 53a-129a (2003); DEL. CODE ANN. tit. 11, § 854 (2004); GA. CODE ANN. § 16-9-121 (Supp. 2004); IOWA CODE § 715A.8 (Supp. 2004); MASS. GEN. LAWS ANN. ch. 266, § 37E (West 2000); MISS. CODE ANN. § 97-45-19 (Supp. 1994); OKLA. STAT. ANN. tit. 21, § 1533.1 (Supp. 2004); 18 PA. CONS. STAT. ANN. § 4120 (West Supp. 2004).

391. *See, e.g.,* ALA. CODE § 13A-8-193(a) (Supp. 2004).

of a unit or level of government by intimidation or coercion, or retaliate against a civilian population or unit of government".[392] It defines "act of terrorism," in part, as

> [a]ny act or any series of two (2) or more acts committed in furtherance of a single intention, scheme, or design that disables or destroys the usefulness or operation of a computer network, computers, computer programs, or data used by any industry, any class of business, or five (5) or more businesses or by the federal government, state government, any unit of local government, a public utility, a manufacturer of pharmaceuticals, a national defense contractor, or a manufacturer of chemical or biological products used in connection with agricultural production.[393]

Connecticut has a "computer crime in furtherance of terrorist purposes" offense.[394] One commits this offense by committing computer crime "with intent to intimidate or coerce the civilian population or a unit of government."[395] Indiana has a similar offense: "computer tampering."[396] "Computer tampering" consists of intentionally or knowingly altering or damaging a computer program or data without the owner's consent.[397] The basic crime is a Class D felony, but it rises to a Class C felony if the computer tampering is committed "for the purpose of terrorism;" and it rises to a Class B felony "if it is committed for the purpose of terrorism and results in serious bodily injury to a person."[398] Illinois simply includes disabling or destroying the usefulness of a computer or computer network in its general definition of terrorism.[399] Georgia makes it a crime to use a computer to disseminate information "relating to terrorist acts."[400]

West Virginia has an "endangering public safety" offense in its computer crimes code.[401] The offense is defined as follows:

---

392. Ark. Code Ann. § 5-54-205 (Michie Supp. 2004).
393. *Id.* § 5-54-201(1)(C).
394. Conn. Gen. Stat. § 53a-301(a) (2003).
395. *Id.*
396. Ind. Code Ann. § 35-43-1-4 (West 2004).
397. *Id.* § 35-43-1-4(b).
398. *Id.*
399. *See* 720 Ill. Comp. Stat. 5/29D-10 (Supp. 2004).
400. Ga. Code Ann. § 16-11-37.1 (1999).
401. W. Va. Code § 61-3C-14 (2000).

Any person who accesses a computer or computer network and knowingly, willfully and without authorization (a) interrupts or impairs the providing of services by any private or public utility; (b) interrupts or impairs the providing of any medical services; (c) interrupts or impairs the providing of services by any state, county or local government agency, public carrier or public communication service; or otherwise endangers public safety shall be guilty of a felony, and, upon conviction thereof, shall be fined not more than fifty thousand dollars or imprisoned not more than twenty years, or both.[402]

G. Miscellaneous Cybercrime Offenses

Some states have a "computer invasion of privacy" crime that typically consists of using a computer to examine "without authority any "any employment, salary, credit or any other financial or personal information relating to any other person."[403] A few make it a crime to introduce false information into a computer system for the purpose of "damaging or enhancing" someone's "data record" or "financial reputation."[404] Some states have a "misuse of computer information" offense that prohibits copying, receiving or using information that was obtained by violating a hacking or cracking statute.[405]

A surprising number of states have an "offense against computer equipment or supplies," which consists of modifying or destroying "equipment or supplies that are used or intended to be used in a computer, computer system, or computer network".[406] A number make it a crime to deny, disrupt, degrade, interrupt or cause the denial, disruption, degradation or interruption of computer services or of access to a computer.[407] A few make

---

402. *Id.*

403. Va. Code Ann. § 18.2-152.5 (Michie Supp. 2004).

404. *See, e.g.,* Alaska Stat. § 11.46.740 (Michie 2000); N.M. Stat. Ann. § 30-45-4 (Michie 1994).

405. *See, e.g.,* Ala. Code § 13A-8-102 (Supp. 2004); Conn. Gen. Stat. § 53a-251 (2003); Fla. Stat. § 815.04 (Supp. 2004); N.H. Rev. Stat. Ann. § 638:17 (Supp. 2004).

406. *See, e.g.,* Ala. Code § 13A-8-103 (1994); Del. Code Ann. tit. 11, § 936 (2004); La. Rev. Stat. Ann. § 14:73.3 (West 1997); Miss. Code Ann. § 97-45-7 (1994); Wy. Stat. Ann. § 6-3-503 (Michie 1999).

407. *See, e.g.,* Cal. Penal Code § 502(c)(5) (West Supp. 2004); Conn. Gen. Stat. § 53a-251(d) (2003); Del. Code Ann. tit. 11, § 934 (2004); Fla. Stat. ch. 815.06 (Supp.

it a crime to destroy computer equipment.[408] Finally, Florida has an "offense against intellectual property" statute that makes it a crime to modify "data, programs or supporting documentation residing" in a computer or computer system.[409]

V. Conclusion

This chapter is concerned only with cybercrime law in the United States. It surveys state and federal laws that target the most frequently-encountered—and therefore most notorious—cybercrimes. As this chapter demonstrates, United States law, at both the state and federal levels, is generally adequate to deal with these basic varieties of cybercrime.

There are certainly areas that could use improvement, however. Many states have not explicitly criminalized denial of service attacks, and others either lack cyberstalking laws or have laws that encompass only conduct that is intended to put the victim in fear of death or serious bodily injury. As to the latter, recent cases demonstrate the havoc an online stalker can create for his victim without resorting to overt threats of death or physical violence.[410] This is also an area in which federal cybercrime law is lacking.

It is important to realize, however, that even though cybercrime law in the United States is generally adequate to allow the investigation and prosecution of cybercriminals, cybercrime, unlike more traditional crime, is not an intrinsically domestic phenomenon. Since cybercrime is not physically-based crime, it can, and does, routinely transcend national boundaries. Because law and law enforcement institutions are territorially-based, this creates new challenges for countries' ability to control cybercrime by apprehending and punishing cybercriminals.[411] Chapter Five deals with the

---

2004); Miss. Code Ann. § 97-45-5 (1994); N.H. Rev. Stat. Ann. § 638:17 (Supp. 2004); Okla. Stat. tit. 21, § 1953 (Supp. 2004); Utah Code Ann. § 76-6-703 (1999).

408. *See, e.g.,* Ala. Code § 13A-8-103(B)(1) (1994); Del. Code Ann. tit. 11, § 936 (2004); N.H. Rev. Stat. Ann. § 638:17(V) (Supp. 2004); W. Va. Code § 61-3C-7 (2000).

409. Fla. Stat. ch. 815.04(1) (Supp. 2004).

410. *See, e.g.,* Paul Shukovsky, *Cyberstalker Just Out of Reach of Law, But, Finally, He Stops,* Seattle Post-Intelligencer (Feb. 11, 2004), *available at* http://seattlepi. nwsource.com/local/160201_cyberstalking11.html (last visited Dec. 9, 2004).

411. *See, e.g.,* Susan W. Brenner, *Toward A Criminal Law for Cyberspace: Distributed Security,* 10 B.U. J. Sci. & Tech. L. 2, 6–11 (2004). Systems must also maintain external order by implementing rules that structure their relationship with their physical and biological environment. *See id.* at 9–10. They must, for example, protect themselves from attacks by competing entities; human societies have traditionally consigned this task to

international dimension of cybercrime and with the efforts that are currently underway to facilitate nation's ability to respond to transborder cybercrime.

---

military forces. *See id.* The discussion in the text above focuses primarily on the need to maintain internal order.

Chapter Three

The Investigation and Prosecution of a Cybercrime

Ivan Orton[*]

In the golden age of cybercrime, from the early 1970s through the early 1990s, the investigation of a cybercrime usually started with the victim's computer. Did the intruder leave some evidence on that computer that could identify him/her? Computer crimes usually involved direct access to the target computer, or, at best, a direct connection over a telephone modem. Tracing the cybercrime back to its origins usually meant identifying who had physical access to the computer or using trap and trace devices[1] or other means of identifying the originating number of a telephonic access.

With the advent of the World Wide Web and the wide spread use of e-mail, instant messaging and other forms of electronic communication over the Internet, the focus of the investigation of cybercrime has shifted. Modern cybercrime often starts with tracing an electronic communication.[2] Be-

---

* Senior Deputy Prosecuting Attorney, Fraud Division, Office of the Prosecuting Attorney, King County (Seattle), Washington. Member of the bar of Washington.

1. A device installed on the victim's telephone line that identified the source of calls coming to that line.

2. Of course not all cybercrime investigations involve tracing electronic communications. The goal of tracing a communication is usually to find the suspect's computer and search that computer. If the location of that computer is known and there is a prov-

cause such communications involve both a receiving computer and a sending computer, both computers are valid sources of investigatory information. The goals in tracing an electronic communication are two-fold: (1) identifying the suspect, and (2) locating the computer from which the communication originated in order to search that computer and seize evidence found there.

This process, of tracing communications, identifying originating computers and obtaining search warrants is the primary investigative method of the cybercrime police officer and prosecutor. It is also fraught with legal and technological jeopardy. This chapter explores that investigative process and the associated perils.

Because this process is often difficult to comprehend in the abstract, we will explore the process in the context of three specific cybercrimes. Both the cases and facts are real, but the names of all parties and companies have been changed.

The first case we will call the Janet Davis case. It is an intrusion and theft of proprietary data case that involves direct access to the target computer. The second case, which we will call the Mel Howard case, is an intrusion and data destruction case, with access to the computer done over direct modem connection and the Internet. The final case, which will be called the Allen Worley case, involves harassment and stalking via e-mail over the Internet. While these three cases do involve some of the more common cybercrimes occurring during the first ten to fifteen years of the Internet, they were selected because, between them, they touch on many of the legal and technological problems a cybercrime investigation will encounter including the use of anonymizing software and transjurisdictional legal issues.

To proceed, the facts of each of the cases will be introduced to the point where law enforcement was contacted. We will then explore tracing e-mail and examine the investigative choices available to the police or prosecutor at that stage of the investigation. We follow that with a discussion of the legal issues involved in obtaining records from third parties. We return to the cases and follow the investigations as they attempt to trace the communications involved back to their source. We will then examine the investigative choices available once the source computer has been identified, including the law relating to the search and seizure of computers and computer records. We return once again to the cases to discuss the steps that

---

able connection between that computer and the crime, there is no need to trace communications back to that computer.

were taken to obtain the suspect's computer and the results of the examination of that computer. We will examine the process of determining what evidence is needed to support the filing of criminal charges. Finally, we return to the cases for a discussion of the actual charges filed, the use of computer evidence in plea negotiations and at trial and the ultimate result in each case.

I. Introduction to the Scenarios

A. Case 1 — Janet Davis

Janet Davis was a senior software engineer at ANDA Software, a mid-level software company. ANDA specialized in providing an easy to use programming language for end users to use in constructing applications.

Due to poor performance evaluations, Janet's employment was terminated. This was on the Friday before the Martin Luther King Monday holiday in January. Janet requested and was granted permission to retain her key card until the following Tuesday so that she could remove her personal possessions. The key card allowed her access to the elevator in the garage and to ANDA's office. Janet cleaned out her office over the weekend and turned in her key card on Tuesday.

About a month later, Carl Rhodes, the head programmer for ANDA, was reviewing his computer. Carl had written what the company hoped would become the key to ANDA's successful future — a new generation compiler. The compiler, code named "Stampede," was such an improvement over existing compilers that, if successfully completed, it would give ANDA a major advantage over their competitors. Its value, thus, was dependent upon it not being disseminated to ANDA's competitors.

Carl was examining his computer and noticed that his F: partition contained a copy of Fastback, a DOS backup utility. He found that curious because, while he had Fastback installed on his computer, it was in the C: not F: partition. He knew that Fastback, when copying files, created a history or log file that displayed the time and date of the backup and the files copied. There was a history file in his F: partition with the date of January 23 — Martin Luther King Day.

Carl examined the history file and, to his dismay, discovered that at 2:16 a.m. on January 23, someone had made a floppy copy of the Stampede source code. Because the source code was very closely held within the company, the only copies were on Carl's computer and in the company safe.

Carl knew he had not made the additional copy of Stampede, but someone had. The code was now possibly outside of ANDA's control.

Carl immediately contacted the President of ANDA and the company's security team. By examining the building's record of key card access they were able to determine that the key card assigned to Janet had been used to access the garage elevator at 1:48 a.m. on January 23 and ANDA's offices three minutes later. Network log files showed that Carl's computer had been logged on to the network at 2:08 a.m. Janet had logged on at 2:12 a.m. The Fastback directory had been created on Carl's computer at 2:14. The backup had started at 2:16 a.m. Armed with this evidence, ANDA's attorney met with the police to see if a search warrant for Janet's house could be obtained.

B. Case 2 — Mel Howard

Mel Howard was the primary software engineer at Cornercave Software. Cornercave was a fledging software company whose principal product was WebUser, a program that would allow companies to use the Internet for internal management. Mel had written most of the code. Because of some disputes between Mel and the President of the company, Mel left the company's employment on June 27. An underling he had been training, Bill Benton, took over the project.

1. Domain Hijacking

On July 29, the company discovered that its domain — www.cornercave.com — had been hijacked. To understand this, one must have a rudimentary knowledge of the role of the domain name system and domain name servers. Typically a user enters a web address, say, www.microsoft.com or enters an e-mail address in the form johndoe@hotmail.com. In each instance the user has specified the domain of the computer he or she wants to connect or send mail to as a word — "microsoft" or "hotmail." Domains are expressed in words because words are easier for humans to remember and use but computers that route traffic on the Internet do not understand domains as words. They understand domains as numbers — specifically numbers in the form of an Internet Protocol or IP address. Every device connected to the Internet must have an IP address for that device to be able to send and receive communications from other devices, just like every telephone must have a telephone number to be usable.

IP addresses have a particular format — a series of four numbers separated by periods, 192.168.0.1, for example. The valid range of numbers within each set is 0–255. Thus the address just given complies with this rule while 192.268.0.1 does not because 268 is greater than 255.

Thus, as far as the computer is concerned, the domain www.microsoft.com is unintelligible—the computer needs an IP address. Users on the other hand are much more comfortable with domain names rather than IP address. So what is needed is a translation device—something to convert domain names to IP addresses so the user can type in www.microsoft.com and the translator can provide the computer with the IP address equivalent. This service is provided by Domain Name Servers ["DNS"] and each computer accessing the Internet has access to such a server. The process is transparent to the end user, but without the translation process, the computer is unable to act on a command to access a webpage or send e-mail.

The DNS in turn rely on a registry of domain names. This registry keeps track of what IP address is associated with what domain name. The registry allows people to sign up for domain names, to transfer ownership of domain names and to change the IP address. The last is what we are concerned with.

If your domain name is www.nextnewthing.com, for example, you will register that domain with one of the recognized domain registry services. As part of that registration you must specify the IP address or range of addresses to be associated with that domain name. If you are a small company with a website you typically rent space from an Internet Service Provider ["ISP"] to host your website, and in such a case the IP address you enter on the registration form will be the IP address assigned you by the ISP.

But what do you do if you wish to change your ISP. You can put your website up at some other ISP but until you change the information provided the domain name registry, all traffic destined for www.nextnewthing.com will not reach your website. It will instead go to your old ISP and, likely, into a blackhole. Users will be unable to contact you or your website. So the domain registry service provides a mechanism for you to tell them that efforts to contact www.nextnewthing.com should not be sent to the old IP address but to the new IP address you have been assigned by your new ISP.

Domain hijacking in its simplest form is the act of providing false change of IP address to the domain registry service. It can be likened to someone else turning in a change of address card for you to the post office. Just like the change of address form will cause all mail intended for one address to be diverted to a different address, a change of IP addresses will cause all electronic communications intended for one address to be diverted to another. While a valid change of address serves a valuable function, a fraudulent change of address can create havoc.

At the time Cornercave was having its difficulty, the process for changing a domain registration was fairly simple. If a change request e-mail was sent from the correct e-mail address, i.e., the address from which the original registration occurred, the change request would be processed.

On July 28, a little more than a month after Mel left the company, Cornercave learned that all traffic for www.cornercave.com was being diverted to an IP address associated with an organization called "Pirates of the Internet." Cornercave quickly regained control of its domain, and in the process learned that unsuccessful attempts to change the domain had occurred on July 16, 23 and 26. The attempts to change the domain, including the successful one, were made via e-mail sent to Network Solutions. Cornercave obtained a copy of the e-mail requesting the transfer. The e-mail for the July 16 request is reprinted below.

Network Solutions Registration Services
    E-mail: hostmaster@internic net

From postmaster@islandermedia.com Wed Dec 31 19:00:00 1969
Received: from rs.internic.net (bipmxo.lb.internic.net [192.168.
120.13]) by opsmail.internic.net (8.9.3/8.9.1) with SMTP id
QAAO17O1 for <hostmaster~internic.net>; Fri, 16 Jul 1999
16:19:46 -0400 (EDT)
Received: (qmail 18559 invoked from network); 16 Jul 1999
20:15:16 -0000
Received: from smtp6.jps.net (209.63.224.103) by 192.168.119.13
with SMTP; 16 Jul 1999 20:15:16 -0000
Received: from [209.63.189.117] (209-63-189-117.sea.jps.net
[209.63.189.117]) by smtp6.jps.net (8.9.0/8.8.5) with ESMTP id
NAA17047;
Fri, 16 Jul 1999 13:19:43 -0700 (PDT)
X-Sender: (Unverified)
Message-Id: <V04003a00b3b475e9299ee[209.63.189.841>
Mime-Version: 1.0
Content-Type: text/plain; charset=~us-ascii
Date: Fri, 16 Jul 1999 13:22:14 -0700
To: hostmaster@internic net
From: Sam Martin <postmaster~islandermedia.com>

Subject: [NIC-990716.l2fcd] MODIFY DOMAIN

1. Comments
2. Complete Domain Name   Cornercave.COM
    Organization Using Domain Name
3a. Organization Name   :PIRATES OF THE INTERNET
3b. Street Address   :666 HELL STREET
3c. City   STOCK
3d. State   CA
3e. Postal Code   :59846
3f. Country   US

2. Massive File Deletions

Before this issue could be addressed, however, Cornercave soon had an even larger problem on their hands. Cornercave's webserver was located at the offices of its ISP—Islander Media. On August 2, shortly before 9:00 a.m., the President of Cornercave, Amy Patterson, found she was unable to access the Cornercave webserver. She contacted Islander Media who checked the server. They discovered that the server was "frozen." When they attempted to reboot the server they were faced with a series of error messages related to missing files. Further examination showed that the server had suffered massive file deletions including much of the Windows NT operating system. Also deleted was the entire source code for WebUser—the main software project.

The President of Cornercave had been concerned for some time about the performance of Bill Benton, the software writer who had replaced Mel Howard. Amy had become convinced that he was in over his head and had expressed this concern to him. Her initial reaction was that Bill had something to do with the problems with the server, either out of anger at her comments or to cover-up problems he had created. In any event, Amy was convinced that she needed to return to the backup made by Mel before he left in June. But when she checked the contents of the Jaz drive where the backup had been made she discovered the disk was blank—there was no backup. The only existing backup was from months earlier.

Nevertheless, Amy set up a new server and installed the company's program on that server. Having learned her lesson from the August 2 incident, she made sure that this server was protected by a firewall.

But logs of that firewall showed that the attacks were continuing. Somehow, someone was gaining access to Cornercave's computers and making changes in the data. Receipts and invoices were missing, changes had been made in employee time sheets—someone had free rein. Clearly, a backdoor existed in the software. Even though the software was close to being ready to release (it was reproduced by updating the old backup), the decision was made to rewrite the software from scratch because of the potential that backdoors would exist on the software when they sold it.

All of this occurred within hours to a few days of the events of August 2. As these events progressed Amy became more and more convinced that this was not a software or hardware malfunction—the damage on August 2 and the continuing access to the server showed that this was the result of someone's malicious action. She called the police. She told the police the suspect was Bill Benton.

C. Case 3—Allen Worley

Bonnie Ronstadt had first met Allen Worley in the mid-eighties, during her sophomore year in high school. He was a senior. He was charming. He paid attention to her. He thought she was pretty. He thought she was smart. She fell for him and for a while it was a dream relationship. But things soon started to change. Allen became emotionally and then physically abusive. Bonnie's grades suffered, but she continued the relationship because she felt Allen was all she had—all she would have.

Overtime, however, as she matured, Bonnie gained self-confidence and began to assert her independence. After a series of false starts, she broke up for good with Allen in the early 1990s and began her own life. She graduated from college, got married and started her career.

And then, in 1998, the nightmare started. Bonnie started receiving correspondence from a woman name Cammie who claimed to have known her in college. Bonnie responded at first but then became suspicious because she had no recollection of Cammie. Cammie, however, had detailed knowledge of Bonnie including where she lived, the name of the bank holding her mortgage and other details of her personal life. One read, "so how are things in richmond? I hope that you like your new house, though I personally think natural bridge road is a silly name. I hope the people at nationsbank were nice to you when you bought it."[3]

At one point in this process Bonnie received an e-mail from her old boyfriend, Allan, in which he claimed a former girlfriend of his was trying to get back at him by harassing Bonnie. His message said:

---

3. All typographical, spelling and grammar errors are from the original e-mail.

It came to my attention last week that you were recently the recipient of harassing e-mails from a former acquaintance of mine. Actually, I was the recipient of harassing e-mail from the same person as well, but since the circle of certifiable lunatics with which I am acquainted has unfortunately? dwindled over the years it didn't take me long to figure out the source. I think the original plan was to make an attempt to torment me, and you were just along for the ride. Anyway, I did a little investigation and wanted to let you know what the deal was.

Apparently, she and her current beau got the idea that it would be big fun to torment me using you as the bait. I had talked about you with her back when she was going through her divorce, and apparently she remembered enough about you to start trying to find you.

Allan explained that in his prior relationship with the person sending e-mail to Bonnie, he'd made the mistake of teaching her how to track down people over the Internet. He also explained that:

About a week ago, I started getting e-mails saying all sorts of crazy things about you and telling me to e-mail you. These e-mails were unsigned, but Cammie hadn't been vigilant enough in her subterfuge to do something to camouflage her real e-mail headers so tracing them back to her was pretty easy.

Bonnie started ignoring Cammie's e-mails, which appeared simply to make Cammie mad. The tone of the e-mails changed:

I guess you think youre just too good for me and want me as an enemy—not only Is it bad karma to have enemies im a bad enemy to have oh well you made your choce and remember now when bad things happen that I just might be behind them

And then:

you have sucseeded in making me mad now I know that you still work at the same place so y dont you write me? oh well it doesnt matter because I think u just want to fight with me yu ought to just be nice so keep your eyes open this week because things might start to happen

Significantly, other things started to happen. The next morning at about 2 a.m., Bonnie's phone rang. When she answered, the person asked if she had just been on line with him. When she said no, he hung up the phone.

Bonnie pressed "*69" and was able to capture the caller's number for the police. When the police contacted the caller, who happened to be a teenager, he said had been in a teen chat room when someone introduced herself as Bonnie. The Bonnie in the chatroom went on to invite the teenager to her house where, the boy was told, he would be having sex with Bonnie and her husband. He was given Bonnie's, home number and asked to call.

Although the police were able to give some assistance in locating the caller, they were ultimately unable to track down Cammie and concluded that the e-mails Bonnie had received did not violate Virginia law. Bonnie was convinced all the e-mails came from Allan but without police assistance she could not do anything.

Things were quiet for a while after that—perhaps because Bonnie went to work with a private company and her e-mail address was not so each to track down over the Internet.

Bonnie moved to Seattle in 2001 and in 2002 accepted a job with a government agency. And soon the e-mails returned.

The first contained the lyrics to a song that had been popular when Bonnie was in high school—one of Bonnie's favorites, in fact. This was followed by an e-mail from the same sender, someone whose name Bonnie did not recognize, asking if he knew her from her past college days—the same approach "Cammie" had taken.

Then the e-mails started flooding in. Between July and November of 2002, Bonnie received at least fifteen e-mails with more or less the same theme. Most were from two men named Adam and Matt who claimed they represented the Honor for Georgia Foundation—an organization set up to preserve the honor of Georgia colleges and universities. Their purpose was to root out alumni of Georgia colleges who were bringing dishonor to those colleges. Bonnie, they claimed, had brought dishonor to her alma mater—a Georgia college.

The e-mails ranged from threats to send information about Bonnie to her husband, to threats to harass other people in her name. All of them demanded that she apologize for her past misdeeds. It was never made clear what she was to apologize for or to whom.

Much of the e-mail was demeaning. The sender had posted her name on a website which allowed people from failed relationships to rant about their ex-spouses or boy/girlfriends, posted a false, extremely unflattering picture of her there and added derogatory comments.

Then, on September 13, the battle escalated. Bonnie received an e-mail from the Honor for Georgia foundation. Copies of the e-mail were sent to her co-workers. The e-mail was a long litany of false allegations against Bonnie, claiming among other things that she:

> may have obtained employment under false pretenses related to her college degree. In addition, this subject has a long record of moral terpitude, sexual deviance, drug use, and psychological infirmity that would seriously call into question her ability to represent the taxpayers of your city.

The laundry list of sins, all false, included:

- Bonnie was suspended from her college on a variety of honor code violations involving lying, alcohol consumption, drug use and deviant sexual behavior;
- She was able to avoid expulsion by offering sexual favors to the faculty;
- She exchanged sexual favors for higher class grades;
- She was removed as editor of the school newspaper after embezzling thousands of dollars for her personal use;
- She was a suspect, although never charged, in other embezzlements;
- She was able to obtain "gifts" of many thousands of dollars from "generous older men";
- She had a history of moral turpitude, sexual deviance, drug addiction and alcohol abuse;
- She had on several occasions moved in with men, taken financial advantage of them and then disappeared;
- She had appeared in pornographic movies and worked as an escort;
- She suffered from a number of psychological problems including kleptomania, nymphomania, and a number of delusional afflictions similar to schizophrenia; and
- The Foundation had been unable to verify that she had a legitimate college degree.

The sender ended by expressing his hope that Bonnie's questionable character would be of interest to her co-workers and the citizens of Seattle and urged the recipients to forward the e-mail to other fellow employees.

Soon after, her co-workers received another e-mail, this one ostensibly from Bonnie herself. In the e-mail "Bonnie" directed the co-workers to a website, posting a clickable URL in the e-mail. In the e-mail "Bonnie" said that the website was "a project of my husband and the sort of activity that we should encourage here in Seattle. He would like to teach Seattle's youngsters about the pleasure of naked wrestling." The URL took the user to a hard core gay pornographic website. Many of Bonnie's co-workers clicked on the website believing the message was from Bonnie and then called her in outrage when the saw the website.

Bonnie also received calls at work asking for her by name. The callers were responding to messages posted on cyber-sex chat boards asking for people to call her to arrange for sexual encounters.

Bonnie went to the police who told her there was nothing they could do. She turned to the FBI who told her to ignore it. She turned to her employer who told her officially that nothing could be done for her. But one person at her job heard her complaint and acted. The head of Information Security at her employment listened and then called me. And I agreed to take a look at her case.

II. Tracing E-mail

Before we continue with the cases, we need to have some basic understanding of how e-mail works and how it can be traced. What follows is a simple explanation of tracing e-mail.[4]

E-mail sent over the Internet usually travels using a set of rules called the Simple Mail Transfer Protocol or SMTP. The SMTP rules prescribe the format of the information that allows e-mail to travel from sender to receiver. Under this format, there is a set of information that travels with the e-mail called "header" information. The header is created when the first computer—a mail server typically—on the Internet handles the e-mail. Other computers handling the e-mail as it is delivered across the Internet add information to the top of the header information, including the last computer that handles the e-mail before its delivery to the ultimate recipient. Much of this information reflects the path taken by the e-mail from

---

4. Numerous more complete explanations can be readily found on the Internet by entering the phrase "tracing e-mail" into a search engine. For example, here are several entries from a Google search, http://www.google.com, run on December 5, 2004:

USUS—tracing e-mail: find out who sent you that e-mail ... How to trace e-mail back to the sender. www.usus.org/elements/tracing.htm

Trace Instant Messages, IM Trace, e-mail Trace, E-mail Tracing ... Trace e-mails and Instant Messages back to their source. www.abika.com/Reports/traceemails.htm.

the sender to the recipient. In most cases it is possible to identify the sender's ISP from this header information.[5]

Only a simple version of the header information is usually displayed when a user sees an e-mail.[6] Significantly, these primary header fields are largely under the control of the sender and can be manipulated to present inaccurate data. Other information, however, is contained in the full headers. The full headers are maintained with the e-mail even if they are not normally displayed. They can be displayed by entering the proper commands to the e-mail program being used.[7]

Much of the information in the full headers is inserted after the e-mail leaves the sender and thus is not under the sender's control. Many of the SMTP trace fields, for example, are added by mail servers handling the e-mail after it leaves the sender's computer. The most important of these are the "Received" fields. Returning to the e-mail in the Cornercave case, the Received fields from the full headers are as follows:[8]

1. Received: from rs.internic.net (bipmxo.lb.internic.net [192.168. 120.13]) by opsmail.internic.net (8.9.3/8.9.1) with SMTP id QAAO1701 for <hostmaster~internic.net>; Fri, 16 Jul 1999 16:19:46 -0400 (EDT)

2. Received: (qmail 18559 invoked from network); 16 Jul 1999 20:15:16 -0000

3. Received: from smtp6.jps.net (209.63.224.103) by 192.168.119.13 with SMTP; 16 Jul 1999 20:15:16 -0000

4. Received: from [209.63.189.117] (209-63-189-117.sea.jps.net [209.63.189.117]) by smtp6.jps.net (8.9.0/8.8.5) with ESMTP id NAA17047; Fri, 16 Jul 1999 13:19:43 -0700 (PDT)

---

5. This is not always easy to do. As will be discussed in more detail below, senders can attempt to disguise the origination of the e-mail in a variety of ways.

6. Using the e-mail we printed earlier attempting to change the Cornercave domain, the simple header fields are:
Date: Fri, 16 Jul 1999 13:22:14 -0700
To: hostmaster@internic net
From: Sam Martin <postmaster~islandermedia.com>
Subject: [NIC-990716.l2fcd] MODIFY DOMAIN

7. The precise method for displaying the full headers varies by e-mail program but usually involves some command to show the full headers or show the source of the message.

8. The lines are numbered 1–4 for our convenience. Those numbers do not actually appear in the header.

It is important to understand three things about these "Received" fields.

First, each server adds them at the top of the existing headers as it handles the e-mail. In the above example Received Field 1 is the information added by the last server handling the e-mail. Received Field 4 is the information added by the first server. Thus if we are trying to trace the e-mail to its source we are most interested in Received Field 4.

Second, the format of a "Received" field is to display from which computer the message was just received and by what computer. Thus, for example, line 3 is read as follows: This message was received from a computer at jps.net with the name smtp6 and the IP address 209.63.224.103 by a computer with the IP address 192.168.119.13. The message was relayed via SMTP at 16 Jul 1999 20:15:16 -0000.[9]

Third, in most instances, the header fields provide an easy to verify path from the sender to the recipient. Each received line, reading up from the bottom, should list the immediately lower received line in the "From" portion. So, for example, line 3, which we just dissected, shows it was received from smtp6@jps.net. The "By" portion of line 4 shows it to be smtp6@jps.net. While not all received lines can be traversed as transparently as this, close examination by a person well versed in SMTP header fields can usually easily detect whether the Received lines do in fact follow or trace from one another.

To identify the source of the e-mail, we would look for the first server handling this which, as just explained, would be the bottom of these received fields—in this case field 4. Received line 4 shows the e-mail was received from IP address 209.63.189.117 on Fri, 16 Jul 1999 13:19:43 -0700 (PDT).[10] Once the IP address associated with the source of the e-mail is identified, it is usually an easy step to identify the entity assigned that IP address. This will usually be an ISP, a business or a government organization.

The information about what entity is assigned a particular IP address is publicly available. The official organizations maintaining this information are called Regional Internet Registries or RIRs. The RIR covering the Amer-

---

9. The "-0000" information shows the time relative to Greenwich Mean Time—in this case the time shown is GMT. Often the time is shown in the timezone of the receiving computer such as PDT or PST in the Pacific time zone, for example.

10. Here is an example of the time being shows as both the deviation from GMT (-700 or 7 hours behind GMT) and the local designator PDT for Pacific Daylight Time.

icas is ARIN (American Registry of Internet Numbers) which can be found at www.arin.net.[11] At the top of that webpage is a box labeled "Search WhoIs". If you enter the IP address in question in that box and hit enter, you are shown the name, address, contacts and phone numbers for the entity assigned that IP address.

Thus far, everything has been easily and publically available. Sometime, though, the information must be obtained from non-public sources. Once we move into the realm of records held by third parties that are not public records, we move into the realm of the law.

III. Obtaining Records from Third Party Record Holders

To understand the law in this area, some background is needed. In *Katz v. United States*,[12] the Supreme Court expressly held that "what a person knowingly exposes to the public, even in his home or office, is not a subject of Fourth Amendment protection."[13] The Supreme Court "consistently has held that a person has no legitimate expectation of privacy in information he voluntarily turns over to third parties."[14]

Thus, at the federal level, any privacy protection in third parties records stems from statutes, not the constitution. Congress has passed a number of laws following the *Smith* and *Miller* decisions[15] to provide statutory privacy protection for bank records,[16] cable television viewing and video rentals.[17] Congress also extended the wiretap statute to provide some privacy protection to records related to electronic communications in the Electronic Communications Privacy Act.[18]

---

11. There are other, more versatile, public sources of this information like www.samspade.org and www.forensicsweb.net.

12. 389 U.S. 347 (1967).

13. *Id.* at 351.

14. Smith v. Maryland, 442 U.S. 735, 743-44 (1979); *see, e.g.*, U.S. v. Miller, 425 U.S. 435, 442-43 (1976); Couch v. U.S., 409 U.S. 322, 335-36 (1973).

15. *See* cases cited in footnote 14, *supra*.

16. Right to Financial Privacy Act, 12 U.S.C. §§ 3401-22 (2000).

17. Cable Privacy Act, 47 U.S.C. § 551 (2000) and the Video Privacy Protection Act, 18 U.S.C. §§ 2710-12 (2000).

18. 18 U.S.C. § 2701-09 (2000).

A. Electronic Communications Privacy Act

The Electronic Communications Privacy Act ["ECPA"] updated the wiretap statute[19] and added the Stored Electronic Communications Act ["SECA"].[20] Although it is common to reference ECPA in discussing limitations on computer searches, most often it is the specific provisions of SECA that are in play.[21]

1. What Does the ECPA Cover?

The act covers the contents of electronic communications while in electronic storage by an "electronic communications service."[22] An electronic communications service is "any service which provides to the users thereof the ability to send or receive wire or electronic communications."[23] The act also covers the contents of electronic communications in a "remote computing service."[24] A remote computing service is one that provides "to the public ... computer storage or processing service by means of an electronic communications system."[25]

2. What Does the ECPA Prohibit?

The act prohibits providers of electronic communication service or remote computing service from disclosing contents of electronic communications or customer records and transactional data to the government, except as provided.

3. When Is a Disclosure to the Government Allowed?

a. Subscriber or Customer Records

All records, except the content and record of real-time communications, can be obtained by a warrant supported by probable cause. Many, but not all records can be obtained by subpoena or court order.

Subscriber or customer records (name, address, telephone toll billing records, telephone number or other subscriber number or identity, and

---

19. 18 U.S.C. §§ 2510-22 (2000).
20. 18 U.S.C.A. §§ 2701-11 (2004).
21. Keystroke monitoring and other real-time monitoring of electronic communications is covered by the wiretap statute, 18 U.S.C. § 2511(1) (2000).
22. *Id.* § 2510(15).
23. *Id.*
24. 18 U.S.C.A. § 2703(b) (2004).
25. *Id.* § 2711(2).

length and type of service for a subscriber or customer) may be obtained by subpoena, warrant or court order.

The USA PATRIOT Act[26] made other subscriber/customer records, such as transaction history, IP logs, etc. available by subpoena. Previously they had been available only by warrant or court order.

Under the PATRIOT Act, a subpoena can be used to obtain basic subscriber information including customer's name; address; length of service; means and source of payment (including any credit card or bank account number); local and long-distance telephone toll billing records; and records of session times and durations, as well as any temporarily assigned network address.[27]

A subpoena can also be used to obtain opened e-mail from a provider if the "customer" or "subscriber" is given prior notice of the disclosure by the government. This disclosure may be delayed for up to ninety days when notice would jeopardize a pending investigation or endanger the physical safety of a person. The issuing court may consider an extension of an additional ninety days. Following the delay notification period, the government must give notice.[28]

Under the ECPA, a court order, sometimes referred as to an "articulable facts order" or "§ 2703(d) court order" may be sought to obtain all other subscriber information except the content of an unopened e-mail that has been stored for 180 days or less. To obtain a "§ 2703(d) court order," there must be specific and articulable facts showing that there are reasonable grounds to believe that the specified records are relevant and material to an ongoing criminal investigation. These records would include complete audit trails/logs, Web sites visited, identities of e-mail correspondents, cell site data from cellular/PCS carriers, and opened e-mail. As a practical matter, a "§ 2703(d) court order" can also be used to obtain basic subscriber information. Notice to the subscriber is only required when the government seeks the content of communications without a warrant.[29]

b. Contents of Electronic Communications

In general, the contents of an electronic communication may be disclosed with the consent of any party to the communication. The consent

---

26. Pub. L. No. 107-56, 115 Stat. 272 (2001).
27. 18 U.S.C.A. § 2703(b) (2004).
28. *Id.* § 2703(b)(B).
29. *See Id.* § 2703(b).

of all of the parties to the communication is not needed—only one party need consent.[30]

A government entity can compel the production of the contents of stored electronic communications by warrant. As previously noted, however, communications in storage for more than 180 days can be obtained by subpoena.

4. *What Is the Remedy for Violation of this Act?*

a.   Criminal Liability

The ECPA provides for criminal liability for one who "(1) intentionally accesses without authorization a facility through which an electronic communication service is provided; or (2) intentionally exceeds an authorization to access that facility; and thereby obtains, alters, or prevents authorized access to a wire or electronic communication while it is in electronic storage in such system."[31] Punishment can be up to two years imprisonment.

b.   Civil Liability

The act creates a civil cause of action for violations, including damages and attorney's fees with punitive damages if the violation was willful. Although one decision held that only the service provider, not the government, was civilly liable for violations[32] a later decision found liability in the government official who obtained the information.[33] The different outcomes in these two cases may be explained by the different sections of the ECPA under which the plaintiffs sued. In *Tucker,* where the plaintiff sued under 18 U.S.C. § 2703(c) (which imposes limits on service providers), the court found no liability on the behalf of the government. In *McVeigh,* where the plaintiff also sued under 18 U.S.C. § 2703(a) and (b) (which impose limits on the government), the court found government liability.

c.   Suppression

Suppression is not a remedy for non-constitutional violations of ECPA.[34]

---

30. See 18 U.S.C.A. § 2511(c) (2004).
31. 18 U.S.C.A. §§ 2701(a)(1) & (2) (2004).
32. Tucker v. Waddell, 83 F.3d 688 (4th Cir. 1996).
33. McVeigh v. Cohen, 983 F. Supp. 215 (D.D.C. 1998).
34. 18 U.S.C.A. § 2708 (2004).

d. Good Faith

Section 2707(e) of the ECPA states that "reliance on ... a court warrant or order, a grand jury subpoena, a legislative authorization, or a statutory authorization ... is a complete defense to any civil or criminal action brought under this chapter."[35] The Tenth Circuit used this provision in *Davis v. Gracey*[36] to reject the defendants' civil claim under ECPA. The court noted that because the officers relied on a warrant supported by probable cause they were entitled to a "good faith" defense.[37]

B. Practical Issues

The ECPA, as just described, puts limits on the government's ability to get access to records of electronic communications including customer records. The requirements for access vary depending on the type of information requested but, at a minimum, require a subpoena for access to customer records including the name and other identifying information related to use of a specific IP address.

Although there is often other useful information in the hands of the ISP, usually the information we are most interested in is that which identifies the individual account holder who was assigned the IP address at issue at the date and time an e-mail was sent.

1. Limitations of Third Party Records

For this process to work, however, there must actually be a record of IP assignment that the government can access. There are at least three obstacles to this.

a. Do the Records Exist

There is no law mandating that any record be maintained of IP assignments for any minimum period of time. Most major ISPs only maintain these records for from thirty to sixty days. Even that may not be enough in some instances where the victim does not know about the crime or does not report the crime for some time. Even when the victim reports the crime promptly, there may be a history of communications, some going back much more than sixty days. Identifying the source of those communica-

---

35. *Id.* § 2707(e).
36. 111 F.3d 1472 (10th Cir. 1997).
37. *Id.* at 1484.

tions may be crucial, particularly where the suspect is assigned a "dynamic" IP address rather than a "static" address. In shorthand, a static address is one that remains constant at least for a substantial period of time. Because the address is static, an ISP's current records are likely to be sufficient to identify the suspect. A dynamic address, on the other hand, is one that can change from Internet access to Internet access. Without the relevant ISP records, discovering the name of the person who was assigned the IP address at the time of the crime will be impossible.

b. Are the Records Useful

For many large institutions like Kinko's and Microsoft, the IP address contained in the header fields is merely the IP address of their proxy server (in the case of Kinko's) serving thousands of the company's computers, or a gateway server (in the case of Microsoft) serving hundreds or thousands of users. The ability to trace such communication back to the originating computer then relies on the maintenance and examination of other log files, such as firewall logs, to determine the originating computer. This is not always possible.

A growing related problem is the availability of truly anonymous Internet connections. Many libraries provide free Internet access without any login or membership requirements. An e-mail that traces back to such a computer provides very little guidance to the identity of the individual using the computer.

Another source of anonymous Internet connections is Internet cafes and other organizations that provide free wireless Internet access. Because the service is free there is little ability to identify the actual sender of the e-mail in question. Equally anonymous are wireless servers that unintentionally are made available to unauthorized (and unidentified) users.[38]

As a side note, however, the diligent investigator should always be aware of the possibility of security videotapes. The premises of many stores providing computer access are covered by security video cameras. If there is a

---

38. See Bill Cotterell, *Student Faces Computer Fraud, Theft Charges*, TALLAHASSEE DEMOCRAT (Dec. 4, 2004), *available at* http://www.tallahassee.com/mld/democrat/2004/12/04/news/local/10335995.htm (last visited Jan. 12, 2005) (The police were able to solve a case involving an unsecured wireless access point, in part because the suspect used the wireless access to make purchases delivered to his apartment. Without the delivery record evidence, the suspect would not likely have been identifiable.).

suspect, these videos can be of enormous value in showing the suspect using a computer at the time an e-mail was sent from that location.

c.   Do the Records Show What They Purport to Show

Even if the records exist, the investigator must consider whether they are spoofed. At the simplest level spoofing is defined as disguising the source of an e-mail so that it appears to originate somewhere other than where it did.

Spoofing can be simple and easy to detect as in the e-mail in the Cornercave case. In that e-mail, the sender configured his e-mail program to show that the e-mail was from Sam Martin at Islander Media. The header information, however, showed the true originating IP address. But spoofing can be more complex. There are freely available programs that enable a user to paste additional header information to her/his e-mail. While the legitimate servers header fields will be posted above these, a careless investigator who merely goes to the last received line will be looking at a received line created by the sender, not one created by the original server.

Spoofing can also be done by using an open e-mail relay. Mail servers can be configured to accept incoming e-mail and send it out as if it originated at that server. Since the mail did in fact come from that server the Received fields will be accurate—they will simply stop at the point of the mail server rather than continuing on to reveal the actual source of the e-mail.

Despite the limits of ISP records and the possibility of spoofing, however, with careful investigatory work (and a little luck), the account information received from the ISP will point toward the actual sender of the communication in question.

2. How to Obtain the Records

The preferred method of obtaining third party records is by search warrant. A warrant has three advantages over a subpoena or a "§ 2703(d)" order.

First, under the ECPA, a search warrant can be used to obtain *any* records held by a third party record holder. This avoids any issue of civil liability under the ECPA.

Second, some states have statutes covering much the same ground as the ECPA.[39] Even if evidence is not suppressible under the ECPA, it may be suppressible under those state statutes.

---

39. See, e.g. VA. CODE ANN. § 19.2-70.3 (Michie 1996).

Third, many states' courts have interpreted their constitution to be more protective of privacy than the U.S. Constitution.[40] It is entirely possible that those states would hold that third party records are protected by the state constitution such that obtaining those records without a search warrant, even if in compliance with the ECPA, would violate the constitution and cause the records to be suppressed.

The two principal reasons for not issuing a warrant are a lack of probable cause and an inability to obtain a warrant for service on an out-of-state record holder. I cannot estimate how much of a problem lack of probable cause creates. I personally have never had an instance where I was prepared to issue process to an ISP for customer identification information where I did not believe I had probable cause.

The second problem—out-of-state record holders—is very real. Some states' statutes or constitutions regarding search warrants are explicit—the warrant may not be served or executed outside the state.[41] Other states statutes or court rules either explicitly or apparently authorize service outside the state.[42] But the majority of states' statutes and rules do not directly address this subject.

Even without specific rules on point, some courts have upheld the service of an extra-territorial warrant.[43] In any case, there is no federal suppression remedy as *United States v. Miller*[44] held that a person has no reasonable expectation of privacy in records held by third parties. The only federal remedy for improperly seized ISP records is statutory under the

---

40. See Utah v. Thompson, 810 P.2d 415, 418 (Utah 1991); Winfield v. Div. of Pari-Mutuel Wagering, 477 So.2d 544, 548 (Fla. 1985); Ill. v. Jackson, 452 N.E.2d 85, 89 (Ill. App. 1983); Charnes v. DiGiacomo, 612 P.2d 1117, 1120–21 (Colo. 1980); Penn. v. DeJohn, 403 A.2d 1283, 1291 (Penn. 1979); N.J. v. McAllister, 840 A.2d 967 (N.J. Super. 2004).

41. See DEPARTMENT OF LAW AND PUBLIC SAFETY, DIVISION OF CRIMINAL JUSTICE, NEW JERSEY COMPUTER EVIDENCE SEARCH & SEIZURE MANUAL 21 (2000) ("a New Jersey court can not authorize a search outside the territorial limits of New Jersey."), *available at* http://www.state.nj.us/lps/dcj/pdfs/cmpmanfi.pdf (last visited Dec. 15, 2004). *See also* N.Y. CRIM. PROC. LAW § 690.20 (McKinney 1995).

42. See, e.g., CAL. PENAL CODE § 1524.2 (West 2000) (requiring out-of-state corporations qualified to do business in California to accept service of and comply with California search warrants). Minnesota and Florida have similar provisions.

43. U.S. v. Bach, 310 F.3d 1063 (8th Cir. 2002) (serving warrant by fax upheld when the court implicitly endorsed treating search warrant execution like the service of a subpoena in a third party record case), *cert. denied*, 538 U.S. 993 (2003).

44. 425 U.S. 435, 442–43 (1976) (involving bank records).

Electronic Communications Privacy Act which does not include a suppression remedy.

While the decision as to whether to use a warrant or other process[45] may be uncertain, once that decision is made, the subsequent steps are clear.

3. Contact the ISP and Then Serve the Warrant/Subpoena

When preparing to serve a warrant or subpoena on a third party record holder identified by IP address, you should always do three things (unless you have previously dealt with this ISP).

First, call the ISP to determine that they, in fact, maintain the records for the IP address in issue. This can help you detect early on where you have made a mistake or there is an error in the header information. It enables you to learn if the IP address has been sub-assigned to another entity, a common practice. It also alerts you to company takeovers or other changes in the IP registration.[46]

Second, ask the ISP if they will accept service by fax and if so what their fax number is.

Third, tell the ISP what information you are interested in and ask them what language the warrant or subpoena should contain to get at that information.[47]

---

45. Alternatives available to a search warrant include: (1) a trial subpoena (if charges have been filed), (2) a grand jury subpoena (pre-filing) which does not have territorial limitations, (3) a trial or grand jury subpoena together with the Interstate Compact on Out of State Witnesses, or (4) a request to law enforcement in the ISP's state for them to obtain a warrant based on an out-of-state affidavit.

46. For example, U.S. West, the local baby bell in the Pacific Northwest was bought out some time ago by Qwest Communications. Qwest took over many of the IP assignments previously held by U.S. West and yet the Regional Internet Registry covering the United States, ARIN.net, still lists U.S. West as the IP assignee for IP addresses assigned to Qwest.

47. For example, AOL suggests the following language for a subpoena: "Any and all AOL and/or AIM records regarding the identification of "XYZ" to include real name, screen names, status of account, detailed billing logs, date account opened and closed, method of payment and detailed billing records (log on & log off times)" and the following language for a warrant: "Any and all AOL and/or AIM accounts for XYZ or screen name "xyz", To include all e-mail, histories, buddy lists, profiles, subscriber information, method of payment, detailed billings records (log on & log off times). AMERICA ONLINE COMPLIANCE AND INVESTIGATIONS, LAW ENFORCEMENT TRAINING MANUAL 4, *available at*, http://www.federaldefender.org/tech/aolmanl.pdf (last visited Mar. 16, 2005).

C. The Case Scenarios

Let us return to the three cases to see what happened in each case regarding obtaining records from a third party record holder.

1. Case 1—Janet Davis

The events in this case occurred before the Internet was widespread. In addition, all of the access to the target computer was made by a person sitting at that computer. Thus, other than the records ANDA obtained from its own building security people about key card use,[48] no third party records were needed or obtained.

2. Case 2—Mel Howard

By the time the police obtained custody of Cornercave's damaged server, it had been altered extensively by Islander Media's efforts to reinstall the operating system and other software and programs. There was no information on that computer useful for identifying who had damaged the computer.

The firewall logs of accesses after August 2 did contain some useful information although that information needed decoding.

There was one piece of evidence, however, that provided a direct lead, at least to the person attempting to hijack the domain. Network Solutions (the company registering domains and handling domain change requests at the time) provided Cornercave with a copy of the e-mail requesting the domain change. That e-mail, displayed earlier, contained the following Received line showing the e-mail's source:

4.   Received: from [*209.63.189.117*] (209-63-189-117.sea.jps.net [209.63.189.117]) by smtp6.jps.net (8.9.0/8.8.5) with ESMTP id NAA17047; Fri, 16 Jul 1999 13:19:43 -0700 (PDT)

Thus, we were interested in the person who was assigned IP address 209.63.189.117 on July 16, 1999 at 1:19:43 p.m., Pacific Daylight Time.

ARIN.net revealed that IP address to be amongst those assigned to a California based ISP called JPS.net. (This confirmed the information contained in the received field showing the same association). The detective prepared

---

48. This did not require a warrant. Even if the defendant had an expectation of privacy in this data (which is extremely doubtful) the Fourth Amendment only applies to searches by government actors or agents. U.S. v. Miller, 688 F.2d 652, 657–58 (9th Cir. 1982); U.S. v. Jennings, 653 F.2d 107, 110 (4th Cir. 1981).

a search warrant for JPS's records of IP assignments for the particular IP in question. One problem: JPS would not agree to accept an out-of-state subpoena or search warrant.[49]

As previously discussed, the need to have a location outside the state searched or to compel the production of out-of-state records is not new and over the years law enforcement has developed mechanisms to accomplish this goal. One is the Uniform Act to Compel the Attendance of Out of State Witnesses.[50] Used most often to force reluctant witnesses in another state to come to your state to testify, the Uniform Act is a fairly cumbersome process, which involves a judge in both your state and the foreign state. It requires the subpoenaed person to appear in the court of the foreign state where they are directed to come to the domestic state (their travel expenses must be tendered in advance). They can be held in custody and transported in custody if they refuse to come voluntarily. The subpoena in question can be a *duces tecum*—a subpoena calling for the production of records, so long as a court hearing is scheduled.

The limits on this process are three: First, as the description implies, it is cumbersome. Second, it is time consuming. This is not a viable process if you need the information or witness quickly. Finally, it requires that the issuing state have a court date at which the witness must appear. If this information is being obtained before the filing of charges, there may not be a court date to which you can direct the witness to appear.

The alternative, relied upon more often when the issue is records rather than witnesses, is for the domestic state to request law enforcement in the foreign state to request a search warrant based on the domestic state's affidavit and for foreign law enforcement to obtain permission to turn the seized information over to the domestic state.

In the Mel Howard case, the detective had already prepared a search warrant affidavit. The easiest course at that juncture was to locate a police agency in California where JPS was located and get their assistance in obtaining a California search warrant based on the Washington affidavit. This was done, and in short order JPS provided the requested information.

JPS records of IP assignments were problematic, however. Instead of a continuous record of assignment, JPS took quarter hour "snapshots" of as-

---

49. This case occurred prior to the enactment of Cal. Penal Code § 1524.2 (West 2000), which would have required JPS to comply with the warrant.

50. Uniform Act to Secure the Attendance of Witnesses from Without a State in Criminal Proceedings (1936), *available at*, http://www.law.upenn.edu/bll/ulc/fnact99/1920_69/uasaw36.pdf.

signment showing who was assigned what address on the hour and 15, 30 and 45 minutes after the hour. Thus if a user connected at 1:10 p.m. and stayed connected until 1:47 p.m., the IP address assigned that user would be shown on the 1:15, 1:30 and 1:45 logs. But if a user signed on at 1:17 and off at 1:28 there would be no record.

We requested information from JPS about the IP assignments for each of the e-mails we had, from July 16, 23, 26 and 28, on the times in question. Only one of these returned a hit from JPS — the July 16 e-mail. JPS records showed that the IP address contained in that e-mail was assigned to Mel Howard:

Date- Username	Address	Time
071699- mhoward	209.63.189.117	1300
071699- mhoward	209.63.189.117	1315
071699- mhoward	209.63.189.117	1330
071699- mhoward	209.63.1B9.117	1345
071699- mhoward	209.63.189.117	1400
071699- mhoward	209.63.189.117	1415

Account Information	
Username:	mhoward
First Name:	Mel
Last Name:	Howard
Address:	xxxxx xxxxx
City:	Kirkland, Washington
E-mail Address:	mhoward@jps.net

There was no record of IP assignments for the other three attempts likely indicating they fell outside the quarter-hour snapshots.

3.   Case 3—Allen Worley

Although the sender of the e-mails professed some knowledge of tracing e-mail[51] and had sent the e-mails in question through anonymizers or anonymous remailers, many of the e-mails he sent contained a crucial clue to the identity of the sender. One of the optional header fields under the SMTP rules is the X-Originating IP field. This field, often inserted by the first server handling the e-mail, is the IP address for the original sender.

---

51. Recall the message from Worley to Bonnie about "Cammie's" e-mails where Worley, referring to e-mail Cammie sent him, noted the "e-mails were unsigned, but Cammie hadn't been vigilant enough in her subterfuge to do something to camouflage her real e-mail headers so tracing them back to her was pretty easy."

While some anonymizers successfully strip out all clues as to the origin of the message, others strip out only "Received" header fields from before the message reached the anonymizer, leaving other information intact including the X-Originating IP and the Message ID. For many of the e-mails that Worley sent through an anonymizing service the X-Originating IP was passed on.

So, despite his efforts to disguise the source of his e-mails, the originating IP address was known. A quick search of arin.net showed this IP address was associated with Kserve, a provider of telephone and cable service in the Southeastern United States. To dig further, we would need a subpoena or warrant, but for what crime? Washington's harassment statute seemed to apply. It covered an act "intended to substantially harm the person threatened ... with respect to his or her physical or mental health or safety."[52] But the Washington Supreme Court has held the "mental health" portion of the statute unconstitutionally over broad and vague.[53] We turned instead to the telephone harassment statute.[54] That statute had been upheld by the Washington Supreme Court and covered a wide variety of acts done via the telephone including anonymous or repeated calls. Although the statute only applied to telephone calls, we knew that many people connected to the Internet via the telephone and thought we had a good faith basis for issuing a subpoena under that statute.

A subpoena was issued to Kserve. Their response identified the IP address as being associated with a cable modem account. The IP address had been assigned the same customer in Charleston, South Carolina from July, 2002, to the date of the subpoena. That subscriber was Allen Worley.

IV. Search Warrants

The ultimate goal of tracing an electronic communication is to be able to identify a location for which we have probable cause to obtain a search warrant and to search that location and any computers at that location for evidence tying the suspect to the crime. The search of computers under a warrant involves a body of law that is evolving from the search warrant law in other contexts. While the law in the computer arena is largely following in the footsteps of the law in other areas, any analysis of computer searches

---

52. WASH. REV. CODE § 9A.46.020 (2002.
53. State v. Williams, 26 P.3d 890 (Wash. 2001).
54. WASH. REV. CODE § 9.61.230 (2002).

must, by necessity, involve an in-depth discussion of the law of search and seizure in the computer arena. Although we are about to take a major detour from the cases we have been discussing to explore search and seizure law, we shall return.

A. Acquisition of Evidence

1. What Crimes?

While this book's focus is on cybercrime, the issues raised in this chapter apply to any case where the evidence is contained within a computer. These cases run the gamut from thefts to drugs, from child pornography to homicide.

2. What Computers?

One of the first questions that must be asked is whose computer are we talking about. These fall into three categories: the victim's computer, the suspect's computer, and a third party's computer. It is important to distinguish between computers in this manner because the law distinguishes between them. For example:

- In most circumstances a suspect has no expectation of privacy in evidence found in the victim's computer.[55]
- The Privacy Protection Act,[56] which sets significant limits on searches of publishers (including computer based publishers), does not usually apply when the alleged publisher is a target.
- The Electronic Communications Privacy Act[57] also sets limits on the access to stored electronic communication, but the limits only apply to records stored on third party service providers, not to records on the suspect's computer.

---

55. See *State v. Townsend,* 57 P.3d 255 (Wash. 2002), however, where the issue was whether the defendant's e-mail and chat messages he had sent to the victim/undercover officer, which were then stored on the undercover officer's computer were "private communications" under the Washington Privacy Act, WASH. REV. CODE § 9.73.030 (2003). The Court held they were private communications but that the very nature of e-mail and chat implies consent to their recording. The case focused on the Privacy Act, not the Fourth Amendment or Article I, § 7 of the Washington Constitution.

56. 42 U.S.C. § 2000aa(a)(1) (2000).

57. 18 U.S.C. § 2701-11 (2000).

• Searches of the suspect's computer will always be subject to the full scrutiny of the Fourth Amendment and other constitutional protections.

3. Legal Limits on Searches

Legal limits on searches flow from three sources: constitutional limits (federal and state), statutory limits, and limits imposed by court rule or the issuing magistrate. These restrictions on searches have different impacts. Searches that violate constitutional protection are likely to be suppressed. Searches that violate statutory restrictions may be subject to suppression, but more typically, while providing a civil remedy to the aggrieved party, do not provide suppression as a remedy. Searches that violate court rules may be suppressed or some lesser sanction may be applied. Each of these limitations will be examined in turn.

a.   Federal Constitutional Limits

The Fourth Amendment guarantees protection against unreasonable searches and seizures.[58] The questions to be asked in the Fourth Amendment context are three: Does the Fourth Amendment apply to the situation, is there a legal warrant, and, if there is not a legal warrant, does the search fall within the exceptions to the warrant requirement?

(1) Does the Fourth Amendment Apply to the Situation?

This involves two separate considerations: Is there a reasonable expectation of privacy and is government action involved?

(a) Is There a Reasonable Expectation of Privacy?

In determining whether there is a reasonable expectation of privacy, courts look at two factors: the subjective expectation of the person asserting a privacy interest and whether society accepts that as objectively rea-

---

58. "The right of the people to be secure in their persons, houses, papers, and effects, against unreasonable searches and seizures, shall not be violated, and no Warrants shall issue, but upon probable cause, supported by Oath or affirmation, and particularly describing the place to be searched, and the persons or things to be seized." U.S. CONST. amend. IV.

sonable.[59] The highest privacy interest is attached to private dwellings.[60] A computer inside a private dwelling will certainly be accorded a similar privacy status. Expectation of privacy in the contents of a computer is less clear when the computer is not in the home or when the contents of the computer are routinely shared with others or members of the public. Consequently, laptops, employer-provided computers and public access computers present distinct issues.

Laptop Computers: Although laptops are similar to automobiles in their mobility, they are dissimilar in the other two ways that courts have used to justify a lower privacy standard for automobiles. First, laptops are not subject to government regulation in the way cars are as their misuse is not immediately and physically dangerous.[61] Second, automobile travel is inherently public in nature while laptop use is not.[62]

Employer-provided computers: Determining whether an employee has a privacy interest in an employer-provided computer is highly fact specific so no universal rule can be stated. As the issues raised by employer-provided computers are the same as those associated with a third party consenting to a search, searches of these computers will be discussed below.

Public access computers: It is highly unlikely a computer that is open to the public would have a legitimate expectation of privacy. Privacy in a public area seems fundamentally contradictory.[63]

(b) Is Government Action Involved?

The exclusionary rule was not intended and does not apply to the actions of private citizens or foreign law enforcement agents.[64] Nor, under the "silver platter" doctrine, does it apply to the actions of non forum-state law enforcement officers.

i) Searches by Non-Forum, State Law Enforcement

The silver platter doctrine arose in the early 1900s when federal search and seizure law was more restrictive than state search and seizure law, and

---

59. Cal. v. Greenwood, 486 U.S. 35, 39 (1988).

60. Welsh v. Wisc., 466 U.S. 740, 748 (1984).

61. S.D. v. Opperman, 428 U.S. 364, 367–68 (1976).

62. Id.

63. See Maryland v. Macon, 472 U.S. 463, 469 (1985) (discussing the absence of a legitimate expectation of privacy in the books displayed to the public in a bookstore).

64. Burdeau v. McDowell, 256 U.S. 465, 475 (1921); Weeks v. U.S., 232 U.S. 383, 398 (1914).

suppression was a remedy for violation of the federal law. When state law enforcement officers conducted a search legal under state law but illegal under federal law, could the fruits of the search be used in federal courts? The answer was yes, if the federal authorities received the fruits on a silver platter, i.e., they were not so involved in the illegal search as to require suppression. "The essential principle underlying the development of this 'silver platter' doctrine is that protections afforded by the constitution of a sovereign entity control the actions only of the agents of that sovereign entity."[65] There is no reason why the same principle should not apply to computer searches.[66]

---

65. N.J. v. Mollica, 554 A.2d 1315, 1324 (N.J. 1989). *Mollica* contains the New Jersey Supreme Court's superb discussion of the history of the silver platter doctrine. *Mollica* involved an FBI investigation of illegal bookmaking being conducted from rooms at Caesar's Palace in Atlantic City, New Jersey. Acting without a warrant the FBI obtained from Caesar's the telephone toll records for the suspect's room for the duration of his stay. The FBI subsequently turned this information over to the New Jersey State Police who used the information to obtain a warrant. Evidence used at trial was discovered during the search. The crucial issues before the New Jersey Supreme Court were whether the seizure of telephone records by the FBI without a warrant was illegal under state law, and if so, whether the products of the state search under a warrant based upon the telephone records should be suppressed.

After concluding that state law prohibited the seizure of toll records without a warrant, the court addressed the second issue. After discussing the history and rationale of the doctrine, court focused on the crucial issue of agency:

> As with the earlier manifestations of the silver platter doctrine, and as seen in the numerous post-*Mapp* [*v. Ohio*, 367 U.S. 643,] examples of interstate transfers of evidence, the salient factor continues to be agency *vel non* between the officers of the respective jurisdictions. The nature of the relationship between the officers participating in the search or seizure and the officers seeking to make use of such evidence is critical.
>
> . . .
>
> This case thus requires us to consider the implications of the silver platter doctrine and its key element: intergovernmental agency. An important aspect of this determination is whether for constitutional purposes the federal agents can be said to be acting under the "color of state law." The assessment of the agency issue necessarily requires an examination of the entire relationship between the two sets of government actors no matter how obvious or obscure, plain or subtle, brief or prolonged their interactions may be. The reasons and the motives for making any search must be examined as well as the actions taken by the respective officers and the process used to find, select, and seize the evidence.

Mollica, at 1328–29.

66. In the Janet Davis case discussed elsewhere in this chapter, a local detective accompanied the U.S. Marshal in the execution of a writ of seizure under the federal Copy-

ii) Searches by Private Citizens

The *Mollica* court viewed a transfer from a federal official to a state official as analogous to a transfer from a private citizen to a state official.[67] Searches by private citizens, not acting as the agent of law enforcement, are not entitled to constitutional protection.[68] The results of searches of computers by private citizens (not acting as agents of law enforcement) should be admissible.

(2) Is There a Legal Warrant?

(a) The Application for the Warrant Must Demonstrate Probable Cause to Believe That Evidence of a Crime Will Be Found in the Place to Be Searched

i) Evidence of a Crime

If there is probable cause to believe both that a crime has occurred and that evidence of the crime will be found at a particular location, then a search warrant may be obtained. In a cybercrime case, where the "victim" or target computer shows the commission of a crime committed via an electronic communication, what we must show is that the sending computer likely contains evidence related to that crime. Further, of course, we must identify the physical location of that sending computer.

Establishing probable cause that the sending computer contains evidence is usually a non-issue. At the very least, evidence of dominion and control of that computer may be evidence of who sent the electronic communication at issue. It is also usually an easy task to show that there is a likelihood that other evidence of the electronic communication will be found on the sending computer in the form of stored sent e-mail, web search history, the

---

right Act. The detective observed, but did not participate in the search. The appellate court reversed the trial court's determination that the detective's mere presence at the search scene made the Marshal his agent, and allowed the evidence under the silver platter doctrine. This issue in the Davis case is discussed more fully later in this chapter.

67. Mollica, 554 A.2d at 1325, 1328.

68. U.S. v. Gomez, 614 F.2d 643 (9th Cir. 1979); U.S. v. Jennings, 653 F.2d 107 (4th Cir. 1981); U.S. v. Entringer, 532 F.2d 634 (8th Cir.), *cert. denied*, 429 U.S. 820 (1976); U.S. v. Sullivan, 544 F. Supp. 701 (D. Maine 1982), *aff'd*, 711 F.2d 1 (1st Cir. 1983); Or. v. Blackshear, 511 P.2d 1272 (Or. App. 1973); N.M. v. Cox, 674 P.2d 1127 (N.M. App. 1983); Wisc. v. Bembenek, 331 N.W.2d 616 (Wis. App. 1983); N.Y. v. Goodman, 380 N.Y.S.2d 768 (App. Div. 1976); Wash. v. Smith, 756 P.2d 722 (Wash. 1988), *cert. denied*, 488 U.S. 1042 (1989).

Internet cache file, other file areas of the computer or in unallocated file space. The computer may also contain evidence as to the individual who actually sent the communication.

The application for the warrant and the warrant itself must state specifically the statute believed to have been violated. This requirement serves as a limit on the search. Courts have held that the failure to state the crime specifically in the warrant itself is fatal, even if the officer executing the warrant knew what crime was being investigated.[69]

Appellate courts have made it clear that failing to establish a nexus between the crime and the items or location to be searched will result in suppression. In a Washington Court of Appeals case,[70] the police were investigating several instances of attacks against young girls and sought to search the suspect's computer. In pertinent part the affidavit said: "[Nordlund] used a computer at this residence to access pornography and to communicate with others via E-mail. Therefore, the computer and any electronic storage media could likely be important evidence in this case regarding intent, dates and locations."[71] The court noted there was no nexus between the alleged crimes and Nordlund's use of the computer to access pornography and send e-mails. "Rather, it appears that the State was fishing for some incriminating document which is precisely what the first and fourth amendment prohibit."[72]

ii) Will Be Found in the Place to Be Searched

The most commonly overlooked element in search warrants is this one. What is the probable cause for believing that evidence of the crime you are investigating will be found in the location you wish to search? This requires articulable facts pointing to the location, not some generic "where else would it be" explanation.

A unique issue arises in the context of computer searches. Assume that you have traced an offending e-mail or computer attack back to a particular IP address and through that to a specific ISP. From the ISP, you obtain account information about whom that IP address was assigned to at the time of the incident in question. The account identifies an individual, a physical address, a telephone number, and other information.

---

69. State v. Riley, 846 P.2d 1365 (Wash. 1993).
70. State v. Nordlund, 53 P.3d 520 (Wash. App. 2002), *petition for review denied*, 70 P.3d 964 (Wash. 2003).
71. *Id.*, 53 P.3d at 525.
72. *Id.*

Clearly you have probable cause to believe that evidence of a crime will be found in the computer used to send the offending e-mail or other message. But do you have probable cause to believe that evidence will be found in the suspect's house?

If the account with the ISP is a dial-up account, the account holder can access the Internet via that account from any number of locations. If you are extremely lucky, and the ISP in question uses caller ID, and the caller ID information for the call in which you are interested in is still on the ISP's system, then you may have sufficient information to search the address associated with the phone number identified by the caller ID system.[73] Otherwise, where the IP address is not necessarily associated with a physical address, other steps must be taken to establish probable cause to search a particular location. In one case with which I was involved, we had traced a suspect to a local ISP. We wanted a warrant to search the suspect's house. But with only the account information from the ISP (a dial-up account), we did not have probable cause to search the suspect's house. The suspect had left copies of sent and read e-mail on the server. We obtained copies of this e-mail. In one message the suspect stated it was after 9:30 (in the morning) and he had to go to class. The police staked out the suspect's house and on several occasions saw him leave his house between 9:30 and 9:45 and drive to a local community college where he was a student.

When the e-mail was coupled with the surveillance results, I was satisfied that we now had probable cause to search the suspect's house. We had evidence that the suspect used the e-mail account in question from his home. This was sufficient to make this a valid search.[74]

Where the IP address is associated with a physical address—a networked computer or a DSL or cable modem connection, for example—the physi-

---

73. In U.S. v. Grant, 218 F.3d 72 (1st Cir.), *cert. denied*, 531 U.S. 1025 (2000), the court upheld a search of the defendant's house based on an IP address that was assigned to the defendant's account, but without specific proof that the account was being used from the address that was searched. The court upheld the search even in the face of evidence showing that one of the accesses to the Internet was to a phone number in Virginia, while the defendant lived in Maine.

74. There are other ways of verifying that the computer law enforcement is interested in, is, in fact, in the location to be searched. *See* U.S. v. Kennedy, 81 F. Supp. 2d 1103 (D. Kan. 2000). After identifying the account associated with a particular IP address, the FBI agent called the suspect and asked him if he was satisfied with his Internet service. The suspect confirmed that he accessed the Internet at his home. Although this was a cable modem service with a physical relationship between the IP address and the physical address, this same technique could be used in a dial-up account case.

cal relationship between the IP address and the physical location to be searched is more reliable.[75]

(b) Signed by a Neutral and Detached Magistrate

The warrant must be signed by a magistrate who has authority to issue the warrant. Obviously, the judge must occupy a position that has been property created and has authority to issue warrants.[76] In addition, and more important for Internet crimes and investigations, the judge must have authority to authorize a search of the location covered by the warrant. As discussed earlier, the statutes and court rules in some states expressly limit a judge's search warrant authority to within that state. A warrant issued by a judge from one of those states, to search an ISP in another state is beyond that judge's authority. If the defendant had a recognizable privacy interest in the evidence provided under the warrant, the evidence is subject to suppression.[77]

In other states, it is less clear that there are such jurisdictional limits on warrants. For example, where a warrant issued under probable cause is being executed like a subpoena (i.e., no "search" takes place — the warrant is served on the third party who then provides the evidence requested by the warrant), it is not clear that jurisdictional limits make such a warrant invalid.

The Eighth Circuit addressed this issue in a circuitous way in a Minnesota case.[78] The Court reversed a decision of the trial court suppressing evidence obtained from Yahoo by a search warrant issued by a state court in Minnesota. The warrant was faxed to Yahoo who complied by sending the requested information to the Minnesota authorities.

---

75. *See* U.S. v. Hay, 231 F.3d 630 (9th Cir. 2000), where the IP address in question was associated with the University of Washington. The University's records showed the IP address was associated with a network port wired to a specific apartment.

76. In Washington, a district court commissioner was found to lack the authority to issue search warrants when the office of district court commissioner was not properly created. State v. Moore, 871 P.2d 1086 (Wash. App. 1994).

77. California has a statute that requires ISPs located in California to accept subpoenas and warrants from out of state as if they were issued in California. Cal. Penal Code § 1524.2 (West 2000). While this requires the California ISP to respond to a non-California warrant, it does not make the warrant valid in the issuing state if the warrant is considered to be outside the issuing judge's authority.

78. United States v. Bach, 310 F.3d 1063 (8th Cir. 2002), *cert. denied,* 538 U.S. 993 (2003).

The trial court, noting that 18 U.S.C. § 3105 requires that an authorized officer be present and acting in the warrant's execution when a third party assists in a search, concluded that the Minnesota officer was not present when Yahoo executed the search and thus the search was improperly executed under § 3105. Although the government argued that § 3105 does not apply to state officers executing state warrants when there is no federal involvement, the court held that the Fourth Amendment provided the same protection. The court stated: "While state officers executing a state warrant without any assistance from federal authorities may not be required to comply with section 3105, protections analogous to those provided for by section 3105 exist under the Fourth Amendment."[79]

The Eighth Circuit, in a footnote, recognized the increasingly common practice of serving search warrants for electronic data by fax, much like subpoenas.[80] The Court noted that since the search warrant standard is more stringent than the subpoena standard, so long as the warrant passes muster under warrant requirements the fact that it is being served like a subpoena is of no significance. The Court, noting that the Fourth Amendment is governed by a "reasonableness" standard, held that official presence is simply one of many factors considered in determining the reasonableness of the execution of a search warrant. The Court also noted that civilian searches are sometimes more reasonable than searches by officer and, if conducted outside the presence of police, may increase the amount of privacy retained by the individual during a search.

The Court noted that no warrant was physically "served", no people or premises were searched in the traditional sense and there was no confrontation between Yahoo technicians and the suspect. Furthermore, the Court observed that the physical presence of an officer would not have aided the search (and might have hindered it), the technical expertise of yahoo's technicians far outweighed that of the officers, the items "seized" were located on Yahoo's property, there was a warrant signed by a judge authorizing the search and the officers complied with the requirements of the Electronic Communications Privacy Act. The Court concluded "All of these factors weigh in favor of the government and we therefore find that the search was constitutional under the Fourth Amendment's reasonableness standard."[81]

---

79. United States v. Bach, 2001 WL 1690055, *3 (D. Minn. 2001), rev'd on other grounds, 310 F.3d 1063 (8th Cir. 2002), cert. denied, 538 U.S. 993 (2003).

80. 310 F.3d at 1066 n.1 (8th Cir. 2002).

81. Id. at 1067.

(c) Reasonably Precise in Describing the Place to Be Searched and the Items to Be Seized

The first thing to understand under this topic is that a reviewing court will look at the four squares of the warrant itself and will not consider information provided in the affidavit in support of the warrant unless the affidavit is incorporated by reference in the warrant.[82]

Does your warrant need to specifically allow the search of a computer before you can search a computer at the search location? If officers are executing a warrant that does not specifically reference computers, may they search a computer if it could contain the item they are authorized to seize, without an additional warrant? Under existing law the answer is clear that they may search the computer without an additional warrant.[83] Despite this, if you anticipate searching a computer, the better practice is to mention that a computer will be searched in your affidavit. After all, the more general your description of the search is and the broader your intrusion into the suspect's private affairs becomes, the more likely it is that your evidence ultimately will be suppressed. Thus, you should articulate with some detail for what you are looking.[84]

---

82. Whether this means you should also leave a copy of the affidavit at the search site along with a copy of the warrant is an open question. U.S. v. Towne, 997 F.2d 537 (9th Cir. 1993), notes the different positions courts have taken on this issue, including: (1) incorporation by reference is by itself sufficient; (2) incorporation is unnecessary if the affidavit was available for the officers executing the warrant to refer to; (3) incorporation is necessary and the incorporated affidavit must accompany the warrant during execution; and (4) the affidavit must be incorporated in and physically attached to the warrant. U.S. v. Hayes, 794 F.2d 1348, 1355 (9th Cir. 1986), *cert. denied*, 479 U.S. 1086 (1987), states the purpose of the accompanying affidavit as both to "limit the officer's discretion and to inform the person subject to the search what items the officers executing the warrant can seize." *See also* State v. Riley, 846 P.2d 1365 (Wash. 1993).

83. *See* U.S. v. Ross, 456 U.S. 798 (1982) ("A lawful search of fixed premises generally extends to the entire area in which the object of the search may be found and is not limited by the possibility that separate acts of entry or opening may be required to complete the search ..."); U.S. v. Hunter, 13 F. Supp. 2d 574, 581 (D. Vt. 1998) (Upholding a search of computers even though the warrant did not specify computers because the items covered by the warrant could be found in the computer. "A finding of probable cause is not predicated on the government's knowing precisely how certain records are stored.").

84. For example here is an excerpt from a warrant I was involved with:
The computers and magnetic media seized may be searched for: Files specific to the King County Library System, such as references to Dynix, the specific operating system used by the library, files containing library records, etc;

If you know computers will be present, you should include them as items to be searched. But what if you do not know if computers will be present? As discussed, computers do not have to be specifically listed for you to be able to search them provided the items you are authorized to seize could be found in the computer. Despite this, should you, as a routine matter, request permission to search any computers that may be at the search site?

There are two views on this. Including this language over time may create a *de facto* requirement that computers have to be listed or they cannot be searched. In an odd way, requesting permission to search computers on the site when you do not have probable cause to believe that computers are there, may cause the search to be invalidated.[85] On the other hand, failure to include the language may lead to suppression, particularly at the trial court level.

My suggestion is to include language like "including any computers and computer media located therein" in your warrant language describing where you are authorized to search. You still run the risk that judges will come to expect this, but by including a reference to computers and media in general rather than a reference to a specific computer you will diminish the likelihood of a *Nafzger* result.[86]

(3) Other Issues Relating to a Valid Warrant

(a) Knock and Announce

In executing a warrant, police are required to knock and announce their purpose. This is both a Fourth Amendment requirement[87] and a statutory requirement in many jurisdictions.[88] The purpose of such a requirement is

---

Files similar or identical to those stored by Phree on the library computer; Messages and other substantive files referencing Phree, KoBK, the library, the method of access, etc; Files showing Higgins dominion and control over the computer(s) being seized; Files relating to Internet usage and familiarity; Files relating to UNIX familiarity.

85. Examine U.S. v. Nafzger, 965 F.2d 213, 215 (7th Cir. 1992), where the warrant authorized the search of a specific stolen truck. The truck in question was in a tool shed. The police entered the shed and found the truck. The evidence was suppressed because there was "a total failure to show probable cause that the truck described could be found" at the location searched. Requesting a search of a computer when you do not show probable cause to believe a computer will be found at the search site may be subject to the same remedy.

86. *See id.*

87. Wilson v. Arkansas, 514 U.S. 927 (1995).

88. *See, e.g.,* WASH. REV. CODE § 10.31.040 (2002).

to reduce the potential for violence to all parties from unannounced entry, prevent unnecessary property damage, and protect the privacy rights of occupants.[89]

The knock and announce requirement can cause difficulty as computer data can be destroyed (or at least made more difficult to recover) in a short period of time. If your jurisdiction allows, you may want to request authorization to execute the warrant without knocking and announcing. You must, of course, justify such a request by the facts of your particular case.

(b) Take Items in Plain View

The plain view doctrine has two components. As an exception to the warrant requirement, contraband and instrumentalities may be seized without a warrant if they are in plain view and the incriminating nature of the item is immediately apparent. Related is the principle that while you are executing a warrant for one item you can seize other items in plain view.

This is discussed in more detail below in the discussion of the plain view exception to warrant requirements below.

(c) Good Faith

The exclusionary rule does not apply in federal court when evidence is seized in reasonable, good faith, reliance on a search warrant that is later found to be unsupported by probable cause. The rationale behind this is that penalizing an officer who has complied, in good faith, with the warrant requirement does not further the deterrent function of the exclusionary rule. The exclusionary rule is, after all, intended to deter police misconduct, not to cure violations of rights. The test is whether the officers acted in objectively reasonable reliance on what turned out to be an invalid warrant.[90]

Some, but not all state courts have adopted the good faith rule. It has also been applied in non-criminal contexts.[91]

(d) Take Computers off Premises to Search

Often (and in these days of multi-gigabyte drives, usually), you will need to take a computer off-site to complete the search. So long as this has been

---

89. Note, *Announcement in Police Entries*, 80 YALE L.J. 139, 140–42 (1970).

90. U.S. v. Leon, 468 U.S. 897 (1984).

91. See the discussion of the Privacy Protection Act and the Electronic Communications Privacy Act below.

justified and requested in the application and approved by the warrant judge, this is generally an accepted practice. As noted by District Court Judge Sessions in *U.S. v. Hunter*, "until technology and law enforcement expertise render on-site computer records searching both possible and practical, wholesale seizures, if adequately safeguarded, must occur."[92]

A recent Colorado case[93] followed the guidance of *Hunter* and other cases, but the dissent raised some issues that must be addressed. In that case, the police executed a warrant at the defendant's apartment, searching for "written or printed material" relating to firearms, explosives, intent to do harm to other people, etc. They seized two desktop computers and five laptop computers and removed them from the premises for offsite searching. They then got a separate warrant to search the computers.

The trial court suppressed the evidence found on the computers because the court was unable to conclude that a computer was analogous to a writing or other type of document — the items that could be seized under the warrant. The Colorado Supreme Court reversed the trial court and ruled the evidence admissible, citing numerous cases found in this chapter and in the Department of Justice's Computer Search guidelines.[94] They viewed the computers as containers which, under well-established law,[95] could be searched if they could contain the evidence for which the warrant authorized seizure. The court specifically approved the procedure of seizing the computers for off-site search.

The dissent argued that computers were not like other containers and that special privacy interests were involved. In particular, the dissent argued that the case law did not support seizing computers to search off-site, even under a second warrant, if the computers were not identified in the first warrant. The dissent also argued that the subsequent search, off-site, should be designed to limit the privacy intrusion.

A related issue to off-site searches is what time limits are there to the off-site search and forensic analysis. These issues are discussed later in this chapter.

---

92. 13 F. Supp. 2d 574, 583 (D. Vt. 1998).

93. People v. Gall, 30 P.3d 145 (Colo. 2001).

94. COMPUTER CRIME AND INTELLECTUAL PROPERTY SECTION, CRIMINAL DIVISION, UNITED STATES DEPARTMENT OF JUSTICE, SEARCHING AND SEIZING COMPUTERS AND OBTAINING ELECTRONIC EVIDENCE IN CRIMINAL INVESTIGATIONS (2002), *available at* http://www.cybercrime.gov/s&smanual2002.htm.

95. See the discussion of *United States v. Ross*, 456 U.S. 798 (1982), earlier in this paper.

(e) Prompt Execution

Finally, a warrant, to be valid, must be executed promptly. What is prompt execution? There are two components. First the warrant must be executed while there is still probable cause to believe that evidence of a crime will be found at the place to be searched—before the information provided in support of the warrant becomes stale. This is a constitutional issue.[96]

A related but separate issue is when laws or court rules require a warrant to be executed within a certain amount of time, setting the outer limits on the time a magistrate may set for the execution of the warrant. This is discussed below in the section dealing with court rules and magistrate imposed restrictions.

(4) If There Is Not a Legal Warrant Does the Search Fall within the Exceptions to the Warrant Requirement?

There are exceptions to the rule that evidence obtained without a warrant is inadmissible. These are, of course, the "few, specific, established, and well-delineated exceptions" developed under the Fourth Amendment.[97]

A few of these exceptions—like consent—may justify the search of a computer without a warrant, but most do not. The more pertinent exceptions are discussed below.

(a) Consent

If the suspect or other person with authority over the property consents to a search, then a warrant is not required. The key questions are: who has the authority to consent, is the consent given voluntarily and intelligently, and is the consent limited?

i) Who May Consent?

Obviously the suspect may consent to a search of his own premises and effects, subject to such consent being given voluntarily and intelligently. As for third party consent, the general rule is that one "who possesses common authority over or other sufficient relationship to the premises or ef-

---

96. *See* Wayne R. LaFave, Search and Seizure, § 4.7 at 584–88 (3d. Ed. 1996).

97. Schneckloth v. Bustamonte, 412 U.S. 218, 219 (1973), *citing* Katz v. U.S., 389 U.S. 347, 357 (1967).

fects sought to be inspected" has the authority to consent to a search.[98] In *United States v. Rith,*[99] the Tenth Circuit stated the *Matlock* test in the disjunctive: A person may give effective consent if they have mutual use of the property by virtue of joint access *or* if they have control of the property for most purposes of it.

The crucial analytical test is whether the defendant has a reasonable expectation of privacy in the premises or effects to which another has consented to be searched. In most instances of shared premises and effects the courts have ruled there is a reduced expectation of privacy in the premises or things shared with another.[100] As the Ninth Circuit stated: "Although there is always the fond hope that a co-occupant will follow one's known wishes, the risks remain. A defendant cannot expect sole exclusionary authority unless he lives alone, or at least has a special and private space within the joint residence."[101] The consent given by a third party may not be valid if the area involved has been set aside, or rented, for the exclusive use of the defendant.[102]

In the computer search context, the issue of consent most commonly arises in searches where an employer, a parent, a spouse, or a co-user has consented to the search of a computer containing evidence against the suspect. In analyzing consent in the computer context it is important to distinguish valid consent to search a room from valid consent to search a container in that room, such as a computer. The *Matlock* factors must apply to the computer itself, not merely the room containing the computer before consent is effective.[103]

a) Employers

1) Private Employers

In non-computer cases involving private employers, the courts have consistently held that the employer has the authority to consent to a search of those areas not set aside for exclusive use by a particular employee.[104] The

---

98. U.S. v. Matlock, 415 U.S. 164, 171 (1974).

99. 164 F.3d 1323 (10th Cir.), *cert. denied,* 528 U.S. 827 (1999).

100. *E.g.,* U.S. v. Ladell, 127 F.3d 622, 624 (7th Cir. 1997).

101. U.S. v. Morning, 64 F.3d 531, 536 (9th Cir. 1995), *cert. denied,* 516 U.S. 1152 (1996).

102. State v. Mathe, 688 P.2d 859 (Wash. 1984).

103. "While authority to consent to search of a general area must obviously extend to most objects in plain view within the area, it cannot be thought automatically to extend to the interiors of every discrete enclosed space capable of search within the area." U.S. v. Block, 590 F.2d 535, 541 (4th Cir. 1978) (While search of the room by consent was okay, search of a footlocker was not.).

104. U.S. v. Gargiso, 456 F.2d 584 (2d Cir. 1972).

rule should equally apply to searches of computers. This is particularly true if the employer has announced a policy that the employer may access such computers at any time, that the employee has no privacy regarding information on the computer, that the employer can consent to a law enforcement search, or other policy explicitly or implicitly putting the employee on notice as to the employer's authority over the computer.[105]

As in other settings, a person with common authority over the area to be searched, such as a co-worker who shares usage of the computer, may also consent to a search.[106]

Of course, if the employer, not acting as an agent of law enforcement, does the search in question, there is no suppression remedy.[107]

2) Public Employers

The first issue is whether a government employee has any reasonable expectation of privacy in their workspace, including computers. This question was answered in the affirmative in *O'Connor v. Ortega*.[108] The Supreme Court held that a government employee does not lose their expectation of privacy merely because they are public employees. The Court did note, however, that the nature of the public workplace could be such that the expectation of privacy is greatly reduced or eliminated in some circumstances. "Some government offices may be so open to fellow employees or the public that no expectation of privacy is reasonable."[109] The expectation of privacy can also be reduced as a result of specific announced policy by the employer.

Thus, the first test under *O'Connor* is whether the facts suggest that an expectation of privacy by the employee is unreasonable. The easiest way to establish this is if the employer has enunciated a policy limiting or eliminating any expectation of privacy in the use of a government provided computer. This can be in the form of an employee policy manual or other written statements limiting employee privacy or in the form of banners or other

---

105. See U.S. v. Simons, 29 F. Supp. 2d 324 (E.D. Va. 1998). The defendant was an employee at the CIA's Foreign Bureau of Information Services. The court held he did not have a reasonable expectation of privacy regarding his Internet use in light of his employer's written policy restricting Internet use.

106. United States v. Longo, 70 F. Supp. 2d 225, 256 (W.D.N.Y. 1999) where the court upheld the authority of a secretary to consent to a search of the employer's computer.

107. See the discussion of the law of private searches earlier in this chapter.

108. 480 U.S. 709 (1987).

109. *Id.* at 718 (O'Connor, concurring).

warnings that are displayed on computers. The two crucial elements of such a policy are (1) that the policy or banner clearly enunciates the absence or limitation of a privacy right, and (2) that the employee in fact is made aware of this policy.

A caution: If the employer explicitly allows (or tolerates) use of such a computer for private purposes and the employee sets aside a separate area of the computer for her/his private files, the question is much closer. If the employee encrypts those files or otherwise restricts access to them, the expectation of privacy is higher still. But the rules are still unclear in this developing area of law.[110]

The O'Connor Court also said that, even where there is a reasonable expectation of privacy, a government employer may search the files and offices of an employee for work-related reasons (to locate a particular document, for example) or to investigate suspected employee wrongdoing.[111]

Two recent cases provide additional insight into the search of public employee computers. In U.S. v. Slanina,[112] the Fifth Circuit held that a city employee's expectation of privacy in his office computer was reasonable because the employer had not notified employees that their computer usage would be monitored and there was no indication that other employees had routine access to Slanina's computer.

The court nevertheless upheld the search under the O'Connor exception permitting warrantless searches by an employer to investigate suspected employee malfeasance. Specifically, a member of the IT staff had accessed Slanina's computer for network installation purposes and had uncovered evidence of pornography. The IT worker brought this to the attention of Slanina's supervisor who happened to be a law enforcement officer with supervision over the fire department where Slanina worked. Child pornography was found on the computer and a criminal prosecution ensued.

The court upheld the search notwithstanding that the employee malfeasance in question also happened to be a crime and notwithstanding that the supervisor was also a law enforcement officer.

In the same week as this decision, the Tenth Circuit ruled that an Oklahoma State University professor did not have a reasonable expectation of

---

110. *See generally* WAYNE R. LaFAVE, SEARCH AND SEIZURE, § 8.6(f) (3d. Ed. 1996).

111. For a computer specific case where a supervisor's seizure of a computer disk containing work related and personal files was upheld, *see* Williams v. Philadelphia Housing Authority, 834 F. Supp. 794 (E.D. Pa. 1993), *aff'd mem.*, 27 F.3d 560 (3d. Cir. 1994).

112. U.S. v. Slanina, 283 F.3d 670 (5th Cir. 2002).

privacy in materials stored on his office computer.[113] OSU had a computer use policy that explained appropriate computer use, warned employees about the consequence of misuse and described how officials administered and monitored the University computer network. This was done via a policy manual distributed to all employees as well as in a banner that was displayed each time the computer was turned on.

b) Parent

Courts generally find third-party consents easier to sustain "if the relationship between the parties — parent to child here, spouse to spouse in other cases — is especially close."[114]

In the computer context, the more the computer is a shared item, both in terms of use and location, the more likely it is that a parent can give a valid consent. Even when the computer belongs to the child or is used by them exclusively and is located in their room or private space, parents can generally consent to a search of such a computer so long as the child is "essentially dependent" on the parent. If the child pays rent or in other ways is independent of the parent, the parent may lack the authority to give valid consent to a search of the child's effects or private space.[115]

c) Spouse

Spouses are generally considered to have joint control and equal right to occupancy of the premises and access to computers on the premises, and so may give a valid consent. If, however, the computer is used exclusively by the non-consenting spouse and is kept in a separate room (especially if locked), the other spouse may not be able to give valid consent.

d) Co-user

A co-user of a computer is much like a co-tenant and should be analyzed the same way. Generally, allowing co-use results in a greatly reduced expectation of privacy. Whether password restricted or encrypted areas are the equivalent of locked bedrooms and thus not subject to a consent search by a co-user is an as yet undecided issue.[116] Until you learn otherwise, how-

---

113. U.S. v. Angevine, 281 F.3d 1130, 1134 (10th Cir. 2002).

114. U.S. v. Ladell, 127 F.3d 622, 624 (7th Cir. 1997).

115. U.S. v. Rith, 164 F.3d 1323 (10th Cir.), *cert. denied*, 528 U.S. 827 (1999).

116. In a very fact specific ruling the court in *U.S. v. Smith*, 27 F. Supp. 2d 1111 (C.D. Ill. 1998) allowed evidence obtained from a computer under a third party consent, not-

ever, I would assume that a co-user can *not* give consent to search such objectively private areas of a computer.

e) Other

When an item has been left in the custody of a third party the courts may find limits on the third party's authority to consent to a search of the item. In *United States v. James*,[117] the Eighth Circuit held the third party did not have authority to consent to the search of a packet of computer CDs left in his possession by the defendant. The court focused on its perception of the defendant's intent and held that the defendant did not intend to give the third party any authority to consent to the search of the disks. He gave them solely for the purpose of storing the disks.

This view of a suspect's ability to limit the scope of authority given to a third party holding the defendant's item conflicts with decisions like *United States v. Falcon*.[118] The defendant left a cassette at his brother's apartment labeled "confidential" and "do not play". Notwithstanding these instructions, the *Falcon* court held the brother's consent to search the cassettes to be effective because the brother "could have played [the tape] at any time, whether by design or by accident."[119]

One way of reconciling these two lines of thought is that in the James case the CDs were contained in a sealed envelope and the envelope was further encased in tape. Thus they could not have been viewed by accident. More importantly, the police came to third party in the *James* case because they intercepted a letter from James to the third party instructing the third party to destroy the envelope and its contents.

Whether the specific facts of *James* will form the basis of future limits on consent searches is unknown, but the case does provide support for the

---

ing that there was no evidence the defendant had password-protected the material seized.

The Fourth Circuit recently held that a search of an individual's password-protected computer files is an illegal search in violation of the Fourth Amendment when consent to the search was given by another individual who had joint access to the computer but did not know the passwords and therefore did not have authority to grant access to the files. Truloch v. Freeh, 275 F.3d 391, 403 (4th Cir. 2001).

117. 353 F.3d 606 (8th Cir. 2003).

118. 766 F.2d 1469 (10th Cir. 1985).

119. *Id.* at 1476.

more widely held view that where the defendant has taken extra steps to insure the privacy of computer files, such as by encrypting or password protecting them, the authority of the third party possessing of having access to the computer containing those files to consent to the search of those files is greatly limited.

ii) Must the Consentor Be Advised of His/Her Right to Withhold Consent

The general rule is that the voluntariness of a consent to search is measured by the "totality of the circumstances."[120] In the Federal system, the burden is on the government to prove voluntariness of consent by a "preponderance of the evidence."[121] In other jurisdictions, like Washington State, a higher standard is required. Consent must be proved by "clear and convincing evidence" from the totality of the circumstances.[122]

Factors to be considered in determining the voluntariness of consent include:

- The age and level of intelligence of the suspect
- Whether the suspect was advised of her/his constitutional rights
- Whether the suspect was in custody or detention and for how long
- Whether physical punishment was inflicted, including denying sleep or food.

None of these factors by themselves are dispositive, but some may be more important than others. "Although the Constitution does not require proof of knowledge of a right to refuse as the *sine qua non* of an effective consent to a search, such knowledge was highly relevant to the determination that there had been consent."[123]

Sometimes an officer will tell a defendant that she/he will ask for a search warrant if consent is not given. Most courts consider that such a scenario does not constitute coercion and consent in such circumstances is valid.[124]

---

120. Schneckloth v. Bustamonte, 412 U.S. 218 (1968).
121. U.S. v. Matlock, 415 U.S. 164 (1974); U.S. v. Mendenhall, 446 U.S. 544 (1980).
122. State v. Werth, 571 P.2d 941 (Wash. App. 1977), *review denied*, 90 Wash. 2d 1010 (1978).
123. U.S. v. Mendenhall, 446 U.S. 544, 558–59 (1980).
· 124. State v. Smith, 801 P.2d 975 (Wash. 1990).

In some jurisdictions there are additional limitations on consent searches when the police have gone to the to-be-searched house on a "knock and talk" mission.[125] In Washington, to be effective, consent obtained as a result of a knock and talk must be preceded by advising the consentor that they need not consent to the entry/search.[126]

iii) Consent May Be Limited and May Be Withdrawn

Consent may be limited and withdrawn. A search of areas for which consent was not given or after consent is withdrawn is invalid.[127]

Some court have held searches invalid when the officers, acting under general consent, broke open locked or sealed containers.[128] Is a search of hidden, password protected or encrypted files under a general consent to search a computer open to the same attack? To the extent that analogy to the physical world is applicable, the answer is probably no. The line of cases represented by *Wells*, focus on the destruction of property necessary to open the sealed or locked container. Since there is no comparable destruction in accessing hidden, password protected or encrypted files, the search may be upheld.

(b) Search Incident to Arrest

"When an arrest is made, officers are allowed to search the person arrested for any weapons or for any evidence on the arrestee's person in order to prevent its concealment or destruction. The officer may also search areas within the arrestee's immediate control for the same purpose."[129] This doctrine would allow an officer to look for computers or computer evidence within the arrestee's immediate control but would not allow them to further search the computers without other legal justification.

---

125. "Knock and talk" is generally understood to mean situations where the police go to a suspect's house without a warrant in an attempt to get the suspect to voluntarily talk to the police and/or consent to a search.

126. State v. Ferrier, 960 P.2d 927 (Wash. 1998). *See also* New Jersey v. Johnson, 346 A.2d 66, 68 (N.J. 1975).

127. *See* Model Code of Pre-Arraignment Procedure § SS 240.3 (1975) (a consent search "shall not exceed, in duration or physical scope, the limits of the consent given"); Mason v. Pulliam, 557 F.2d 426 (5th Cir. 1977).

128. Florida v. Wells, 539 So.2d 464 (Fla. 1989), *aff'd*, 495 U.S. 1 (1990).

129. Chimel v. California, 395 U.S. 752, 762–63 (1969).

(c) Exigent Circumstances

The exigent circumstances exception allows a warrantless search of premises where the officer has probable cause and exigent circumstances exist. The determination of whether exigent circumstances exist includes an examination of many factors.[130]

> We have long recognized that the imminent destruction of evidence may constitute an exigency excusing the failure to procure a warrant. This risk is particularly weighty where narcotics are involved, for it is commonly known that narcotics can be easily and quickly destroyed.... We held that a police officer can show an objectively reasonable belief that contraband is being, or will be, destroyed within a home if he can show 1) a reasonable belief that third persons are inside a private dwelling, and 2) a reasonable belief that these third persons are aware of an investigatory stop or arrest of a confederate outside the premises, so that they might see a need to destroy evidence.[131]

In the context of computer searches, the important thing to understand about this exception is, like a search incident to arrest, it does not justify a

---

130. *See* U.S. v. Brown, 52 F.3d 415, 421 (2d Cir. 1995), *cert. denied*, 516 U.S. 1068 (1996) ("Our court has looked to six touchstones for determining the existence of exigent circumstances. Those are: '(1) the gravity or violent nature of the offense with which the suspect is to be charged; (2) whether the suspect is reasonably believed to be armed; (3) a clear showing of probable cause ... to believe that the suspect committed the crime; (4) strong reason to believe that the suspect is in the premises being entered; (5) a likelihood that the suspect will escape if not swiftly apprehended; and (6) the peaceful circumstances of the entry.' Those factors are 'merely illustrative, not exhaustive, and the presence or absence of any one factor is not conclusive.'" (citations omitted)).

U.S. v. Rico, 51 F.3d 495, 501 (5th Cir.), *cert. denied*, 516 U.S. 883 (1995) ("In evaluating whether exigent circumstances existed, we have found relevant the following factors: (1) the degree of urgency involved and amount of time necessary to obtain a warrant; (2) [the] reasonable belief that contraband is about to be removed; (3) the possibility of danger to the police officers guarding the site of contraband while a search warrant is sought; (4) information indicating the possessors of the contraband are aware that the police are on their trail; and (5) the ready destructibility of the contraband and the knowledge 'that efforts to dispose of narcotics and to escape are characteristic behavior of persons engaged in the narcotics traffic.'" (citations omitted)) .

131. U.S. v. Dawkins, 17 F.3d 399, 405 (D.C. Cir. 1994).

search of computer. It might allow for a search for and seizure of a computer to preserve evidence under the right facts, but a separate legal justification to search the computer must be provided.

(d) Inventory

While inventory searches are generally thought of as searches of vehicles, one type of an inventory search that might apply to computers is a booking search.[132] While such a search, like a search incident to arrest or an exigent circumstances search, is probably limited to removing a computer (such as a laptop or other portable computing device) from a suspect's person as opposed to searching the computer itself, in some circumstances a search of the computer to ascertain or verify a defendant's identity may be appropriate.[133]

(e) Stop and Frisk

"[A] law enforcement officer, for his own protection and safety, may conduct a pat-down to find weapons that he reasonably believes or suspects are then in the possession of the person he has accosted."[134] While any computing device found during such a frisk which is contraband may be seized, this exception to the warrant requirement is generally not applicable to computer based evidence search cases.

(f) Mobility

An officer with probable cause to search a vehicle he/she has lawfully stopped, may conduct such a search without a warrant because the automobile's ready mobility constitutes an exigency sufficient to excuse failure to obtain a search warrant.[135] There may be a case where probable cause exists to search a vehicle for an item which could be found in a computer, thus allowing a warrantless search of a computer under this doctrine but there are no reported decisions involving such a case. As stated earlier, there

---

132. *See generally* Illinois v. Lafayette, 462 U.S. 640, 648 (1983); U.S. v. Thomas, 11 F.3d 620, 628 (6th Cir. 1993), *cert. denied*, 511 U.S. 1043 (1994).

133. *See* Illinois v. Lafayette, 462 U.S. at 646 (Discussion of inventory searches in general).

134. Ybarra v. Illinois, 444 U.S. 85, 93 (1979).

135. LaBron v. Kilgore, 518 U.S. 938, 940 (1996).

is little likelihood that a laptop computer could be searched without a warrant under this justification.

(g) Plain View

The rationale of the plain view doctrine is that if contraband is left in open view and is observed by a police officer from a lawful vantage point, there has been no invasion of a legitimate expectation of privacy and thus no search within the meaning of the Fourth Amendment—or at least no search independent of the initial intrusion that gave the officers their vantage point.[136] This exception has three requirements when applied in the computer evidence search context:

- The incriminating nature of the item in plain view must be immediately apparent.
- The officer must be lawfully located in a position from which he or she can plainly see the item.
- The officer must not change the focus of her/his search as a result of discovering the plain view item.

The first two of these rules come from the development of the plain view doctrine in the non-computer context.[137] The third comes from the unique aspects of a search for computerized evidence.

For example, if a search protocol calls for examining all files sequentially on a computer, then every file may be examined.[138] If incriminating evidence outside the scope of the warrant is observed in one file (such as child pornography) and then, still following the search protocol, other files are examined which also contain incriminating evidence outside the scope of the warrant, all qualify as plain view evidence.

On the other hand, however, if the search is for records of business transactions and the search protocol calls for a key word search and an examination of the directory and file structure, but not the examination of each

---

136. Minnesota v. Dickerson, 508 U.S. 355, 375 (1993).

137. U.S. v. Bradshaw, 102 F.3d 204, 211 (6th Cir. 1996), *cert. denied*, 520 U.S. 1178 (1997).

138. This and subsequent examples assume the officer has a valid warrant allowing her/him to be at the location, with the object they are authorized to seize being such that it could be found in a computer.

individual file, then the discovery of a possibly incriminating file name ("babyfuk.jpg," for example) does not justify the opening of that file. Furthermore the discovery of child pornography, in plain view and outside the scope of the warrant, does not justify a change in the search protocol or search focus.[139]

With a solid search protocol, the police can follow that protocol, even if they discover incriminating evidence outside the scope of the warrant, and be confident that the evidence will be admissible. Without such a protocol, or if the new evidence creates the need to go outside the protocol, the best practice when outside-the-scope-of-the-warrant evidence is discovered is to stop the search and get a new warrant based on the plain view evidence discovered.

b. State Constitutional Considerations

Some states' constitutions are more restrictive or have been interpreted in a more restrictive manner than the federal constitution. Many states do not allow a good faith exception to the requirements of a valid warrant. Some states provide more protection to occupants of vehicles and the vehicles themselves than do the federal courts. Obviously any consideration of whether a search of a computer is allowed must take the constitutional requirements of the forum state into account.

c. Statutes

The Electronic Communications Privacy Act, previously discussed, is one example of a statute that sets limits on the acquisition of computer related information. Another is the Privacy Protection Act.[140]

---

139. U.S. v. Carey, 172 F.3d 1268 (10th Cir. 1999). The defendant, who was under investigation for narcotics violations, consented to a search of his apartment. Two computers were seized and a warrant was issued allowing the computers to be searched for information relating to the sale and distribution of controlled substances. In conducting this search of the computer the police discovered child pornography. The officer testified that while he did not originally believe the jpg files he examined contained child pornography, after he saw the first one he had probable cause to believe the others contained child pornography. He continued to examine the jpg files, finding more child pornography. He did this examination on another computer because the files could not be viewed on the suspect's computer. The court interpreted this continued examination of the jpg files as an expansion of the scope of the search to include items outside the warrant's parameters.

140. 42 U.S.C. § 2000aa (2000).

(1) Privacy Protection Act

The Privacy Protection Act ["PPA"], was passed in response to *Zurcher v. Stanford Daily*.[141] In that case, officers executed a search warrant at the offices of the *Stanford Daily*, a student newspaper, to search for pictures of a demonstration. The newspaper and some of its staff brought a 42 U.S.C. § 1983 action against the officer who conducted the search and others. The Supreme Court, in *Zurcher*, held that other than applying warrant requirements with particular exactitude, there were no limitations on warranted searches where First Amendment interests are involved.[142]

The PPA, imposed limitations based on First Amendment concerns. It prohibits searches and seizures of material that an individual intends to publish or broadcast and "documentary material" possessed by a person in connection with a purpose to publish or broadcast the material.[143] Such material must be obtained by subpoena. There are exceptions, however:

- The law does not apply to material that constitutes contraband, fruits of a crime, or property designed or used to commit a crime
- It does not apply to searches and seizures needed to prevent imminent death or injury
- It does not apply when the material is possessed by the target of the investigation[144]
- It does not apply to child pornography.

In addition, for "documentary material," the law does not apply if there is a reason to believe that the possessor of the material would destroy, alter or conceal the evidence if a subpoena was issued, or if there is a finding that the materials have not been produced as directed under a subpoena and further delays would threaten the interests of justice. Further, the act only applies when there is a reasonable belief of the subject's intent to publish the material.

Most law enforcement professionals who did computer searches were unaware of this act until the *Steve Jackson Games* case. In March, 1990, Secret Service agents executed a search warrant at the offices of Steve Jackson

---

141. 436 U.S. 547 (1978).

142. *See id.*

143. *See* 42 U.S.C. § 2000aa(b) (2000).

144. In an exception to the exception, this exception does not apply when the alleged crime is the receipt, communication, or withholding of such evidence unless the material relates to national defense/is classified.

Games, Inc. ["SJG"], searching for a computerized text file containing information about Bell South's emergency call system. SJG published books, magazines, role-playing games and other related products. SJG also hosted an electronic bulletin board system which, among other things, allowed customers to send and receive private e-mail. Among the items seized in the search was the computer that operated the Bulletin Board System. There were 162 items of unread, private e-mail on this system.

In 1991 SJG filed suit[145] against the Secret Service claiming violations of the Privacy Protection Act and the Electronic Communications Privacy Act. The trial court held that the Secret Service violated the PPA and awarded damages of $51,040. The court also found a violation of the ECPA and awarded statutory damages of $1,000 to each individual plaintiff. It also awarded SJG over $250,000 in attorney fees and costs.

The court found that although the Secret Service may not have known that SJG was a publisher at the time of execution of the warrant, they were aware of this by the day after the execution of the warrant. Although SJG asked for the prompt return of the material seized, and, the court found, the material could have been copied and returned "within a period of hours and not more than eight days," the material was not returned for several months. It was the failure to return the seized property that exposed the Secret Service to liability.

The decision makes several things clear. First, a computer "publisher" is protected under the PPA. Second, even if there is no knowledge of publisher status at the time a search is executed, if the seized material shows publisher status, the seizing agents may be liable for their actions following their presumed acquisition of knowledge of publisher status. Finally, the decision also makes it clear that a lack of familiarity with the Privacy Protection Act can be costly.

Of course, SJG was not itself a target in the investigation. Had the company been the target, the results might have been different. The Act applies almost exclusively to third party search situations. When you seek to search your target's computer you are usually (but not always) outside the parameters of the PPA.

Subsequent decisions to *Steve Jackson Games* suggest that the PPA will not be applied broadly where the suspect's computer is involved. In *Guest v. Leis*,[146] the Sixth Circuit decided a civil case brought, *inter alia,* under the

145. Steve Jackson Games, Inc. v. U.S. Secret Service, 816 F. Supp. 432 (W.D. Tex. 1993), *aff'd*, 36 F.3d 457 (5th Cir. 1994).

146. 255 F.3d 325 (6th Cir. 2001).

PPA, involving the search and seizure of computer bulletin board systems containing obscene material. The court held that

[W]hen protected materials are commingled on a criminal suspect's computer with criminal evidence that is unprotected by the act, we will not find liability under the PPA for seizure of the PPA-protected materials. We emphasize, though, that police may not then search the PPA-protected materials that were seized incidentally to the criminal evidence.[147]

(a) Suppression

A violation of the Privacy Protection Act is not a basis for suppressing the evidence obtained. "[E]vidence otherwise admissible in a proceeding shall not be excluded on the basis of a violation of this chapter."[148]

(b) Civil Liability

Civil liability can result from a violation of the Privacy Protection Act. The PPA states that an aggrieved person has a cause of action:

(1) Against the United States, against a State which has waived its sovereign immunity under the Constitution to a claim for damages resulting from a violation of this chapter, or against any other governmental unit, all of which shall be liable for violations of this chapter by their officers or employees while acting within the scope or under color of their office or employment; and

(2) Against an officer or employee of a State who has violated this chapter while acting within the scope of or under color of his office or employment, if such State has not waived its sovereign immunity as provided in paragraph (1).[149]

---

147. *Id.* at 342 (footnote omitted).

148. 42 U.S.C. § 2000aa-6 (2000). In Oklahoma *ex rel.* Macy v. One Pioneer CD-Rom Changer, 891 P.2d 600 (Okla. Ct. App. 1994) (*cert. denied*, Feb. 15, 1995), the state sought to forfeit computer equipment used in the distribution of pornography. The system owner claimed a violation of the PPA because the material seized contained non-offending material that was intended for publication on CDs. The court rejected this defense, noting that even if the PPA had been violated, this did not preclude a forfeiture so long as the equipment was seized pursuant to an otherwise lawful search and seizure.

149. 42 U.S.C. § 2000aa-6(a) (2000).

It was this provision that provided the legal basis for the liability found in the *Steve Jackson Games* case discussed above.[150]

(c) Good Faith

Good faith reliance on an otherwise valid search warrant is a defense against civil liability under the PPA. In *Davis v. Gracey*,[151] the plaintiff sued law enforcement officers and entities involved in a search and seizure of a computer system involved in the distribution of pornography. The plaintiff contended the police seized materials that the defendant intended to publish on a CD, thus violating the PPA. The district court granted summary judgment to the defendants, holding that the defendants were entitled to the good faith defense of 42 U.S.C. § 2000aa-b(b) because the police had acted in reliance on a valid warrant.[152]

(2) State Privacy Statutes

Several states have laws imposing greater restrictions on the recording or interception of communications than federal law. One example is Washington's Privacy Act.[153] That Act has been called one of the most restrictive in the nation.[154] While the Act has historically been applied in the context of aural communications, a recent case states clearly that electronic communications are protected by the act as well.[155]

(3) Court Rules and Magistrate Imposed Restrictions

(a) Court Rules—
Time within Which Search Must Be Completed

Some jurisdictions have statutes or court rules that require a search warrant to be executed within a specified period of time after it was issued.

---

150. Liability was also found under the ECPA, discussed earlier.

151. 111 F.3d 1472 (10th Cir. 1997).

152. On appeal, the Tenth Circuit dismissed the suit because of an absence of subject matter jurisdiction. All of the entities had been previously dismissed leaving only the individual officers. The Court held that the PPA only allowed actions against governmental entities unless the state had not waived sovereign immunity. Since Oklahoma had waived immunity, only the government, not the individual officers could be sued. *Id.*

153. WASH. REV. CODE §§ 9.73.010–9.73.230 (2003).

154. State v. O'Neill, 700 P.2d 711 (Wash. 1985).

155. State v. Townsend, *supra* note 55.

Some courts hold a violation of such statutes or court rules to require suppression.[156] Other courts have held that absent a Fourth Amendment violation (i.e., probable cause still existed when the warrant was executed), suppression is not appropriate even when the statute or court rule time limit was exceeded.[157]

In the context of computer searches, the more problematic issue relates to the off-site search of a computer following the execution of the warrant. It is important to understand that even if your application justifies and the warrant approves an off-site search of a computer, the off-site search of the computer must be done within the same time limits set for the search of the premises where the computer was located.

If a computer is contraband or an instrumentality, it may be seized. If it is a container of evidence it may be "seized" solely for the purpose of searching it off-site. There is no other legal basis for retaining the computer. Thus, if the warrant sets a three day deadline on the execution of the warrant, and the computer is not searched within that three day period, arguably there is no longer any justification for police to hold the computer and there is no authority for a search outside that three day period. Even if the issuing judge is willing to allow additional time to search a computer off-site, the court rules discussed earlier may be an absolute limit on the judge's authority to extend that time.

Some argue that the justification for magistrate imposed and statute/rule imposed deadlines is to insure that a warrant will be executed before the information on which it is based becomes stale. Since the computer was seized during the required time, and since the information in that computer will not change between that seizure and the ultimate search of the computer, there is no staleness issue. This is a fine argument in principle and may be successful in many cases. If, however, you have a court that considers the magistrate/statute/rule deadline to be absolute, then this argument may not be successful.

For example, in *United States v. Syphers*,[158] the trial judge rejected a suppression motion based on a seven month's delay in analyzing computer evidence seized under a warrant. Analogizing to the seizure of suspected heroin (which is not lab analyzed for several months), the trial judge held

---

156. Sgro v. U.S., 287 U.S. 206 (1932) (holding a warrant void under the federal National Prohibition Act, 27 U.S.C. § 39 (repealed)).

157. U.S. v. Gerber, 994 F.2d 1556 (11th Cir. 1993).

158. 296 F. Supp. 2d 50 (D.N.H. 2003).

there is no Fourth Amendment violation where probable cause has not dissipated because the item previously seized has been in control of the police since the seizure.

The thrust of the *Syphers* decision is that while federal warrants must be executed within a specified time no longer than ten days,[159] this does not impose a deadline to analyze evidence already seized. If police seize evidence consistent with Rule 41 and the Fourth Amendment, any delay in the analysis of such evidence (whether it be a hard drive or a filing cabinet full of documents) is not of constitutional concern.

Nevertheless, where a computer has been seized solely as a container of evidence to be searched offsite, it begs the question to claim that the subsequent examination is an "analysis" not a search. If the only justification for seizing the computer was to search it offsite, there is a strong argument that the search has not occurred until the computer is examined.

In a Washington case involving bank records, the detective obtained a search warrant for bank records and served it on the bank the same day. The warrant directed that the premises be searched within ten days.[160] The bank provided the documents covered by the warrant seventeen days later. The defendant objected to the admission of the bank records, arguing that they were obtained outside the ten-day limit of the warrant and rules.

The Court of Appeals first noted that the constitutional requirement that a warrant be served before the probable cause becomes stale was met in this case. The court held that the service of the warrant on the bank initiated the bank retrieval process and involved the

> records of a disinterested business entity whose daily operations involve the creation, storage and retrieval of the records themselves. In these circumstances, service of the warrant begins the search. Therefore, the search began before the warrant expired, and so long as probable cause continues to exist through completion of the search, the search is constitutionally timely.[161]

The court then addressed the specific requirement of Wash. Cr. R. 2.3(c) and held that this was concerned only with the staleness of probable cause issue, already decided.[162] The admission of the evidence was affirmed.

---

159. Fed. R. Crim. P. 41(e)(2)(A).

160. *See* Wash. Cr. R. 2.3(c).

161. State v. Kern, 914 P.2d 114, 116 (Wash. App. 1996).

162. *See id.* at 117.

What I advise the police to do is to make some search of the computer within the prescribed time sufficient to identify some contraband on the computer. Once that is done, you are no longer holding the computer solely as a container which might contain evidence and which you will search in the future. You are now holding the computer as a container of actual identified contraband. Any subsequent review of the computer will be separating the wheat from the chaff—separating the contraband from non-contraband. If you do not find contraband within that time period, your choices are to request an extension (which may not be effective if your statute or court rule sets a maximum limit) or, if you continue to have probable cause, request a new warrant.

Both of these arguments are stopgap measures until some change is made that recognizes the reality of the length of time it takes to search multi-gigabyte drives.

(b) Magistrate Imposed Restrictions

The magistrate issuing the warrant may impose deadlines for the search of computers seized during the execution of the warrant that are different from the date by which the warrant itself must be executed. If those deadlines are not complied with, the evidence may be suppressed. In *United States v. Brunnette*,[163] the warrant was approved on February 4 and executed on February 9, within the time set by the warrant. The government requested thirty days to examine the computer seized in the warrant, and subsequently requested a thirty-day extension. The magistrate granted both requests. Notwithstanding this deadline of April 8 to examine the computer, the search of the computer was not started until April 10. Finding no good reason for this delay, the court suppressed the evidence from the search of the computer.

B. Analysis of Evidence

1. At the Search Location

It is beyond the scope of this chapter to discuss all of the technical details of what should be done at the search location. Other sources should be referenced for this information.[164] I will touch on a few legal issues, however.

---

163. 76 F. Supp. 2d 30 (D. Me. 1999).

164. *E.g.,* KENNETH ROSENBLATT, HIGH-TECHNOLOGY CRIME, INVESTIGATING CASES INVOLVING COMPUTERS (1995); FRANKLIN CLARK & KIN DILIBERTO, INVESTIGATING

a. Who Should Accompany the Officers Executing the Search?

(1) Should an Expert Accompany the Officers?

At the federal level, 18 U.S.C. § 3105 (2000) precludes anyone other than the officer being present at the search except for a person "in aid of the officer." The statute has been interpreted to allow experts, specifically provided for in the warrant, to accompany and participate in the search.[165] In *Wilson v. Layne*,[166] the Supreme Court noted that it is well established that the presence of third parties for purposes related specifically to the execution of the warrant is appropriate even when not specifically authorized by the warrant. Other courts have made it clear that such persons are there to assist the peace officer executing the search.[167]

A somewhat different issue may arise where computers have been taken off-site for searching and an expert who is not a peace officer conducts that search. Although I am unaware of any cases bearing directly on this, it is my recommendation that, in the application, you justify and request permission for this person to examine the computer under peace officer supervision (i.e., the officer will be instructing the expert in what to look for), and that permission for this activity be specifically provided for in the warrant.[168] It is important to understand that this requesting and receiving permission process is dictated by the fact that the off-site examination is a continuation of the execution of the warrant, not merely the evaluation of already legitimately seized information where no special permission is needed.

This suggests that any time the presence of an expert will be useful (and an expert is available, of course), you should justify and request that the expert be allowed to accompany the officers and participate in the search.

COMPUTER CRIME (1996); UNITED STATES SECRET SERVICE, BEST PRACTICES FOR SEIZING ELECTRONIC EVIDENCE (2002), *available at,* http://www.secretservice.gov/electronic_evidence.shtml.

165. U.S. v. Schwimmer, 692 F. Supp. 119 (E.D.N.Y. 1988).

166. 526 U.S. 603 (1999).

167. Commonwealth v. Sbordone, 678 N.E.2d 1184 (Mass. 1997); U.S. v. Clouston, 623 F.2d 485 (6th Cir. 1980).

168. If you decide, after the search, to use a non-peace office expert to examine the computer, I recommend you file a supplemental affidavit with the warrant judge requesting permission for that person to search the drive.

(2) Should a Representative of the Victim Accompany the Officers?
But What If the Only Expert Is a Representative of the Victim?

Justifying the presence of an independent expert is merely a matter of explaining why an expert's assistance is needed. Justifying the presence of a representative of the victim is a more difficult task, and, even if approved in the warrant, the presence of a victim representative always creates a credibility issue. The strongest argument in favor of having a victim representative present is that they can quickly identify specific items covered by the warrant and thus minimize the intrusion and inconvenience to the suspect. (Of course, the victim representative's unique familiarity and ability to recognize offending material is also the reason why their presence is particularly invasive.)

If you do request the presence of a victim representative, you must explain why only that person or other victim representative can do the identification necessary. You should stress that the person's ability to recognize offending evidence on sight will likely reduce the extent and time of the search. Further, the officers should be advised that notwithstanding this permission, they are the ones conducting the search, not the victim. To the extent possible the role of the victim representative should be clearly delineated in the application.

The problems associated with allowing a victim to accompany warrant executing officers is illustrated by a recent case in Washington, *In re U.S. Computer Corporation.*[169] In that case, the trial judge discussed some of these problems:

> It is without question that private entities should be encouraged to support public law enforcement through a variety of means. The insurance industry does so in valuable ways and various reward programs have been quite successful. Private entities' financial support for a law enforcement effort is not, by itself, tantamount to private entities seeking to perform the law enforcement function.
>
> What is called for, it would seem, is that this public/private relationship remain somewhat at arm's length. Some distance is essential both to the police agency's ability to maintain its loyalty solely to the broad public and also to that public's confidence that

---

169. No. 98-118 (Super. Ct., Kings County, Jun. 23, 2000).

such is the case. Although it may sound Pollyannaish, the theory is that the police officer works at once for the suspect as well as the victim. A private security officer serves but one master.

If, for example, company "A" were to suspect itself to be being victimized by company "B" through illegal means, it would logically be motivated by a strong desire to gather confirmation. One approach would be to file a civil lawsuit and utilize the discovery process in hopes of gaining information. A second alternative would be for A's security personnel to travel to B's headquarters and announce "We'd like to come in and poke around a little bit and also ask your employees a few questions about your illegal activities."

The first alternative is slow and laborious and subject to obstructionism. The second is laughable in its chances of success; acting on their own, the security personnel would never get across the rival's threshold.

In this case, it was entirely appropriate for Hewlett-Packard security personnel to accompany law enforcement officials as they (the law enforcement officials) served this court's warrant to search USCC. A role for the "victim" in helping to identify stolen property for which there is probable cause to search, was contemplated by this court and is fully consistent with established law. *See, e.g., Wilson v. Layne,* 526 U.S. 603 (1999).

The role played by such a citizen participant in the service of a search warrant must be narrowly circumscribed. To the extent that his role is expressly or impliedly authorized in the warrant, he is acting under color of state law. Any actions beyond that, however, constitute "a frolic of his own" and cannot be countenanced.

In the service of this search warrant, the role for citizen participants that was impliedly authorized was to aid in identifying stolen memory modules bearing fictitious or no serial numbers. Actions beyond that were not authorized.

When private citizens necessarily accompany law enforcement personnel on the execution of a search warrant, it must be expected that the police officers—familiar with the requirements of the law—will ensure that the civilians do not engage in any unlawful conduct. It may very well be that the close relationship (financial and otherwise) between the entities involved in this search

provides some explanation for the blurring of what should have
been more clearly defined roles.[170]

b. What Can Be Seized[171]

So long as you have a valid basis for an off-site search, storage devices
that could contain the evidence you are authorized to seize may themselves
be seized for searching off-site. But what about all the other computer
"stuff" at the search location? Can you seize the CPU box as opposed to removing the hard drives from the box? What about the monitor, printers,
cables or manuals?

The general rule is that you can request and seize those items necessary
to achieve the core purpose of your search. If you seize floppies for searching offsite, then you may request permission to and seize floppy drives. The
same rationale applies to other storage media that require particular devices to be useable — tape drives for tapes, DVD or CD players for DVD or
CD media, etc.

A hard drive contains both the media and the device to read the information. May you nevertheless seize the CPU box and its contents — cards,
memory, cables, etc? I am not aware of any decisions answering this question, but my answer is yes.

On one level you can seize the box and its contents to show that the defendant had an operating computer, a computer capable of connecting to
the Internet, a computer capable of displaying a certain quality of video
image, etc. On a more fundamental level, you do not search a hard drive by
examining it with a magnifying glass. You search it by having it connected
to an operating computer system, including a monitor. While you can
search the drive by removing it from the suspect's system and inserting it
into another system you are not required to do this. So long as you can justify why an object is necessary to achieve the core purpose of your search
you can seize that object. Manuals and other instructional material, and cables and cords connected to the computer would also be covered by this rationale.

Can printers, scanners, digital cameras, and other peripheral devices be
taken? The answer is less clear. If you have an incriminating printout that
you want to tie to a particular printer, then you may have a basis to seize

---

170. *Id.* at 8–11.
171. This discussion is limited to situations where you are seizing computers as containers of evidence.

the printer. If you want to show the suspect had the capability to input images into a computer, you may have a basis for seizing a scanner or a digital camera.

c. When to Get an Additional Warrant

The simple answer is you get an additional warrant when you have probable cause to believe the evidence, not covered by your current warrant, may be found in a computer. In fact, as discussed in the plain view section earlier, even if you develop probable cause to believe that evidence outside the scope of your warrant will be found in the computer you are searching, you need not get an additional warrant to take note of such additional evidence, so long as you follow your search protocol.

The safest course, however, is to request an additional warrant for the new information. You can do that by stopping your valid search to get the new warrant, or by completing the search authorized by the warrant, and then applying for a new warrant to complete the search with the new category of evidence as your focus.

2. Offsite/Detailed Analysis

Even more important than having an expert at the search scene is having an expert available to examine a seized computer. If there is a capable, trained and available police computer forensics expert, that is your first choice. Often, however, there is no such person or that person is busy on other cases. The next best choice is an independent investigator, paid for by the police. Much further down the choice list is a representative of the victim or an expert provided or paid for by the victim. The last option is to examine the data without an expert. To do so, however, runs the risk of damaging or altering data, making evidence inadmissible and overlooking key evidence.

a. Make a Forensic Copy

In olden days, when I first started prosecuting computer crime, we actually worked with the original data. This was justifiable, at first. The data was on floppy drives, the write protect tab could be set on the floppy so no alterations would be made. But even when the first hard drives started appearing in our cases, we worked with the original drives.

Then the conventional wisdom became to make a backup before working with the data. That way you could always compare the original, even if modified, to the backup. We slowly moved from just making a backup to actually installing the backup on a new hard drive and doing our analysis on that drive.[172]

Making a backup, however, had a major weakness. Backups, as we think of them, back up files and directories, i.e., they recognize what the operating system recognizes as data. But there is much information on a drive that is not recognized by the file or operating systems. Deleted files are a common example. The operating system does not recognize deleted data, but if the area on the drive where the file existed has not been overwritten, the data still exists.

Even if the file has been overwritten, unless the new file takes up all of the cluster allocated to the old file, remnants of the old file will be found in the part of the cluster following the new file. Often the areas of a drive not recognized as data by the operating system—slack space, ambient space—contain the most incriminating information.

So always make a foresic copy—a copy of all magnetic information on the drive. There are several programs that have established their validity in court for making accurate mirror images.[173]

b. Search/Analysis Protocol

It is critical to have a search protocol for analyzing the drive. First a protocol is important to insure that you have exhaustively examined the drive. Second, it is important to establish the validity of your examination and the expert's report. Finally, it is important to demonstrate that your examination of the computer was as minimally invasive of the owner's privacy as possible.

While the general structure of the protocol will be the same in most cases, it will almost always vary in detail from case to case. The protocol will often be a dynamic process, changing as you examine the computer and gather information.

---

172. We did not do that from the first because of time, cost (prior to the early 1990s, typical capacity hard drives cost $400 or more), and lack of an expert (often I was my only expert).

173. *E.g.*, SafeBack by New Technologies, Inc., *available at* http://www.forensics-intl.com/safeback.html (last visited Dec. 28, 2004); Encase by Guidance Software, Inc., *available at* http://www.guidancesoftware.com (last visited Dec. 28, 2004). Useful tools to use in conjunction with these programs are available from New Technologies of Portland, Oregon, *available at* http://www. forensics-intl.com (last visited Dec. 28, 2004)) and AccessData, *available at* http://www.accessdata.com/Product04_Overview.htm (last visited Dec. 28, 2004)).

Think of a protocol as crime scene investigation techniques. Modern law enforcement officers know not to disturb the crime scene. Modern detectives and medical examiners follow certain sets of procedures in examining a dead body. You should have similar protocols for investigating computer scenes and computers.

Examination of the directory and file structure and initial examination of only those directories and files that appear relevant on their face is an appropriate first step. Subsequent action may be based on what your initial examination reveals. For example, examination of other directories and files may be justified if the names of the directories and files you do examine do not match their contents.

Most investigators I work with use key word searches of all of the drive's binary data (obtained from the forensic copy) as an initial first step. This is a useful way to determine if evidence exists (which allows you to retain the computer—recall the discussion on the time limits on the execution of warrants.) This also helps you focus in on suspect directories and files. But framing the search terms requires the assistance of someone who is familiar with the information for which you are searching—often a representative of the victim.

Having a search plan can also help insulate law enforcement against a claim of undue invasion of privacy. Although most courts view computer searches like any other container search (where you can search the entire container for what you are authorized to seize), the *Gall*[174] case suggests that some court may be willing to afford more privacy protection to a computer than ordinary containers.

In practice, however, most forensic examinations of computers cannot follow a pre-written script. What the examiner should do is keep detailed notes of what examination was undertaken and the reasons for each part of the examination. This practice was commented on favorably in the trial court's ruling on the motion to suppress in *United States v. Triumph Capital Group, Inc.*[175] This is a rapidly developing area of law, however, and some federal magistrates are requiring the government to submit an acceptable (to the magistrate) search protocol along with the affidavit for a search warrant.[176]

---

174. *See* note 93, *supra* with accompanying text.
175. 211 F.R.D. 31 (D. Conn. 2002).
176. *See* In the Matter of the Search of 3817 W. West End, First Floor, Chicago, Illinois, 321 F. Supp. 2d 953 (N.D. Ill. 2004) (Schenkier, M.J.).

3. What Must Be Returned and When

Occasionally, the return time is dictated by the warrant itself. The magistrate may instruct you to complete the examination of the computer and return items not covered by the warrant within a certain amount of time. Other times the defendant or other owner of the computer may request—or demand—its return. In other situations you may want to return items not covered by the warrant on your own, particularly if this is a third party's equipment or data and you need their continued cooperation.

So, what do you do when the computer owner wants the original items returned? There may be times when the prudent course is to return the original computer, or, more particularly, the original hard drive, to the owner. Courts may be more inclined to view your search more generously, and to give you more leeway as a defendant in a civil case, when you have made every effort to accommodate the reasonable requests of the original computer owner. If the computer is the center of an ongoing legitimate business, even the defendant's own legitimate business, you should make efforts to return enough of the data you seized to allow the business to continue. One could argue that the Secret Service was treated more harshly than they otherwise would have been in the *Steve Jackson Games* case because they held on to the defendant's e-mail that was crucial to the operation of his business for several months, despite the owner's repeated requests for its return, and despite the e-mail's irrelevance to the case the Secret Service was investigating.

a. Stipulation

If you are returning original evidence, whether it is just the hard drive or the complete computer system, you should be careful to get a stipulation from the defendant, eliminating any objections as to authenticity or foundation, before returning the evidence. If the defendant refuses to so stipulate, you have a valid reason for hanging on to the original evidence. Some suggested language would be:

> [suspect], in the interest of expediting the searching and seizing of records and other evidence as authorized by Search Warrant #_____, signed by _____, Judge, on _____, 2005, so as to minimize interruption of the normal computing activities of [suspect or suspect's company], stipulate to the following terms applicable to the records, equipment and evidence itemized in the attached Inventory, incorporated by reference:

[suspect] is satisfied that the backup or mirror image copies. made on _____, 2005, are complete and accurate copies of the entire contents of the systems searched as of that date. [suspect] will not contest the accuracy, reliability or source of any record copied, printed out or derived from those backups/mirror image copies. [suspect] waives any objection as to best evidence, authenticity or foundation as to any record copied, printed out or derived from those backups/mirror image copies.

b.   What If the Computer Owner Is Not the Suspect?

What if the person from whom the computer was seized, and who wants it back, is not the suspect? The suspect has no incentive to stipulate in this context and the owner of the computer cannot stipulate to admissibility of evidence against the defendant. In this case, try to reach a compromise with the owner. In most cases, returning a mirror image on a different drive will be sufficient.

If the owner must have the original, and the suspect will not stipulate, so long as you have a valid forensic copy and an expert who can testify as to its creation, you should be safe in returning the original even without a stipulation. The absence of a stipulation does not make your forensic copy and evidence from that copy inadmissible; it simply raises your admissibility hurdle.

c.   Contraband on Computer

Unless a computer is forfeited, there will come a time when you must return the computer to its owner. That may be early in the case when you determine there is no useful evidence on the computer or when a court orders the return of non-evidentiary items. It may occur when you have mirrored the hard drive and are returning the original under a stipulation as described earlier. It may occur when you have seized a business computer or a third party computer and wish to get it back to a non-suspect owner.

But what if there is contraband on the computer? Must you return it? Must you destroy it?

(1) Obvious Contraband

There are certain items that are contraband *per se* and should never be returned. On a computer, the most likely contraband is child pornography. While it should not be returned, neither should they be destroyed arbitrarily. Often the "owner" of the contraband has the right to challenge your retention of this material and you face the possibility of civil liability for destroying the items without authority. Seek permission from the judge issuing the warrant (or your own legal advisor) before deleting this material.

(2) Suspected Stolen Property—
No Irreversible Harm in Returning

Where there is a legitimate question as to ownership of property, you may have the right to withhold the property in question until a court has determined ownership. For example, if you have what appears to be pirated software, can you withhold the software from the person you seized it from until they prove their ownership? While this may vary from case to case, I would be very careful in presuming software to be pirated and withholding it from the purported owner. In these days of buying software online, there may be no books or documentation, no specially produced CD or floppy disk, and the software is still legitimate. If you have concerns, you can contact the Software Company and alert them to what you've found. They have seizure remedies available to them under the Federal Copyright Act.

(3) Suspected Stolen Property—Irreversible Harm in Returning

But what if the property about which there is a dispute is proprietary information—information that if returned to the defendant could be copied or transmitted to others. Any after-the-fact remedy by the true property owner may be too late. In this instance the cautious approach is to hold on to the property until the warrant judge has directed what is to become of the property.

(4) Other Types of Contraband—Passwords, Hacking Programs

Often computer criminals have cybercrime-related contraband on their computers—passwords of others, hacking programs, utilities for cracking password accounts, etc. What can/should you do with those? Passwords of others, under federal law and most state law, are "access devices." Access devices in the names of two or more different people besides the possessor are presumed, in many jurisdictions, to be stolen. You are, if your law is comparable, entitled to treat this like any other clearly identified stolen property. You keep it and return it to the lawful owner.

Hacking programs, like burglar tools, are different. Just like many non-criminals own crowbars, many non-criminals own hacking programs. Such tools and programs serve many legitimate purposes and cannot be considered contraband *per se*. In addition, most hacking programs can be easily found on the Internet. Deleting such a program simply delays its subsequent acquisition by a few minutes.

C. The Case Scenarios

1. Case 1 — Janet Davis

As noted earlier there were no third party records utilized in this case. The company had identified Janet Davis as the likely suspect based on the fact that her key card was used to access ANDA's offices at the time the illegal copying was done. The FASTBACK history showed a backup was made so there was evidence of the crime somewhere. ANDA's attorneys suggested searching Janet Davis' house. Someone had observed a computer at her house approximately three months earlier while attending a party there.

When presented in this form it is clear that there was not probable cause to believe the disks would be found at Janet Davis' house other than "where else would they be." While that may be sufficient in some instances in the presence of other supporting facts, there was nothing else supporting this conjecture. In addition, the discovery of the unlawful copying occurred a month after the actual incident.

I told the assigned detective that there was not sufficient probable cause for a warrant. He passed the information on to ANDA's attorneys. They then informed the detective and me that they were going to obtain a writ of seizure under the Federal Copyright Act.

Shortly afterwards, ANDA registered its copyright with the Copyright Office. The same day ANDA filed a lawsuit in United States District Court for the Western District of Washington, claiming, *inter alia,* copyright infringement. Pursuant to 17 U.S.C. § 503(a) (2000), ANDA sought a writ of seizure to enter the residence of the defendant and seize any materials belonging to ANDA. The court issued the writ that day, directing the U.S. Marshal to enter Janet Davis' residence and seize any material belonging to ANDA.

The writ was executed the following day. At the invitation of ANDA's attorneys, the detective they had originally consulted about a warrant accompanied the U.S. Marshal and ANDA's attorneys. The detective attended the execution, observed the search and left. During the search the floppy disks containing the backup of Stampede were discovered as were hundreds of other diskettes containing proprietary Stampede information and information what appeared to be proprietary information from several of Davis' former employers. The information was seized by the Marshal and turned over to ANDA's attorneys. ANDA obtained a civil judgment against Davis and referred the matter to the police for criminal prosecution. The items obtained under the copyright writ were delivered to the prosecutor in response to a subpoena.

2. Case 2—Mel Howard

The third party records showed that the e-mail in question had been sent from an account associated with the suspect Mel Howard. But this was a dial up account and could be accessed anywhere. Thus, I told the investigating detective that we needed additional information showing there was a computer in Howard's house and that he used that computer to access the Internet via his JPS account.

As previously discussed there were several options available to the detective to obtain this information. He chose the most direct. He called Mr. Howard and invited him to the police station for a voluntary interview. In the course of the interview, he asked if the defendant had a computer in his house. He did. Did he access the Internet from his house? Yes. Who was his Internet Service Provider? JPS. Did he access his JPS account from anywhere other than his house? No. Did anyone else at his house use his computer? No.

"Now", the detective politely inquired of me, "do we have enough for a warrant for his house?" The answer was yes.

A warrant was obtained and Mr. Howard's house was searched the day after the interview. Howard's computer was seized and taken off site for examination.

The examination showed that Howard's Internet Explorer and Netscape history cache, reflecting web activity for the past twenty days, was still intact. That history cache reflected numerous accesses to the Cornercave website. The history cache only went back to about two weeks after the destruction of records on Cornercave's server, however, and thus did not provide any clues as to that incident.

3. Case 3—Allen Worley

When we left this case we had just discovered that the e-mails originated at a cable modem account in the name of Bonnie Ronstadt's former boyfriend, Allen Worley. But Allen Worley lived in South Carolina. How could we get a warrant to search in South Carolina? More fundamentally, as we knew this was not a telephone dial-up account, was sending an e-mail via a cable modem the making of a telephone call? Was there a crime?

Fortuitously, at the same time this case was coming to fruition, the Western Washington Cybercrime Task Force was coming into existence. This group, combining the investigative resources of state and federal law enforcement and working with state and federal prosecutors, had been in the formative stages for several months and was now looking for some cases on which to cut their teeth.

In discussing the case with this Task Force, it appeared that federal prosecution was a viable alternative. The federal telecommunications harassment statute[177] appeared to cover e-mail communications. The statute, among other things, makes illegal the use of a telecommunications device to initiate the transmission of obscene, lewd, lascivious, filthy or indecent communication with the intent to annoy, abuse, threaten or harass another person.[178] It also makes illegal the making of a telephone call or the use of a telecommunications device anonymously with the same intent or makes repeated telephone calls or use of a telecommunications device solely to harass the person receiving the communication.[179] Although the term "telecommunication device" is not specifically defined, the fact that it is included in addition to telephone calls in the statute implies greater coverage consistent with the phrase "telecommunication device."

The local U.S. Attorney's Office and FBI agreed to take on the case. Over the next two months, the FBI put together their own investigation which mirrored what the state had done. In February, 2003, it sent an affidavit and search warrant application to South Carolina for the local U.S. Attorney's Office to present to a federal magistrate.

The magistrate agreed there was probable cause to believe that evidence of a crime would be found in Worley's house. He did not, however, feel the matter was of such a nature that the federal government should be involved. He declined to authorize the search.

Everybody was frustrated. The U.S. Attorney was still committed to prosecuting the case but they needed to get Worley' computer to complete the evidentiary trail.

While alternative plans were being formulated, Bonnie Ronstadt continued to receive harassing e-mail. In early January, 2003, she received an

---

177. 47 U.S.C. § 223 (2000).
178. *Id.* § 223(a).
179. *Id.*

e-mail containing a story about hard core gay sex involving famous sports players and broadcasters. The story could readily be found on the Internet. Four days later, another message was received by Bonnie asking for Bonnie and her husband to join the e-mail sender in a threesome and including a graphic photo. She received additional derogatory communications from the Anti Bonnie Fan Club—the ABFC. More derogatory information was posted about her in a publicly available web page. Once again, she started receiving calls at work asking for her by name and referencing a recent on-line chat or a message posted on a cyber-sex bulletin board.

A new plan was conceived. First, a Washington protection order would be obtained and served on Worley in South Carolina. Second a pen register would be installed on Worley's account which would record the outgoing destination of all e-mail. Then, if Worley violated the protection order, the magistrate in South Carolina would be approached with the new information.

Worley was served with the protection order. Two days later he sent an e-mail to Bonnie. His reaction ranged from sympathy to outrage and disdain:

> I've just received a visit from our local sheriff who has served me with a restraining order of some sort.... I'm sorry that you're having problems that necessitate such an action.
> I hate to tell you this but you're barking up the wrong tree.
> It's pretty insulting that you think that I would act in such a manner in the first place.
> I'm going to send this to my attorney and may end up challenging your order on general principles.
> I've got some business associates in Seattle and could easily take a tax write-off on a trip. I'm not sure it's worth the time and effort ...

This e-mail was a clear violation of the protection order. There was something more important about the e-mail however. This e-mail, coming directly from Worley to Bonnie, had the same originating IP address as all the harassing e-mails sent to her through anonymizers. Although there had previously been little doubt that Worley was behind the harassment, the matching IPs eliminated any doubt.

Armed with the violation of the protection order and the new harassment Bonnie had undergone since February, an assistant U.S. Attorney from the Seattle office went herself to South Carolina to present the request for a search warrant. There were two surprises. First, the magistrate, for un-known reasons, recused himself. Thus the matter went to a district court judge. Surely this judge would recognize the separation of powers doctrine and not try to impose his views on what matters should be investigated and prosecuted on the U.S. Attorney representing the executive branch whose duty it was to make such decisions.

The Judge did not argue that the case was not important enough for fed-eral prosecution. What he stated, however, was that the sending of harass-ing e-mail was not covered by the federal statute. The assistant U.S. Attor-ney was stunned. She had not anticipated this since the legislative history was clear. To make sure she had not misread that history, she researched the matter overnight. Her recollection was correct. The legislative history showed that Congress' intent was to update the prior telephone harassment provisions to address new technology.

She returned to the Judge the next day and shared the results of her re-search. He was unmoved. She returned to Seattle without a warrant.

The resolve of the U.S. Attorney to prosecute this matter was still high but the obstacles created by the judiciary in South Carolina were eroding the U.S. Attorney's ability to procure Worley' computer. Until that com-puter could be obtained the case was not going to be prosecuted.

And so we were back to where we were six months earlier. In fact, be-cause of the e-mail directly from Worley to Bonnie, we were in an even stronger position. But we needed his computer. Since it was not going to happen at the federal level, I returned to thinking how it could be obtained in a state investigation. I had spoken with a South Carolina prosecutor and there was little doubt they could obtain a South Carolina warrant based on our affidavit.

The obstacle was the absence of a crime. Now that we knew this was a cable modem our argument that the sending of the e-mail was a telephone call was flawed. There were still no threats to Bonnie's physical safety. We appeared to be at a dead end.

But something had happened since I had first evaluated the possible laws governing Worley' behavior. To understand this, we need to bring in one more case—the case of the retributive students.

Five months earlier, in January, 2003, a story ran in a Seattle paper about a school teacher whose life was in disarray. Someone was posting messages in his name on electronic and physical bulletin boards.

Phillips and his wife started getting several calls daily about ads offering to buy and sell items on the online auction site eBay.

Phillips didn't place the ads, but they listed his name, address and phone number. Callers expected him to buy and sell paintings, pets, collectibles, even sexual favors. Some calls came late at night, in response to an ad asking people to phone after 11 p.m.

The most recent ad linked to Phillips, which appeared on SeattleInsider.com, offered puppies for sale and said those that didn't sell would be destroyed.[180]

Phillips had gone to the police but they had told them there was nothing they could do. I was not so sure. A burglary detective was interested in working on the case.[181] I asked him to see if Phillips had any e-mail from the suspect. He did. There was one e-mail from the University of Science and Technology in China. It was a bizarre message—a quote from Stephen Crane about a beast eating its own heart. But it was to prove to be enough.

The e-mail header contained the originating IP address. That address belonged to an ISP who had subleased the address to another company who had in turn subleased it to a third person. Following this chain required a search warrant at each link. The third person explained that he let a friend of his run an alumni e-mail service at that address. A search warrant to that person revealed that it was a free service, much like Hotmail, that no sign-up information was verified or retained. But like other web based e-mail services, the alumni service did maintain a log of originating IP addresses.

The originating IP address for the e-mail in question came back to AT&T WorldNet. Believing we were close to the answer, a warrant was served on AT&T. They told us they had recently been bought out by Comcast. And Comcast required a separate warrant. But that warrant, the last in a long line, led to a cable modem account at a residence in the name of a family the teacher recognized. He had had problems with two kids from that family several years earlier.

A search warrant was executed at the residence. The "kids"—now adults—were present and confessed.

But, you ask, where is this heading? How is this any different from Bonnie? After all the "kids" did not threaten Phillips with damage to his person or property. I turned again to the statutes and I discovered a crucial difference between the harassment statute and the stalking statute. The harass-

---

180. The names of the parties have been changed and the source of the quotation is omitted to preserve the individuals' privacy.

181. Phillips' home had been burglarized a few months earlier and a personal computer had been taken. Phillips believed the person had obtained the personal information contained in the ads from the computer.

ment statute required a threat to damage a person or their property. The stalking statute made illegal the repeated harassment of a person where the person *perceived* a threat to their person or property. The word "harassment" in the stalking statute had a different definition than in the harassment statute. The stalking statute referenced the definition of harassment in the civil protection order statute. The definition was broad:

> "Unlawful harassment" means a knowing and willful course of conduct directed at a specific person which seriously alarms, annoys, harasses, or is detrimental to such person, and which serves no legitimate or lawful purpose. The course of conduct shall be such as would cause a reasonable person to suffer substantial emotional distress, and shall actually cause substantial emotional distress to the petitioner.
>
> "Course of conduct" was defined as a pattern of conduct composed of a series of acts over a period of time, however short, evidencing a continuity of purpose. "Course of conduct" includes, in addition to any other form of communication, contact, or conduct, the sending of an electronic communication.[182]

So we met the first test of stalking—the electronic communications by the students constituted harassment. But the statute also required the victim to perceive a threat to their person or property and that had to be a "reasonable" perception.

It was clear that the teacher was very fearful after the puppy ad. His name and address had been in the ad where he purportedly threatened to kill puppies. He was concerned about possible threats to himself or to his home because of the ad. Under the circumstances, that was a reasonable perception.

So the crime of stalking applied, but it was a gross misdemeanor. Returning yet again to the statutes, I examined the identity theft statute. That statute makes it a crime to:

> obtain, possess, use, or transfer a means of identification or financial information of another person, living or dead, with the intent to commit, or to aid or abet, any crime. "Means of identification"

---

182. WASH. REV. CODE § 10.14.020 (2002).

means information or an item that … is personal to or identifiable with an individual or other person, including: A current or former name of the person, telephone number …[183]

Did the students possess a means of identification of Phillips? They had his name and telephone number. Did they use that means of identification with the intent to commit another crime? Stalking would apply. Identity theft, under these circumstances, was a felony. The students were charged with identity theft and, in December, 2003, pled guilty.

And so, as I pondered the case of the vindictive students, I wondered if those statutes could be used in Bonnie's case. My concern was that the stalking and identity theft statutes had worked in the Phillips case, but he had legitimately feared damage to himself or his property. What did Bonnie fear?

Did she fear that Worley was going to come to Seattle and harm her or ransack her residence? No, she had no such fear. What she feared was that he was going to continue to mentally torment her, but that was not enough under the statute. She feared he would continue to send e-mail to her co-worker, which was equally insufficient. She feared her ability to concentrate at work would be effected and between that and the e-mail to her co-workers, she might lose her job. But even that appeared inadequate to satisfy the statute.

Or was it? Numerous courts have held that a property right under the Due Process Clause exists to employment.[184] While Washington courts rejected the blanket existence of a property right in public employment, they did recognize such a right in certain circumstances.[185] Maybe a fear of losing her job was good enough. For if Bonnie had a property interest in her job and Worley' e-mails were intended to and had the effect of creating in Bonnie the reasonable fear that she might lose her job, then the crime of stalking applied. And if Worley had used Bonnie's name and telephone number in chat rooms and online bulletin boards with the intent to stalk Bonnie, then the crime of identity theft, carrying a felony label, applied.

---

183. WASH. REV. CODE § 9.35.005 (2003).

184. *See, e.g.,* Perry v. Sinderman, 408 U.S. 593, 601 (1972) ("A due process property interest exists 'if there are such rules or mutually explicit understandings that support [an individual's] claim of entitlement to the benefit and that he may invoke at a hearing.'").

185. *See* Punton v. Seattle Public Safety Comm'n, 650 P.2d 1138 (Wash. App. 1982).

After discussing this with my boss it was agreed that we could justify requesting a search warrant based on that theory.

A draft affidavit was sent to South Carolina. They responded they would seek a warrant based on that affidavit. So the formal affidavit was prepared and witnessed by a Washington Superior Court judge. But in this case of delays and false starts there was another hitch. The day the affidavit was signed, Hurricane Isabel was threatening the South Carolina coast near Charleston. We delayed sending the affidavit until the storm passed.

Now, however, we were in the final stretch. I anxiously awaited the call from South Carolina saying the warrant had been executed and Worley' computer seized. Then the call came. The investigator explained that the previous day he and some colleagues had done some pre-search reconnoitering of the search location, determining the number of exits, the number of vehicles and other factors aimed at making the execution of the warrant a smooth and safe process. As they surveyed the house the mail carrier arrived and they asked him about the number of people in the house who obtained mail — how many occupants might they expect. The carrier detailed the people at the house receiving mail. Worley was not on the list. They asked about him. "I think he's moved," the mailman said. "He turned in a change of address card a month ago to have his mail forwarded to Columbia, South Carolina."

The investigator said to me the words that were already forming on my lips. "We no longer have probable cause to search this house." We no longer had a basis for believing Worley's computer was there if he was not. This case seemed doomed for failure.

V. The Use of the Seized Material and the Final Results

A. Case 1 — Janet Davis

1. Items Found During the Execution of the Writ

Among the items found were:

- Two floppy disks containing the FASTBACK produced copies of the Stampede files;
- Personnel files relating to Davis and other employees including peer reviews of her performance;
- A file showing the salaries of ANDA employees;

- A file detailing financial arrangements between ANDA and its distributor;
- spreadsheet comparing company projections with sales to date, inventory information, sales commission compensation schemes and other financial data;
- Source code for virtually all ANDA commercial products and products in development;
- Training material and program documentation for many of ANDA's products; and
- A large number of diskettes—more than 800—with the label of Davis' employer before ANDA.

Many of the ANDA files, according to the date of the file's creation, showed that Davis had copied them shortly before her termination.

Steve Carlson, a senior software engineer at ANDA, was asked to evaluate the data found during the writ execution. In his opinion, the ANDA material found in Davis' possession could be used to produce new products in competition with ANDA products. The potential impact on ANDA of the release of this material to competitors would be massive. The work represented by this material involved tens of person-years of work.

After the writ was executed, Davis asked that two disks be returned to her. She claimed they pertained to projects independent of ANDA. Carlson was asked to determine if any ANDA material was on those two disks. Carlson determined that Davis had taken ANDA files, deleted certain history portions of them, slightly changed their names and changed the Copyright notice from ANDA to a corporation owned by Davis. This corporation, among other things, consults with major multimedia companies. Davis' corporation had created a prototype for a multimedia product. The Stampede was for use in multimedia development.

2. Davis' Deposition in the Civil Case

Davis' deposition was taken in the civil case with ANDA. In the deposition:

- Davis expressed the opinion that Carl Rhodes terminated her because he found her both professionally and personally threatening.
- She acknowledged visiting ANDA's offices on the evening/morning when the backup copies of Stampede were made. She guessed that the visit was approximately one to two hours in length. The purpose of that visit was to clean up her office, get all her affairs squared away,

etc. She acknowledged that she was in possession of her access card continuously from her termination on Friday until she turned it in the following Tuesday.

- Davis denied turning on any computers other than her own during this visit. She denied entering Carl Rhodes' office. She denied that she took computer files that had been developed by anyone at ANDA while she was employed there. She denied ever copying any files from Rhodes' computer.
- Davis acknowledged that she was familiar with FASTBACK. She denied using FASTBACK to copy files from Rhodes' computer.
- When asked to explain how the diskettes containing the information copied from Rhodes' computer got into her house, Davis stated that her house was broken into after she left the company but before the writ was executed. It was her belief that the incriminating items found in her house during the execution of the Writ of Seizure were planted in her house during the break in. Davis further stated that she believed the materials were placed by somebody either hired by, employed by or somehow connected with ANDA.

3. The Criminal Case

a. Trial

At trial, the defense attorney moved to suppress all evidence found during the execution of the Writ. The argument narrowed down to the following:

- Washington's exclusionary rule applies only to searches conducted by Washington law enforcement officers. Under the "Silver Platter" doctrine, evidence legally seized by law enforcement officers of other jurisdictions is not covered by the exclusionary rule and such evidence may be presented to Washington authorities "on a silver platter" even if it could not have been seized legally under Washington law. (There was some case law suggesting that even if the evidence was seized *illegally* by officers of another jurisdiction it may be admissible in Washington courts.)
- If, however, the "foreign" law enforcement officers were acting as agents for Washington officers, then the exception provided by the silver platter doctrine does not apply. If the search does not pass muster under Washington law in those circumstances, then the evidence will be excluded.

The trial judge suppressed all evidence found during the execution of the writ, concluding that the detective's mere presence made the U.S. Marshal his agent. A motion for reconsideration was denied. The case was dismissed and appeal of the suppression and dismissal was made.

b. The Appeal

In the appellate brief, I was able to demonstrate that in countless other decisions, including some in Washington, involving local police action far more intrusive than that of the detective in this case, the courts had never found agency or a violation of the silver platter doctrine. About two minutes into argument at the Court of Appeals one of the judges asked "Is there any evidence that the detective did anything but stand there?" to which I replied, "No." He then said, "Doesn't that decide the issue before us?" to which I said, "To me it does, and if I had any indication the other two judges on the panel feel the way you do I'd probably sit down." At that point a second judge pointed out that the three of them had met the day before to discuss this case and that the first judge's question accurately summarized the feelings of the panel. The third judge agreed. Wisely I shut up and sat down.

The suppression and dismissal was reversed in an unpublished opinion and the case was remanded for trial.

c. The Second Trial

I had numerous witnesses from ANDA prepared to testify about the meaning of the evidence found in Davis' possession. I had an expert witness available to explain to the jury how a computer worked (pulling out of his pocket a motherboard, a hard disk, a floppy disk, etc.), how DOS works, and how Fastback works, including an in court demonstration of a backup that produced results like those found on Rhodes' computer. I had witnesses available to explain that the time and date stamps on the files found at Davis' residence belied her claim that they had been planted during a burglary.

After much of our case had been presented, and in the midst of testimony about how she had altered ANDA's code to make it her own, Davis decided to plead to our original 30-month recommendation.

Why did she decide to plead guilty? I was not told, except indirectly and by implication. Davis' defense had been announced by her attorney to the jury as being a combination of her being fired because Carl Rhodes felt she was personally threatening to him, that unnamed ANDA employees (presumably including Rhodes) wanted to retaliate against her (for what was never stated), and someone planted all the incriminating evidence in a burglary five days prior to the search.

That defense, as incredible as it was at first glance, essentially fell to pieces as the trial progressed. The trial judge ruled that the peer reviews which led to Davis' termination (and which had been found at Davis' house in the search) were admissible. Those reviews, while balanced in structure in terms of positive and negative comments, were essentially uniformly negative. Her prior review had emphasized that she must improve in the very areas these peer reviews found her deficient. It was clear that the basis for her termination was her performance.

Furthermore, the evidence showed that the burglary (yes a burglary actually did occur five days before the search) involved an audible alarm with a response time by the police of less than thirty minutes. This would mean that those planting the evidence would have had to complete their work in less than thirty minutes, not knowing when the police were going to arrive. The extent of the incriminating material found at her house, the fact that significant portions of it were on her hard disks, the interweaving of incriminating information with routine files, the structure and time and date stamps of the incriminating information—all of these showed a process that would have taken weeks to have created and far more than thirty minutes to have planted.

In addition, I was prepared to show that some of the incriminating files had creation or modification dates after the burglary. (Weren't those burglars clever? Not only did they plant the files; they planted some post-dated files, but not too post-dated so as to be dated after the search.) Finally, why in the world would ANDA plant Stampede and the numerous other proprietary source code items and other material found at Davis' house, just so they could spend countless thousands of dollars on attorney fees and tie up their senior software engineer's time, to get the items back. It made no sense.

My own sense was that Davis could see the futility, and indeed, the humiliation of testifying to such an incredible scenario. Many of the fraud defendants I have prosecuted in the past have had no difficulty lying in the face of logic and the facts, but, to her credit, Davis did not want to go through that exercise.

The only real issue was how much was the program she took actually worth? Estimates ranged from $25,000 to $15 million. The program was never completed. The programmer working on the program left ANDA and no comparably skilled programmer was found to replace him. In addition, ANDA had moved in a different direction with their software than they planned in 1991. But ANDA spent more than $155,000 trying to recover and protect what they called "the family jewels."

The defendant had been charged with computer trespass and theft. We accepted a guilty plea to one count of theft. The standard range for that crime was up to ninety days incarceration.[186] We recommended thirty months based on the low-end estimate of the value of the stolen product and on the cost ANDA incurred to regain the product.

The judge did not find the state's evidence of value to be persuasive, believed this to be a *de minimis* offense, and sentenced the defendant to thirty days of home detention. That sentence was consistent with the fairly minimal sentences handed out in my prior cybercrime prosecutions. That trend toward minimal punishment was about to change, however.

B. Case 2 — Mel Howard

We had four different sources of evidence. We had the history files on Howard's computer showing the dates and times he went to specific pages at Cornercave's website stored on the server. We had JPS's log files showing the dates and times Howard's account was used. We had the logs stored on the firewall after the August attack. And we had the logs stored on the damaged NT server.

1. Comparing the History/Log File Data

a. Comparing JPS Logs with the NT Server Logs

JPS log files showed:

6/23/99   0:45:00   Howard was assigned IP 209.63.189.149

Cornercave's log files showed:

6/23/99   0:49:17   209.63.189.149 [136]USER chris 331
6/23/99   0:49:17   209.63.189.149 [136]PASS
6/23/99   0:50:34   209.63.189.149 [136]sent /WebAdvisor/_
                        derived/_vti_cnf/search.htm0.htx 22
6/23/99   0:50:39   209.63.189.149 [136]sent /WebAdvisor/_
                        derived/search.htm0.htx 226
6/23/99   0:50:43   209.63.189.149 [136]sent /WebAdvisor/
                        backgrounder.asp 226

---

186. Washington has a determinate sentencing law.

6/23/99	0:50:48	209.63.189.149 [136]sent /WebAdvisor/ BUCKET/README.TXT 226
6/23/99	0:50:51	209.63.189.149 [136]sent /WebAdvisor/ common_data.asp 226
6/23/99	0:51:21	209.63.189.149 [136]sent /WebAdvisor/ Connect.mdb 426
6/23/99	0:51:44	209.63.189.149 [137]USER chris 331
6/23/99	0:51:44	209.63.189.149 [137]PASS -230
6/23/99	0:52:14	209.63.189.149 [137]sent /WebAdvisor/_ derived/_vti_cnf/search .htm0.htx 226
6/23/99	0:52:19	209.63.189.149 [137]sent /WebAdvisor/_ derived/search.htm0.htx 226
6/23/99	0:52:23	209.63.189.149 [137]sent /WebAdvisor/ backgrounder.asp 226
6/23/99	0:52:27	209.63.189.149 [137]sent /WebAdvisor/ common_data.asp 226
6/23/99	0:52:27	209.63.189.149 [137]ABORT - 225
6/23/99	0:52:29	209.63.189.149 [137]sent /WebAdvisor/ Connect.mdb 426
6/23/99	0:52:31	209.63.189.149 [137]sent /WebAdvisor/ CREDITS.ASP 426

Several things can be discerned from this comparison of the JPS and server log files:

- Howard's JPS account was assigned a particular IP address on June 23 at 12:45 a.m. (This was the morning after Howard left the company.)
- Access was made to the Cornercave server from the IP address assigned to Howard on June 23 at 12:49 a.m.
- The person accessing Cornercave logged in as user "Chris". There was no legitimate authorized user "Chris". This user and password had been created prior to Howard's departure from the company. Creation of usernames and passwords was one of Howard's duties at Cornercave.
- Numerous accesses were made during this session to various parts of Cornercave's website.

b. The Firewall Logs

The firewall logs showed numerous accesses made or attempted to the Cornercave server after the August file deletions. (The server was not

brought inside the firewall until after those deletions.) Here's an example
of the firewall logs shortly after the August 3 file deletions:

8/4/99	22:30:00	209.63.189.127
8/4/99	22:34:56	FTP Attempt - allow in 209.63.189.127
8/4/99	22:45:06	FTP Attempt - denied
8/5/99	14:15:00	209.63.189.116
8/5/99	14:28:01	FTP Attempt - allow in 209.63.189.116
8/6/99	22:30:00	206.63.189.30
8/6/99		"unauth"
8/6/99		"206.63.189" [a JPS address]

While the IP address associated with these accesses could not always be tied
to Howard's account (likely because of the quarter hour snapshots), there
were numerous accesses from within the range of IP addresses controlled
by JPS.

c. Howard's History Files

Howard's history files showed repeated accesses to the Cornercave server.
For example, one history line showed that Howard had accessed the time
sheet of a particular employee at Cornercave on a particular date within a
portion of the webpage that allowed changes to employee time records.
Cornercave had experienced some problems with their employee records
post the August file deletions. Here is one excerpt from Howard's history
file documenting access to a password protected internal webpage dealing
with making changes in employee time records.

8/17/99   21:50:24   Default@http://www.cornerstonesw+
C63.com/products/webuser/track/
AdmTimesheetChg.asp?employee=118&
gotodate=8/12/99[187]

Another attempt was made in late August to hijack Cornercave's domain.
Howard's history files show that he made repeated "whois" requests to Network Solutions to identify Cornercave's domain at this time. If one were attempting to hijack a domain, one way to determine if the attempt was successful would be to make a "whois" request regarding that domain.

Cornercave's president believed that someone was gaining access to e-
mail sent to the company. One of the history files shows that Howard was

---

187. In the actual cache file this is read as one long line.

using a search engine to research how to forward e-mail from a Windows NT server. Cornercave's server ran Windows NT.

One of the most damning history results was the record of searches made by Howard upon his return from the interview with the detective. The search warrant was executed the next day. History files seized during that search showed that within a half hour of ending the interview Howard was doing an Internet search on the word "hacking" followed by a search on the words "computer trespass." Twelve minutes later Howard visited the attorney directory site, Martindale-Hubbel and searched under the phrase "hiring lawyer." The post interview history files also showed that Howard revisited the Cornercave site that evening, this time going through an anonymizer.

The combination of these four sources of evidence clearly established that Howard was the party responsible for the attempts to hijack the Cornercave domain and had made repeated accesses to Cornercave's server and to password protected pages of Cornercave's website both before and after the August deletion incident.

2. Gaps in the Evidence

What those records did not show was whether Howard was responsible for the blank backup JAZ drive and whether he was responsible for the August 2 break-in and file deletions. His history cache did not go back that far. The firewall was not in place then. JPS records showed some Howard activity during that time period but there were no records that could be tied to those IP addresses. The only tools available were the log files on the NT server that was attacked.

Normally those log files might be a treasure lode of information about activity immediately preceding the file deletions. That was not to be true in this case, however. Apparently the same security laxness that caused the server to be set up outside the firewall also allowed NT to only have two default log files enabled—AdminEvent and SysEvent.

An outside expert was brought in to evaluate those files. Nothing useful was found in the AdminEvent log. The SysEvent log revealed something troubling:

8/2/99	9:01:58 AM	Disk Error	None	15	N/A	CRWEBSRV
8/2/99	9:02:19 AM	Disk Error	None	15	N/A	CRWEBSRV
8/2/99	9:02:20 AM	Disk Error	None	15	N/A	CRWEBSRV
8/2/99	9:02:20 AM	Disk Error	None	15	N/A	CRWEBSRV
7/30/99	1:46:04 PM	Disk Error	None	15	N/A	CRWEBSRV

6/4/99   1:32:39 PM   Disk Error   None   41   N/A   CRWEBSRV
The file system structure on the disk is corrupt and unusable. Please
run the chkdsk utility on the device \Device\Harddisk0\Partition2 with
label "Web".

The expert's conclusion: "I cannot rule out that the massive file deletions
were not the result of a hard disk failure." The expert did not believe that
was at all a likely explanation of the deletions but he could not rule it out.
That opinion, coupled with other weaknesses in the case, caused us to limit
our planned charges to the many unauthorized accesses to Cornercave's
computers before and after August 2 and the changes and alterations to files
before and after August 2 and to the attempts to hijack the domain.

3. Determining Damages

Our biggest problem was the calculation of Cornercave's loss amount
based on the crimes we intended to charge. It was clear that Cornercave had
suffered a major loss as a result of the events of August 2. Cornercave's insurance company had paid the policy limits of more than $150,000 for the
damage. Cornercave estimated its actual loss at a nearly $900,000, but we
could not include that loss unless it was related to the activity that we were
going to charge. We knew that, even with the file deletions, had there been
a valid backup Cornercave could have restored the software in short order.
But even with a valid backup, the repeated accesses after August 2, which
were attributable to Howard, showed that the code was likely permeated
with backdoor accesses.

4. Resolution

The end result? A pragmatic compromise. There was no objective way
of setting the precise amount. We intended to ask for a twelve-month jail
sentence. Our sentencing standards call for a recommendation of one
month in jail for each $5,000 in loss in the lower loss brackets. A twelve-
month sentence would represent a $60,000 loss. So we calculated the loss
at $60,000. Had this amount been contested, we might not have been suc-
cessful in proving that loss amount, but it was our offer in a plea recommendation. Plead guilty to two felony counts of computer trespass (one for
before August 2, one for afterwards) and two felony counts of malicious
mischief (again, one before and one after August 2) with agreed restitution
of $60,000 and we would recommend twelve months in jail. The defense
would be free to make whatever recommendation they wanted. Reject the
plea and we would file one count of computer trespass and one count of

malicious mischief for each incident we could prove. We had 119 known unauthorized accesses we believed could be attributed to Howard.

The defense made a counteroffer. Reduce the charges from felonies to gross misdemeanors and we will join in the twelve-month recommendation.

Our decision was easy. For purposes of sending a message to the community of the consequences of computer crime, a sentence of twelve months spoke far louder than the felony label. After all, our previous longest cybercrime sentence had been a thirty-day home detention sentence. And so we agreed to the defense proposal.

There was another condition, however. The victim was concerned about continued access to her computers by the defendant. We considered a ban on computer or Internet use but quickly rejected that as impractical. The defense offered to have logging software installed on the defendant's computer with reports automatically e-mailed to me. The software was designed to show if it was tampered with. We agreed and that condition became part of our plea offer.

At the defendant's sentencing, the State recommended twelve months jail on each of the four counts, to be served concurrently, $60,000 in restitution and the installation of logging software. The defense joined in that recommendation. The judge was troubled by that recommendation. His reasoning was that twelve months was the maximum sentence for a gross misdemeanor. Imposition of the maximum sentence meant that if the defendant violated any of the conditions of his sentence—failed to pay restitution, disabled the logging software, etc.—the judge would not have any additional punishment he could mete out.

The judge's solution—he would impose a nine-month sentence on each of the counts so that he had additional jail time in reserve in case of a sentence violation. But the judge had one more card up his sleeve. The time on the two computer trespass counts would be concurrent with each other. And the time on the two malicious mischief counts would be concurrent with each other. But the two computer trespass counts and the two malicious mischief counts would be *consecutive* to each other—a total sentence of eighteen months.

The times had changed. In the six years between the Davis sentencing and the Howard sentencing, the Internet had become a public commodity. Cybercrime was starting to be viewed as the serious threat it was. Deterrence had gained a valuable ally in the court system.

C. Case 3—Allen Worley

Although relaying the ups and does of this case to Bonnie had never been easy, the phone call I made following the discovery that Worley had moved from Charleston and we no longer had probable cause to search his house was particularly difficult. This had been our final hope and we had seemed to be on the verge. Bonnie was crushed. But not for long. She had remained silent for all these months, granting the legal system a full opportunity to provide her with some relief. It had let her down. Not the individual prosecutors or investigators but the system had let her down. She decided to break her silence. She wrote to the media. She wrote to her government representatives. She detailed what she had endured and that, in the end, there was no remedy.

And things started happening. Legislation was proposed in the Washington legislature to create an electronic communication version of the telephone harassment statute. The legislation moved forward without any meaningful opposition. It was signed by the governor and enacted into law with an immediate effective date.[188] A front-page newspaper story ran about her ordeal, championing Bonnie's courage. Although it appeared she was not to receive any relief in her own case, she made the path much easier for those in similar circumstances who trod after her.

But in the meantime, while the legislation was working its way forward, the FBI and U.S. Attorney were not sitting idle. Worley was confronted about this. He denied any involvement but agreed to allow the FBI to take and examine his computer. Based on that examination and the long history of e-mails Worley was charged with violation of the federal telecommunications harassment statute.

Worley ended up pleading guilty to two counts of use of a telecommunications device with intent to annoy, abuse, threaten or harass. (This was the criminal charge of harassment using a telecommunications device brought under that statute). His sentence included restitution of $12,297.23 to Bonnie's employer for expenses associated with the case and 500 hours of community service. The government had asked for only 160 hours but the judge, citing Worley's lack of remorse, imposed the longer sentence.

---

188. See WASH. REV. CODE § 9.61.230 (2003).

VI. Conclusion

As these three scenarios demonstrated, there is often a telltale line connecting electronic communications from their source to their destination. Uncovering and legally following that line is a central part of most modern cybercrime investigations for, while the line is rarely sufficient in and of itself for a criminal prosecution, it can often lead to evidence sufficient to sustain a criminal charge and a successful prosecution.

Finding and following that trail requires police and prosecutors to become well versed in both technology and the law relating to that technology. Familiarity with the technology and the law can lead to satisfying results in otherwise difficult to solve cases.

Chapter Four

Defending Cybercrime Cases: Selected Statutes and Defenses

Joseph F. Savage, Jr. with Darlene D. Moreau and Dianna Lamb[*]

I. Introduction

In August 2004, the Department of Justice announced Operation Web Snare, the biggest federal crackdown on cybercrime to date.[1] Operation

---

[*] Joseph F. Savage, Jr. is a partner in the Boston law firm of Goodwin Procter, LLP where he represents clients in complex white collar criminal defense matters as well as civil litigation. He is a former federal prosecutor in Boston, New York, West Virginia and Missouri. Mr. Savage has lectured extensively, particularly on issues relating to the high tech economy and is the author of more than 40 articles on white collar crime issues.

Darlene D. Moreau is an associate in the Trial Group at Duane Morris, LLP and Dianna Lamb is an associate in the Litigation Group at Fried, Frank, Harris, Shriver & Jacobson LLP.

The authors express their appreciation to David Goldstone, counsel in the Trial Department at Goodwin Procter, LLP and a former federal prosecutor in the Computer Crime and Intellectual Property Section of the Criminal Division of the U.S. Department of Justice, for his assistance.

1. Operation Web Snare involved 36 U.S. Attorneys; Offices, the Criminal Division of the Department of Justice, 37 of the FBI's 56 field divisions, 13 of the Postal Inspec-

Web Snare included more than 160 investigations, 140 search and seizure warrants, and the arrest or conviction of more than 150 individuals.[2] The Operation targeted online crimes such as identity theft, fraud, computer intrusions, intellectual property theft, and cyber-extortion. Attorney General John Ashcroft stated that, "Operation Web Snare shows that America's justice community is seeking to anticipate, outthink and adapt to new trends in Internet crime."[3] Operation Web Snare is one example of how law enforcement is responding to recent increases in computer crimes. With the government's current zeal towards investigating and prosecuting computer crimes, it is increasingly a challenge for the defense bar to ensure that defendants' rights are protected and the government is playing by the rules.

This chapter addresses the elements of, and defenses to, some of the more significant statutes pursuant to which alleged cyber criminals are prosecuted. These statutes fall into three major categories that address (1) unauthorized access to computers, (2) cyberfraud, and (3) intellectual property crimes. Following the discussion of the specific statutes, this chapter will address general defenses that arise in a variety of cases involving computer crime.

---

tion Service's field divisions, the FTC and a variety of other federal, state, local and foreign law enforcement agencies. Press Release, U.S. Dept. of Justice, Justice Department Announces Operation Web Snare Targeting Online Fraud and Crime (Aug. 26, 2004), *available at* http://www.usdoj.gov/opa/pr/2004/August/04_crm_583.htm. *See generally* Computer Crime and Intellectual Property Section of the Criminal Division of the U.S. Department of Justice at http://www.cybercrime.gov.

   2. *Id.*
   3. *Id.*

II. Category 1: Unauthorized Access

While there is no single standard computer crime, the most common computer-related criminal activity centers around the transmission of, or unauthorized access to, information stored on a computer.[4] "Hackers" have been depicted as the typical computer criminal and described as "skilled computer users who penetrate computer systems to gain knowledge about computer systems and how they work."[5]

As with computer crimes, there are also different brands of computer criminals. Pure hackers[6] are outsiders who access systems, without any authorization, for their own interest and not for economic profit,[7] and traditionally lack the criminal intent to damage systems.[8] Another breed of computer criminal is the "cracker," who is described as "a hacker with criminal intent" because he or she intends to access a system to steal information or otherwise damage the system.[9]

Over the last two decades, Congress has responded to the increase in computer-related crimes by enacting statutes that specifically target computer criminals. With the passage of the Counterfeit Access Device and Computer Fraud and Abuse Law in 1984, Congress began handling computer-related crimes as discrete offenses.[10] Since then, Congress has enacted

---

4. *See* Joseph M. Olivenbaum, *Ctrl-Alt-Delete: Rethinking Federal Computer Crime Legislation* 27 SETON HALL L. REV. 574, 577 (noting computer criminal activity involves distribution of information on one computer by means of software operating on another remote computer).

5. *See* Eric J. Sinrod, *Cyber-Crimes: A Practical Approach to the Application of Federal Computer Crime Laws* 16 SANTA CLARA COMPUTER & HIGH TECH. L.J. 177, 181–83 (A significant challenge is presented due to the overlapping nature of many terms. For example, the individual who defeats the copyright protection of pirated software is called a cracker. U.S. v. Rothberg, No. 00 CR 85 (N.D. Ill. Nov., 1999) (Special November 1999 Grand Jury Indictment of Rubin Rothberg). The term hacker appears to have originated in the 1960s to describe the hacker prankster culture surrounding certain students at the Massachusetts Institute of Technology) [hereinafter Sinrod, *Cyber-Crimes*].

6. Hackers have been depicted as the typical computer criminal. *See id.*

7. Haeji Hong, *Note: Hacking Through the Computer Fraud Abuse Act*, 31 U.C. DAVIS L. REV. 283, 289 (1997) (Hackers access systems generally out of curiosity and to learn) [hereinafter Hong, *Hacking*].

8. *See* Sinrod, *Cyber-Crimes* at 185 (Recreational hackers break into computer networks for the thrill of the challenge or for bragging rights in the hacking community).

9. *See id.* at 182.

10. Pub. L. No. 98-473, Title II, Chapter XXI, § 2102(a), 98 Stat. 1837, 2190 (1984) (current version at 18 U.S.C. § 1030 (2000)). This approach differs from that taken by

additional statutes aimed at facilitating the prosecution of cybercrime and resulting in harsher penalties for computer criminals.

A. Computer Fraud and Abuse Act

The primary federal statute aimed specifically at combating computer crime is the Computer Fraud and Abuse Act ["CFAA"].[11] The CFAA was originally directed at individual theft of information from government computers.[12] Since its enactment, Congress has amended the Act three times, substantially broadening the scope of the CFAA.[13]

After replacing "federal interest computer" with "protected computer" in 1996, Congress expanded the scope of the CFAA to include every computer linked to an interstate communications line, including the Internet. Therefore, access to a private computer within the same state will still fall under the CFAA if either computer is linked to interstate commerce in any way.[14] In 2001, Congress expanded this definition further in the USA PATRIOT Act[15] to include foreign computers that affect interstate commerce or communications of the United States.[16]

---

many states where traditional theft and trespass statutes are used to address such offenses.

11. *See* 18 U.S.C. § 1030(a)(1)-(a)(7)(2000).

12. *See* Joe D. Whitley & William H. Jordan, *Computer Crime*, ABA White Collar Crime Inst. at E-4 (1999).

13. For more discussion on the evolution of the Computer Fraud and Abuse Act, *see*, Reid Skibell, *Cybercrimes & Misdemeanors: A Reevaluation of the Computer Fraud and Abuse Act*, 18 BERKELEY TECH. L.J. 909 (2003).

14. National Information Infrastructure Protection Act of 1996, Pub. L. No. 104-294, Title II § 201, 110 Stat. 3488, 3491–94 (1996); John J. Falvey, Jr. & Amy M. McCallen, *Crimes Online in 2* INTERNET LAW AND PRACTICE ch. 26 (2005).

15. USA PATRIOT Act, Pub. L. No. 107-56, 115 Stat. 272, § 814 (2001).

16. *Id;* 18 U.S.C. § 1030(e)(2) (2000). The CFAA now defines the term "protected computer" as a computer

(A) exclusively for the use of a financial institution or the United States Government, or, in the case of a computer not exclusively for such use, used by or for a financial institution or the United States Government and the conduct constituting the offense affects that use by or for the financial institution or the Government; or

(B) which is used in interstate or foreign commerce or communication, including a computer located outside the United States that is used in a manner that affects interstate or foreign commerce or communication of the United States;

The CFAA also prohibits any attempts to commit the offenses contained in §1030(a).[17] The CFAA contains seven main subsections aimed at specific computer-related criminal conduct.[18]

1. Section 1030(a)(5)

a. Provisions

Section 1030(a)(5) is the principle anti-hacking subsection in the CFAA. The statute makes it a crime to intentionally damage a protected computer through the "transmission of a program, information code, or command."[19] The offender must act without, or in excess of, authorization.[20] Insiders with authority are responsible only for the intentional damage that they cause. Outsiders are culpable if they cause damage, regardless of intent.[21]

Damage is defined by the statute as "impairment to the integrity or availability of data, a program, or information."[22] To be liable under section 1030(a)(5), the defendant's conduct must cause, or would have caused if successful, loss to one or more persons during a one year period aggregating at least $5000 in value.[23] In 2001, Congress defined loss as "any reasonable cost to any victim."[24] This cost includes any cost incurred in responding to an offense, conducting a damage assessment, remedying any system damage, and any revenue lost, cost, or consequential damage incurred because of an interruption in services.[25]

Alternatively, an offender will be liable under section 1030(a)(5) if the defendant's conduct causes damage that: (1) potentially or actually modi-

---

17. 18 U.S.C. § 1030(b) (2000).

18. *Id.* § 1030(a)(1)-(a)(7). The CFAA creates six felony offenses and five misdemeanors.

19. *Id.* § 1030(a)(5).

20. *Id.*

21. *Id.*

22. *Id.* § 1030(e)(8).

23. *Id.* § 1030(a)(5)(B)(I).

24. *Id.* § 1030(e)(11). Prior to the 2001 amendments, the term "loss" remained undefined and ambiguous. *See,* U.S. v. Pierre-Louis, 2002 WL 1268396 at *2 (S.D. Fl.), *aff'd,* 2002 WL 31719473 (11th Cir. 2002)).

25. 18 U.S.C. § 1030(e)(11) (2000); USA PATRIOT Act, Pub. L. 107-56, 115 Stat. 272, § 814 (2001). Through the amendments, Congress endorsed the definition of loss enunciated by the Ninth Circuit in *U.S. v. Middleton,* 231 F.3d 1207 (9th Cir. 2000). In *Middleton,* the Court included the cost of damage assessments and lost revenue incurred due to an interruption in service.

fied or impaired medical treatment; (2) causes physical injury; (3) threatens the public health or safety; or (4) damages a computer used by or for a government entity in furtherance of the administration of justice, national defense, or national security.[26]

b. Defenses

In general, the 1996 Amendments to the CFAA sought to greatly limit the defenses available under section 1030. Also, the amendments under the USA PATRIOT Act broaden the scope of culpable conduct under section 1030 and eliminate certain intent requirements to allow for easier prosecutions.

(1) Intent

In 1994, this subsection was amended to require evidence of an "intent to damage" for a felony conviction while recklessly causing damage became a misdemeanor.[27] Congress amended the statute in 1996 and again in 2001, to redefine the different *mens rea* requirements for a felony and a misdemeanor.[28] Under the amended section 1030(a)(5)(A)(iii), a defendant may be convicted of a misdemeanor even absent the intent to damage if there is intent to access.[29] Once it is shown that a defendant intentionally accessed a protected computer, it is no longer a viable defense that the damage caused was beyond the intent of the offender.[30]

Previous statutory ambiguities under section 1030(a)(5) appeared to allow defendants to challenge the proof of intent by arguing that an intent to *damage*, and not merely an intent to access, was required. In *United States v. Morris*,[31] the defendant was convicted for intentionally accessing a "federal interest computer" and thereby causing damage after releasing a destructive program onto the Internet. The defendant did not intend to cause

---

26. 18 U.S.C. § 1030(a)(5) (2000); USA PATRIOT Act, Pub. L. No. 107-56, 115 Stat. 272, § 814 (2001).

27. Pub. L. No. 103-322, § 290001, 108 Stat. 1796 (1994) (codified, as amended at 18 U.S.C. § 1030(a)(5)(A)-(B) (2000)).

28. 18 U.S.C. §§ 1030(a)(5)(A), (B), & (C) (2000).

29. *Id.* § 1030(a)(5)(A)(iii).

30. *See* Michael Hatcher, Jay McDannell & Stacy Ostfeld, *Computer Crimes*, 36 AM. CRIM. L. REV. 397, 407 (1999) ("[O]nce a prosecutor proves intentional access, courts will reject a defense claiming that the effects of a program exceeded the programmer's intentions.") [hereinafter Hatcher, *Computer Crimes*].

31. 928 F.2d 504 (2d Cir.), *cert. denied*, 502 U.S. 817 (1991).

any damage, but only to point out defects in the computer network's security.[32]

The defendant argued that the statute required intent to cause damage and not merely intent to access. The Second Circuit disagreed. While recognizing the ambiguity in the wording of the statute, the Court affirmed the defendant's felony conviction concluding that the "intentional" element only applied to accessing a system and not to causing damage.[33]

(2) Lack of Damage under CFAA

Section 1030(e)(8) defines damage as "any impairment to the integrity or availability of data, a program, a system, or information" that causes a loss of at least $5000 in a one-year period.[34] This provides a fact specific argument about the consequence of an intrusion. Courts have used different methods to calculate the aggregate losses. In *United States v. Sablan*, the court calculated damages by looking at losses "directly resulting" from the defendant's criminal conduct.[35] The court in *United States v. Middleton*, on the other hand, calculated damages to include the time employees expended in identifying, investigating, and correcting the damage caused by the defendant.[36]

In 2001 Congress amended the CFAA to define "loss" as any reasonable cost to the victim, thereby limiting the extent to which a defendant may argue lack of damage.[37] The new definition of loss includes the cost of responding to, conducting a damage assessment of, and repairing the damage caused by an offense.[38] Loss also includes any lost profits or other consequential damages as a result of any interruption of service caused by the offense.[39]

c. Penalties

The CFAA's sentencing provision is found at section 1030(c), which was amended in 1996 and 2001.

---

32. *See id.* at 505.
33. *Id.* at 506–09.
34. 18 U.S.C. § 1030(e)(8) (2000). Congress amended the CFAA in 2001 to define the term "loss." See *supra* note 44 with accompanying text.
35. 92 F.3d 865, 870 (9th Cir. 1996).
36. 35 F. Supp. 2d 1189 (N.D. Cal. 1999).
37. 18 U.S.C. § 1030(e)(11) (2000).
38. *Id.*
39. *Id.*

Under the Federal Sentencing Guidelines,[40] a defendant convicted of violating 1030(a)(5), causing a loss of more than $5000,[41] would receive a sentence of four to ten months. This sentence may be satisfied by a term of imprisonment, but more likely will result in a combination of imprisonment and supervised release or of probation and community or home confinement.[42] The advisory sentence will increase if the defendant knowingly and intentionally caused the damage under §1030(a)(5)(A)(i). This is significant not only because the length of the sentence will increase to 12 to 18 months, but because the sentence can no longer be satisfied by a term of probation or a form of home or community confinement. Furthermore, if the defendant actually caused a substantial disruption of a critical infrastructure, the guidelines recommend a sentence of 51 to 63 months.

Previously, a person convicted under the CFAA received an enhanced sentence if on a prior occasion she was convicted of violating any subsection of 1030(a).[43] Today, a person convicted under the CFAA will receive an enhanced sentence if any she has a prior conviction under a 1030(a) subsection or a state statute punishable by one or more years in which unauthorized access to a computer is an element of the offense.[44]

2. Section 1030(a)(2)

a. Provisions

Section 1030(a)(2) prohibits *obtaining*, without, or in excess of, authorization, information from a financial institution, the federal government, or a "protected computer" involved in interstate or foreign communica-

---

40. While the federal sentencing guidelines are no longer mandatory, they remain advisory and must be considered by the sentencing court as one factor in determining the appropriate sentence. *See*, U.S. v. Booker, 125 S. Ct. 738 (2005).

41. The guidelines increase the base level of the offense according to the amount of loss involved. For violations of 1030(a) that result in loss under $5000 the sentence is not increased. However, the sentence increases incrementally depending on the amount of loss.

42. If the offense involved a computer system used to maintain a critical infrastructure, in furtherance of the administration of justice, national defense, national security, or with the intent to obtain personal information the sentence may be increased by two months (6–12 months).

43. Prior to the 1996 amendments, a repeat offender only received enhanced sentences if they violated the same subsection of 1030(a) under which they were previously convicted. After the 1996 amendments, a repeat offender received an enhanced sentence if they subsequently violated any other 1030(a) subsection. 18 U.S.C. § 1030(c) (2000).

44. *Id.*

tion.[45] Merely reading the information is "obtaining", as the subsection does not require that the information be copied or altered.[46]

Thus, a defendant may be convicted under section 1030(a)(2) simply for viewing the information, where the information is obtained from a financial record of a financial institution, from any department or agency of the United States, or from a protected computer involved in interstate or foreign communication.[47]

b. Penalties

If there are no aggravating factors, a violation of 1030(a)(2) is a misdemeanor and the guidelines recommend a sentence of 0 to 6 months, which may be satisfied by a term of probation.[48] A violation of 1030(a)(2) becomes a felony if committed for commercial gain, committed in furtherance of a crime, or caused a loss of over $5000. In the case of a felony violation the defendant may be sentenced to up to five years in prison.

3. Section 1030(a)(7)

a. Provisions

Section 1030(a)(7) prohibits online extortion through the transmission of any threats to cause damage to a protected computer with the intent to extort something of value.[49] Violators of this section will most likely be prosecuted under the Hobbs Act[50], a separate federal extortion statute, which will result in more severe penalties.

b. Penalties

The sentencing guidelines provide a range of 27 to 33 months for violations of 1030(a)(7), which must be served by a term of imprisonment. The

---

45. *Id.* § 1030(a)(2).

46. *See* Hatcher, *Computer Crimes, supra* note 30, at 404 n.39 ("Since there is no requirement that information be transported or copied, merely reading the information may be considered 'obtaining'... Merely reading information, however, is not considered 'obtaining something of value' for purposes of ... 18 U.S.C.A. § 1030(a)(4) (Supp. 1998).").

47. 18 U.S.C. § 1030(a)(2) (2000).

48. The sentence remains zero to six months even if the offense involved a computer used to maintain the critical infrastructure, in furtherance of the administration of justice, national defense or national security, or used to obtain personal information.

49. 18 U.S.C. § 1030(a)(7) (2000).

50. Hobbs Act, 18 U.S.C. § 1951 (2000).

sentence may increase depending on the amount of money demanded or the actual loss to the victim.[51] If the offense involved damage to a computer affecting a critical infrastructure, or used in the administration of justice, national defense or national security, the recommended sentence will range from 37 to 46 months.[52]

4. Section 1030(a)(6)

a. Provisions

The CFAA prohibits trafficking in passwords that could be used to access a protected computer, where it is done knowingly and with intent to defraud, in section 1030(a)(6).[53] This provision is most applicable in a case of online identity theft, where passwords are stolen to obtain personal information.[54]

b. Penalties

The guidelines provide for a sentence of zero to six months, which may be satisfied by a term of probation or other form of confinement. If the offense resulted in a monetary loss the guideline sentence will increase incrementally depending on the amount of loss.[55] If the sale of the password resulted in the disruption of a critical infrastructure the guideline will recommend fifteen to twenty-one months that must include a term of imprisonment.

5. Section 1030(a)(4)

a. Provisions

Section 1030(a)(4) prohibits access to a protected computer, without or in excess of authority, with the intent to defraud or obtain anything of value.[56] If the only thing obtained or taken is computer time, the value of

---

51. The recommended sentence does not increase if the amount was below $10,000; after $10,000, the base level increases.

52. Again, the guideline sentence will increase depending on the amount of money demanded or the amount of loss caused. U.S. Sentencing Guidelines Manual § 2B3.2 (1998).

53. 18 U.S.C. § 1030(a)(6) (2000).

54. See discussion of identity theft below in section III(A), *infra*.

55. *See* Table, U.S. Sentencing Guidelines Manual § 2B1.1(b)(1) (1998).

56. 18 U.S.C. § 1030(a)(4) (2000).

the use obtained must exceed $5,000 in any one-year period to violate the section.[57]

b. Defense: Obtain Anything of Value

Before a defendant can be found guilty under section 1030(a)(4), the prosecution must demonstrate that the offender knowingly and with fraudulent intent accessed a protected computer, without or in excess of authority, and *obtained anything of value*.[58] A defendant may raise the defense that she did not "obtain anything of value" when she only viewed the information on a computer screen, but did not actually take something. This defense was successfully raised in *United States v. Czubinski*.[59]

In *Czubinski*, the defendant was convicted on four counts of computer fraud under section 1030(a)(4) when he carried out unauthorized computer searches and viewed confidential taxpayer information.[60] On appeal to the First Circuit, the defendant argued that he had not violated section 1030(a)(4) because he merely viewed information and did not obtain anything of value.[61] The Court agreed and reversed the conviction, emphasizing that "merely viewing information cannot be deemed the same as obtaining something of value for the purposes of this statute."[62] This defense is valid where a defendant has not in some way used, recorded or printed the information obtained.[63] However, in *U.S. v. Ivanov*, the court concluded that the defendant obtained something of value within the meaning of section 1030(a)(4) where he obtained root access to a protected computer.[64] As in *Czubinski*, the defendant did not actually use or alter the data contained on the computer, but the Court found that by obtaining root access the defendant obtained intangible property of the victim and therefore, obtained something of value.[65] Therefore, the defendant's physical relation-

---

57. *Id.*

58. *Id.*

59. 106 F.3d 1069 (1st Cir. 1997).

60. *Id.* at 1071 (defendant also convicted of nine counts of wire fraud under 18 U.S.C. §§ 1343 & 1346 (2000)).

61. *Id.* A defendant could not raise this argument under § 1030(a)(2) where merely viewing is considered obtaining information. *See supra* note 25 with accompanying text.

62. Czubinski, 106 F.3d at 1078; U.S. v. Ivanov, 175 F. Supp. 2d 367, 371 (D. Conn. 2001).

63. Czubinski, 106 F.3d at at 1078.

64. Ivanov, 175 F. Supp. 2d at 371.

65. *Id.* at 371–72.

ship to the data may affect the court's analysis regarding whether the defendant obtained something of value.[66]

c. Penalties

For a violation of 1030(a)(4), where the loss exceeded $5000, the sentence recommendation is between zero to six months. The guideline range will increase incrementally depending on the exact amount of loss and other aggravating factors.

6. Section 1030(a)(3)

a. Provisions

Under section 1030(a)(3), the CFAA protects government computers and prohibits intentionally accessing a nonpublic computer of a U.S. department or agency without authorization.[67] The 1996 Amendments removed the requirement that the access "adversely" affect the government's use and, consequently, a possible defense that the access was harmless was also eradicated.

b. Penalties

A violation of 1030(a)(3) is punishable generally by zero to six months. The sentence may increase depending on the amount of loss caused by the invasion and the type of government computer involved.[68]

7. Section 1030(a)(1)

a. Provisions

The first of the CFAA's subsections, section 1030(a)(1), prohibits the knowing access of a computer, without authorization or in excess of authorization,[69] and the subsequent transfer of classified government information.[70] Information is protected if it *could* be used to injure the United

---

66. *See*, Skibell, *supra* note 13 at 925.

67. 18 U.S.C. § 1030(a)(3) (2000).

68. *See* U.S. Sentencing Guidelines Manual § 2B2.3 (1998).

69. 18 U.S.C. § 1030(a)(1) (2000). The CFAA defines the term "exceeds authorized access" as access to a computer "with authorization and to use such access to obtain or alter information in the computer that the accessor is not entitled to obtain." *Id.* § 1030(e)(6).

70. *Id.* § 1030(a)(1).

States, eliminating a pre-1996 requirement that the offender have knowledge that the information "is to be used" to injure the United States.[71]

b. Penalties

If top-secret information is involved, absent other aggravating factors, the guidelines recommend a sentence between seven and nine years; if not top secret, four to five years.

B. Electronic Communications Privacy Act

The Electronic Communications Privacy Act ["ECPA"] was enacted in 1986 and extends privacy protections to electronic communications.[72] In general ECPA (1) criminalizes the unauthorized interception of electronic communications by private entities and (2) provides prerequisites to government access of electronic communications. ECPA is divided into two main chapters: the "Wiretap statute"[73] and the Stored Wire and Electronic Communications and Transactional Records Act.[74]

1. The Wiretap Statute

The Wiretap statute prohibits the interception and disclosure of wire, oral, or electronic communications.[75] The broad definition of "electronic communication" includes within the statute electronic mail, voicemail, cellular phones and satellite communications. Interception of electronic com-

---

71. *Id.*
72. Electronic Communications Privacy Act (ECPA), Pub. L. No. 99-508, 100 Stat. 1848 (1986) (codified as amended at 18 U.S.C. §§ 2510-21, 2701-10 (2000)).
73. 18 U.S.C. §§ 2510–22 (2000 & Supp. II 2003).
74. *Id.* §§ 2701–11.
75. Under *id.* § 2510(12), an "electronic communication" is defined as
   any transfer of signs, signals, writing, images, sounds, data, or intelligence of any nature transmitted in whole or in part by a wire, radio, electromagnetic, photoelectronic or photooptical system that affects interstate or foreign commerce, but does not include—
   (A) any wire or oral communication;
   (B) any communication made through a tone-only paging device;
   (C) any communication from a tracking device (as defined in section 3117 of this title); or
   (D) electronic funds transfer information stored by a financial institution in a communications system used for the electronic storage and transfer of funds.

munication can include anything from tapping telephones to intercepting e-mails. Violations under this section can result in a fine and a recommended sentence of four to ten months. If the defendant commits the offense for commercial gain the recommended sentence may increase to ten to sixteen months.[76]

For a person to be convicted under § 2511, the interception must occur while the communication is transmitted, or the conduct may fall instead under the provisions of the Stored Wire and Electronic Communications Act, which prohibits access and disclosure of information stored electronically. However, it is difficult to determine when a communication is "in transit" because electronic communications, such as e-mails or voicemails, are only transmitted for milliseconds and stored on different servers as they are routed.[77] At least one court has grappled with this precise issue.

In *U.S. v. Councilman*,[78] the defendant questioned the meaning of "transmission." The defendant in *Councilman* operated a system that intercepted e-mails sent to amazon.com and made a copy of the e-mails before Amazon received them. In dismissing the indictment against the Defendant under the Wiretap Act, the Court found that the e-mails were in a form of electronic storage, even if only temporarily, as opposed to real time interception while the e-mails were being transmitted.[79] The Court commented that, "[i]t may well be that the protections of the Wiretap Act have been

---

76. *See* U.S. Sentencing Guidelines Manual § 2H3.1 (1998).

77. *See* Joe D. Whitley & William H. Jordan, *Computer Crime, White Collar Crime: Business and Regulatory Offenses, reprinted in* White Collar Crime 2000 at E9 (1999) [hereinafter Whitley, *Computer Crime*] ("For example, an e-mail message is typically typed on one computer, stored on the sender's e-mail server, transmitted over the Internet through a series of routers to the destination, stored on the recipient's e-mail server, delivered to that persons e-mail account at which time it may, depending on the configuration, be stored on the recipients hard drive. Thus, there is only a fraction of a second when the e-mail is actually in transit between the sender and the recipient.").

78. U.S. v. Councilman, 373 F.3d 197 (1st Cir. 2004). *See also* Konop v. Hawaiian Airlines, Inc., 302 F.3d 868 (9th Cir. 2002), *cert. denied*, 537 U.S. 1193 (2003); Fraser v. Nationwide Mut. Ins. Co., 352 F.3d 107 (3rd Cir. 2003); Steve Jackson Games, Inc. v. U.S. Secret Service, 36 F.3d 457 (5th Cir. 1994).

79. Councilman, 373 F.3d at 203 ("'At all times that sendmail and procmail performed operations affecting the e-mail messages at issue, the messages existed in the random access memory (RAM) or in hard disks, or both, within Interloc's computer system.' When defendant obtained the e-mails, they were in temporary storage in Interloc's computer system.").

eviscerated as technology advances."[80] According to the Department of Justice, the ruling creates an unintentional loophole in Internet wiretapping laws.[81]

2. Stored Wire and Electronic Communications Act

Section 1207 prohibits access to electronic communications while they are in storage.[82] Section 2701 exempts from its prohibitions conduct that is authorized by the entity providing the service or by the user of the service, where the communication was intended for that user.[83] As such an employer who provides its employees with electronic communication services to be used in the course of employment cannot be liable for accessing the communications. In addition, where a governmental entity follows the procedures delineated in the statute for accessing such information, its conduct is exempted from section 2701.[84]

A public provider may disclose information about its users if certain statutory exemptions are met. The provider may disclose user information if the user gives his or her consent,[85] or if the provider feels it is necessary to protect its own rights and property.[86] A public provider may also disclose the contents of communications that are inadvertently obtained and pertain to the commission of a crime. Lastly, a public provider may disclose user information lawfully if the provider reasonably believes an emergency involving danger of death or serious physical injury requires disclosure without delay.[87] Additionally, private providers of electronic communica-

---

80. *Id.*

81. The Department of Justice asked the First Circuit to review their decision, and on October 5, 2004 the Court agreed to rehear the appeal, which remains undecided as of January, 2005. U.S. v. Councilman, 2004 U.S. App. LEXIS 20756 (1st Cir. 2004). Legislation has been introduced in the House of Representatives to redefine "interception" in the Wiretap Act as a result of this decision. *See* E-Mail Privacy Act of 2004, H.R. 4956 (the bill has been referred to the Subcommittee on Crime, Terrorism, and Homeland Security).

82. *See* 18 U.S.C. § 2701(a) (2000).

83. *See id.* § 2701(c)(1)-(2).

84. *See id.* § 2701(c)(3).

85. For example, through the use of banners stating that by using the service you consent to the providers' disclosure of certain information.

86. 18 U.S.C. § 2702(b)(5) (2000).

87. Id. § 2701(c)(4).

tion services may disclose transactional data and user information without violating section 2701.[88]

The criminal penalties under section 2701 include a fine or imprisonment of not more than one year, or both, if the offender obtains the unauthorized access for "commercial advantage, malicious destruction or damage, or private commercial gain."[89] In the absence of any aggravating factors, the guidelines generally call for a sentence of zero to six months for a violation of § 2701.[90] Repeat offenders may also be fined, imprisoned for a maximum of two years, or both.[91] Other cases of unauthorized access are punishable by a fine, imprisonment for up to six months, or both.[92]

III. Category 2: Cyberfraud

A. Identity Theft

According to the government, identity fraud is one of the fastest growing crimes in the United States. The Federal Trade Commission estimates that identity thieves victimized almost ten million people in 2002 and as many as twenty-seven million in the last five years.[93] In the last year, victims of phishing scams,[94] the latest trend in identity theft, allegedly lost over $1.2 billion. "Phishing" is the term for the scam in which an individual sends an e-mail or creates a website that appears to come from a well-known legitimate business, such as a bank, in order to trick people into disclosing personal and financial information. The phisher then uses that information to steal the victim's identity. According to the Anti-Phishing Working Group, phishing attacks increased by 800% in the first six months of 2004, from 176 in January 2004, to 1,422 in June, 2004.[95] Enforcement activity targeting phishing scams stealing the identities of individuals and

---

88. *See id.* § 2702.

89. *See id.* § 2701(b)(1)(A).

90. *See* U.S. Sentencing Guidelines Manual § 2B1.1 (1998).

91. *See* 18 U.S.C. § 2701(b)(1)(B) (2000).

92. *See id.* § 2701(b)(2).

93. U.S. Dept. of Justice., *Special Report on Phishing, available at* http://www.usdoj. gov/criminal/fraud/Phishing.pdf (last visited May 5, 2005).

94. "Phishing" is the general terms used to describe the creation and use of e-mail messages and websites to dupe Internet users into providing bank or financial account numbers and other personal data.

95. Anti-Phishing Working Group, *Phishing Attack Trends Report* (2004), *available at* http://www.antiphishing.org/APWG_Phishing_Attack_Report-Jul2004.pdf.

businesses have increased. Additionally, in July 2004, President Bush signed legislation increasing the penalties for identity theft and associated crimes.[96]

The Identity Theft and Assumption Deterrence Act of 1998, ["ITAD"][97] makes it a federal crime to knowingly transfer, possess, or use, without lawful authority, a means of identification of another person with the intent to commit, or to aid or abet, or in connection with, any unlawful activity that constitutes a violation of Federal law, or that constitutes a felony under any applicable state or local law.[98]

The Identity Theft Penalty Enhancement Act ["ITPEA"] adds two years to the prison sentence received by any individual convicted of an enumerated felony who unlawfully transfers, possesses, or uses a means of identification of another person.[99] The ITPEA adds five years to the sentence received by a defendant convicted of identity theft in connection with an act of terrorism.[100] Additionally, several legislators have introduced legislation to specifically criminalize phishing.[101] The ITAD has been used extensively to prosecute more traditional types of identity theft. However, there have

---

96. *See* 18 U.S.C.A. § 1028A (2004).

97. *Id.* § 1028.

98. *Id.* § 1028(a)(7). The statute also punishes anyone who:

(1) knowingly and without lawful authority produces an identification document or a false identification document;

(2) knowingly transfers an identification document or a false identification document knowing that such document was stolen or produced without lawful authority;

(3) knowingly possesses with intent to use unlawfully or transfer unlawfully five or more identification documents (other than those issued lawfully for the use of the possessor) or false identification documents;

(4) knowingly possesses an identification document (other than one issued lawfully for the use of the possessor) or a false identification document, with the intent such document be used to defraud the United States;

(5) knowingly produces, transfers, or possesses a document-making implement with the intent such document-making implement will be used in the production of a false identification document or another document-making implement which will be so used;

(6) knowingly possesses an identification document that is or appears to be an identification document of the United States which is stolen or produced without lawful authority knowing that such document was stolen or produced without such authority.

99. *Id.* § 1028A(a).

100. *Id.*

101. In July 2004 Senator Patrick Leahy introduced legislation called the Anti-phishing Act of 2004, S. 2636, 108th Cong. (2004).

been few cases involving phishing scams yet. Although, law enforcement activity in this area increased dramatically in 2004. In May 2004, a United States District Judge from the Southern District of Texas sentenced one phisher to four years in federal prison for his scheme to defraud consumers.[102] In October 2004, the U.S. Secret Service, in conjunction with various domestic and foreign law enforcement agencies, arrested twenty-eight individuals accused of using the Internet to steal and forge identification documents.[103] The suspects, targeted by Operation Firewall, are alleged to have stolen over 1.7 million credit card numbers.[104]

B. Can-Spam Act

The Controlling the Assault of Non-Solicited Pornography and Marketing Act of 2003 ["CAN-SPAM"] prohibits fraud and related activity in connection with e-mail.[105] CAN-SPAM applies to e-mails that are sent in bulk,

---

102. Zachary Keith Hill sent out spam e-mails to people purportedly from America Online and Paypal asking for customers to confirm or update account information. Mr. Hill used the replies to his phony e-mails to access 473 credit card numbers, 152 sets of bank account and routing numbers, and 566 usernames and passwords for Internet service accounts. For more details, see U.S. Dept. of Justice, *Fraudster Sentenced To Nearly Four Years In Prison In Internet 'Phishing' Case* (2004), *available at* http://www.usdoj.gov/criminal/cybercrime/hillSent.htm.

103. Press Release, U.S. Secret Service, U.S. Secret Service's Operation Firewall Nets 28 Arrests (Oct. 28, 2004), *available at* http://www.ustreas.gov/usss/press/pub2304.pdf. The Department of Justice indicted 19 individuals in connection with the arrests alleging the individuals conspired to create "shadowcrew," a website designed to facilitate identity theft. *See*, Press Release, U.S. Dept. of Justice, Nineteen Individuals Indicted in Internet 'Carding' Conspiracy (Oct. 28, 2004), *available at* http://www.cybercrime.gov/mantovaniIndict.htm.

104. U.S. Secret Service, *Operation Firewall, supra* note 103.

105. 18 U.S.C.A. § 1037 (2004). Specifically, the Act holds liable an individual who

(1) accesses a protected computer without authorization, and intentionally initiates the transmission of multiple commercial electronic mail messages from or through such computer,

(2) uses a protected computer to relay or retransmit multiple commercial electronic mail messages, with the intent to deceive or mislead recipients, or any Internet access service, as to the origin of such messages,

(3) materially falsifies header information in multiple commercial electronic mail messages and intentionally initiates the transmission of such messages,

(4) registers, using information that materially falsifies the identity of the actual registrant, for five or more electronic mail accounts or online user accounts or two or more domain names, and intentionally initiates the trans-

unsolicited by the receiver, and commercial in nature. There has only been one criminal conviction for a violation of the CAN-SPAM Act to date. On September 38, 2004, an individual pled guilty to gaining unauthorized access to a computer to send multiple spam e-mails.[106] The defendant admitted to "wardriving," driving around in a car in order to find "hot spots" for wireless access to the Internet, and sending spam from various locations. The defendant faces a maximum of three years in prison.[107]

IV. Category 3: Intellectual Property Crimes

A. The Economic Espionage Act

1. Overview of the Statute

The Economic Espionage Act of 1996 ["EEA"][108] was drafted to protect information guarded by "reasonable" secrecy measures, valuable because of its secrecy, and "related to or included in a product" in interstate commerce.[109] President Clinton heralded the Act as crucial to preserve "the competitiveness of critical U.S. industries" and to protect the trade secrets of all businesses operating in the United States from economic espionage and trade secret theft.[110] At a time when twenty-six states did not have criminal trade secrets statutes in effect, the Act criminalized the theft of trade secrets and authorized the United States Department of Justice ["DOJ"] to prosecute employees and businesses, and even seize companies for stealing trade secrets.

---

mission of multiple commercial electronic mail messages from any combination of such accounts or domain names, or

(5) falsely represents oneself to be the registrant or the legitimate successor in interest to the registrant of 5 or more Internet Protocol addresses, and intentionally initiates the transmission of multiple commercial electronic mail messages from such addresses, or conspires to do so.

106. Press Release, Debra Wang, Guilty Plea by Local 'War-Spammer' is First-Ever Conviction Under CAN-SPAM Act (Sept. 28, 2004), *available at* http://www.usdoj.gov/usao/cac/pr2004/131.html.

107. *Id.*

108. 18 U.S.C. § 1831-39 (2000).

109. *See id.*

110. For further discussion of this topic, *see* Joseph F. Savage, Jr., Matthew A. Martel, & Marc J. Zwilling, *Trade Secrets: Conflicting View of the Economic Espionage Act*, 15 A.B.A. Crim. Just., Fall 2000 at 10.

Prior to the EEA's enactment, the only federal statute directed at economic espionage was the Trade Secrets Act.[111] Private citizens handled trade secret theft through civil litigation, but in the criminal context, the government was forced to make creative use of other statutes.

The EEA filled the gap, and several cases prosecuted under the EEA contain examples of trade secret theft effected through the use of computers, and, more specifically, e-mail. In *United States v. Ho*, an employee of one company sent an e-mail to an employee of a competitor's company, which outlined and requested information relating to the competitor's technology.[112] Unfortunately for the employee making the request, the competitor's employee cooperated with the FBI and provided information that ultimately led to the employee's arrest.[113]

In *U.S. v. Martin*, the First Circuit affirmed an EEA conviction that arose "out of an electronic mail 'pen-pal' relationship between a dissatisfied Maine chemist ... and a California scientist."[114] Camp, a chemist in Maine, was interested in leaving her current employment.[115] Accordingly she sent a resume and began corresponding with a competitor, Martin.[116] In the course of correspondence, Camp repeatedly sent confidential company information to Martin (some at his urging).[117] On Camp's last day, she inadvertently sent a message to the global marketing manager of her current employer, discussing a package of confidential information that she had sent to Martin.[118] Martin was ultimately convicted by a jury of conspiracy to steal trade secrets under the EEA.[119] From 2000 to 2003, the Department of Justice reports that it prosecuted twenty-six EEA violations, twelve of which involved ex-employees.[120]

---

111. 18 U.S.C. § 1905 (2000).

112. *See* 155 F.3d 189, 192 (3rd Cir. 1998).

113. *See id.* at 192–93.

114. U.S. v. Martin, 228 F.3d 1, 6 (1st Cir. 2000).

115. *Id.*

116. *See id.* at 6–10.

117. *See id.* at 7–10. Although Martin told Camp only to send public information, he encouraged her to accumulate relevant knowledge and used the word "spy."

118. *See id.* at 10.

119. *See id.*

120. Computer Crime and Intellectual Property Section, Criminal Division, U.S. Dept. of Justice, *Economic Espionage Act (EEA) Cases*, *available at* http://www.cybercrime.gov/eeapub.htm (last updated Nov. 24, 2003).

The EEA proscribes two types of trade secret theft: foreign economic es-pionage[121] and commercial theft of trade secrets.[122] Section 1831, used to

121. *See* 18 U.S.C. § 1831 (2000). Section 1831 provides in full:
    (a) In General—Whoever, intending or knowing that the offense will ben-efit any foreign government, foreign instrumentality, or foreign agent, know-ingly—
    (1) steals, or without authorization appropriates, takes, carries away, or conceals, or by fraud, artifice, or deception obtains a trade secret;
    (2) without authorization copies, duplicates, sketches, draws, photographs, downloads, uploads, alters, destroys, photocopies, replicates, transmits, deliv-ers, sends, mails, communicates, or conveys a trade secret;
    (3) receives, buys, or possesses a trade secret, knowing the same to have been stolen or appropriated, obtained, or converted without authorization;
    (4) attempts to commit any offense described in any of paragraphs (1) through (3); or
    (5) conspires with one or more other persons to commit any offense de-scribed in any of paragraphs (1) through (3), and one or more of such per-son do any act to effect the object of the conspiracy, shall, except as provided in subsection (b), be fined not more than $500,000 or imprisoned not more than 15 years, or both.
    (b) Organizations—Any organization that commits any offense described in subsection (a) shall be fined not more than $10,000,000.
122. *See Id.* § 1832. Section 1832 provides in full:
    (a) Whoever, with intent to convert a trade secret, that is related to or in-cluded in a product that is produced for or placed in interstate commerce, to the economic benefit of anyone other than the owner thereof, and intending or knowing that the offense will injure any owner of that trade secret, know-ingly—
    (1) Steals, or without authorization appropriates, takes, carries away, or conceals, or by fraud, artifice, or deception obtains such information;
    (2) Without authorization copies, duplicates, sketches, draws, photographs, downloads, uploads, alters, destroys, photocopies, replicates, transmits, deliv-ers, sends, mails, communicates, or conveys such information;
    (3) Receives, buys, or possesses such information, knowing the same to have been stolen or appropriated, obtained, or converted without authoriza-tion;
    (4) Attempts to commit any offense described in paragraphs (1) through (3); or
    (5) Conspires with one or more other persons to commit any offense de-scribed in paragraphs (1) through (3), and one or more of such persons do any act to effect the object of the conspiracy, shall, except as provided in sub-section (b), be fined under this title or imprisoned not more than 10 years, or both.
    (b) Any organization that commits any offense described in subsection (a) shall be fined not more than $5,000,000.

indict a defendant for the first time in 2002, criminalizes the theft of trade secrets with the intent or knowledge that the offense will benefit a foreign entity.[123] Section 1832[124] criminalizes commercial theft of trade secrets, regardless of who receives the benefits.

The EEA presents potential issues for those accused of criminal trade secret theft both because of its breadth and because the elements of the statute are not clearly defined. The necessity of computer use in the workplace increases the implications of the Act. An employee can more easily depart her workplace with a disk full of confidential information than with an armload of hard copies.

2. *Wide Expansion of Trade Secret Prosecution*

Section 1832 of the EEA requires the government to establish that: (1) the defendant stole, or without authorization of the owner, obtained, destroyed or conveyed information; (2) the defendant knew that this information was proprietary; and (3) the information was in fact trade secret information.[125]

The EEA encompasses not only the removal of property from the owner's physical possession, but also less-traditional methods of misappropriation (often computer assisted). These include, among others, copying, duplicating, replicating, transmitting, delivering, sending, communicating, or conveying, thereby fulfilling Congress' intention "to ensure that the misappropriation of intangible information is prohibited in the same way that the theft of physical items are protected."[126]

The government must further prove that a Defendant under the EEA acted "without authorization" from the owner of the property. "[A]uthorization is the permission, approval, consent or sanction of the owner" to obtain, destroy or convey the trade secret.[127] The EEA only protects against knowing misappropriation of trade secrets.[128] The government must es-

---

123. *See* Press Release, U.S. Dept. of Justice, First Foreign Economic Espionage Indictment; Defendants Steal Trade Secrets from Cleveland Clinic Foundation (May 8, 2001), *available at* http://www.cybercrime.gov/Okamoto_SerizawaIndict.htm. In *U.S. v. Okamoto*, the government charged the defendants misappropriated information related to DNA research for the benefit of RIKEN, an instrumentality of the Japanese government.

124. *See* U.S. v. Lange, 312 F.3d 263 (7th Cir. 2002) (employee stole computer data from employer and attempted to sell to competitor).

125. *See* 18 U.S.C. §§ 1831 & 1832 (2000).

126. S. Rep. No. 104-359 at 16 (1996).

127. 142 Cong. Rec. S12,202, S12,212 (daily ed. Oct. 2, 1996) (Managers' Statement for H.R. 3723).

128. 18 U.S.C. §1832(a) (2000).

tablish that the defendant was aware or substantially certain that he was misappropriating a trade secret.[129] Trade secrets have been traditionally limited to scientific or technical information, but the EEA's definition of a "trade secret", as written, purports to be broader than the scope of the Uniform Trade Secrets Act ["UTSA"], upon which many state criminal trade secrets statutes are based.[130] In addition, the government must show the defendant intended or knew the offense would injure the trade secret owner.[131]

Finally, the owner must have "taken reasonable measures to keep such information secret," and the information must derive economic value from not being generally known to or readily ascertainable by the public.[132]

3. Defending against Liability under the EEA

Most EEA cases to date have involved theft by "insiders," that is, company employees stealing employee trade secrets.[133] Several employment situations seem uniquely poised for scrutiny and potential liability for both a company and an employee under the EEA: (1) A company hires an employee who has substantial knowledge of his former employer's intellectual property; (2) a company buys a business that has employees who recently worked for another employer in the industry; (3) a company uses consultants who are privy to industry technical and marketing information because of their work with competitors. When a company hires a new em-

---

129. Computer Crime & Intellectual Property Section, Criminal Division, U.S. Dept. of Justice, *Federal Prosecution of Violations of Intellectual Property Rights (Copyrights, Trademarks and Trade Secrets)* 73 (Jan., 2001), http://www.cybercrime.gov/ipmanual.htm [hereinafter U.S. D.O.J., *Prosecution of IP Crime*].

130. The UTSA covers "information, including a formula, pattern, compilation, program, device, method, technique, or process...." under 18 U.S.C. § 1839(3) (2000). The EEA's definition of trade secrets includes:

> all forms and types of financial, business, scientific, technical, economic, or engineering information, including patterns, plans, compilations, program devices, formulas, designs, prototypes, methods, techniques, processes, procedures, programs, or codes, whether tangible or intangible, and whether or how stored, compiled, or memorialized physically, electronically, graphically, photographically or in writing.

131. 18 U.S.C. § 1832(a) (2000).

132. Id. § 1839(3)(A)-(B).

133. Computer Crime & Intellectual Property Section, Criminal Division, U.S. Dept. of Justice, *Economic Espionage Act (EEA) Cases*, available at http://www.cybercrime. gov/eeapub.htm (last updated Nov. 24, 2003). From 2000 to 2003, only five of twenty-six prosecutions for violations of the EEA involved outsiders.

ployee who brings along her former employer's confidential information, the employee and employer are both at significant risk of criminal liability under the EEA, regardless of whether the employer is aware of the employee's inside information.

a. The Prosecutors' Perspective on Defenses

The Department of Justice has identified four categories of defenses which companies and employees may use to try and avoid liability under the EEA: Parallel development, reverse engineering, general knowledge, and the First Amendment. The DOJ attempted to train prosecutors about how to respond to challenges.[134]

(1) Parallel Development

The owner of a trade secret does not have an absolute, sole right to possession of a trade secret. Other companies and individuals can discover or invent the same trade secret through their own research and work.[135] A defendant in an EEA prosecution can therefore assert as a defense that his possession of another's trade secret was derived through independent work. The government must disprove this possibility beyond a reasonable doubt, as this defense is implicit in the statute's *mens rea* requirement.[136]

(2) Reverse Engineering

Reverse engineering refers to the practice of taking something apart to determine how it was made or manufactured.[137] The EEA itself does not mention reverse engineering, but the legislative history states: "[T]he important thing is to focus on whether the accused has committed one of the prohibited acts of this statute rather than whether he or she has reverse engineered. If someone has lawfully gained access to a trade secret and can

---

134. U.S. D.O.J., *Prosecution of IP Crime, supra* note 129, § VIII(B)(6)(a).

135. *See* Kewanee Oil Co. v. Bicron Corp., 416 U.S. 470, 490–91 (1974) ("If something is to be discovered at all, very likely it will be discovered by more than one person....").

136. *See* 18 U.S.C. § 1832(a) (2000).

137. *See* Kewanee Oil Corp., 416 U.S. at 476; Joseph F. Savage, Jr., *Federal Criminalization of Trade Secret Theft: An Update on the Economic Espionage Act*, Mass. C.L.E. (2000).

replicate it without violating copyright, patent, or this law, then that form of 'reverse engineering' should be fine."[138]

Although the EEA suggests that reverse engineering can serve as a valid defense to the misappropriation of trade secrets (since no trade secret is being taken), it is not enough for a defendant to claim that the trade secret *could have been* discovered through reverse engineering.[139] The defense of reverse engineering therefore rests on the means actually used to develop the purported "trade secret."[140]

In *U.S. v. Lange*,[141] the defendant argued that all data obtainable by reverse engineering another product are "'readily ascertainable ... by the public," and therefore not trade secrets.[142] The prosecutor argued that "the public" does not have the ability to reverse engineer. The Court engaged in a lengthy discussion regarding whether the "public" referred to in section 1839(3)(B) references the general public or some specific category of people to whom the information would be a source of economic value. The Court declined to rule on the correct interpretation, but decided that the information obtained and sold in this case was not readily ascertainable to "the general public, the educated public, the economically relevant public, or any sensible proxy for these groups."[143]

(3) General Knowledge

"The government can not prosecute an individual for taking advantage of the general knowledge and skills or experience that he or she obtains or comes by during his tenure with a company. Allowing such prosecutions to go forward and allowing the risk of such charges to be brought would unduly endanger legitimate and desirable economic behavior."[144] The defense of general knowledge applies particularly to the situation where an employee changes employers or starts his own company within the same industry. That employee cannot be prosecuted merely because he was exposed

---

138. 142 CONG. REC. S12,201, S12,212 (daily ed. Oct. 2, 1996) (Managers' Statement for H.R. 3723).

139. *See* Telerate Sys., Inc. v. Caro, 689 F. Supp. 221, 232 (S.D.N.Y. 1988).

140. *Id.*

141. 312 F.3d 263 (7th Cir. 2002).

142. *Id.* at 266.

143. *Id.* at 267.

144. 142 CONG. REC. S12,201, S12,213 (daily ed. Oct. 2, 1996) (Managers' Statement for H.R. 3723).

to the first employer's trade secret information, unless the government can establish that the employee stole or misappropriated a trade secret.[145]

(4) First Amendment

Freedom of speech can serve as a defense to a claim of misappropriation of trade secrets if a defendant acts to serve or educate the public; however, if the government can establish the element of the EEA that a defendant intended his misappropriation to economically benefit a third party and harm the secret's owner, that defendant will not succeed with a claim of First Amendment protection for his actions.[146] The First Amendment does not protect speech made for economic gain with intent to harm another. In a related context, one court noted,

> [t]he defense is further unavailable if the speech itself is the vehicle of the crime. [T]he court finds no support for [the defendant's] argument that the criminal activity with which he is charged … is protected by the First Amendment. Interpreting the First Amendment as shielding [the defendant] from criminal liability would open a gaping hole in criminal law; individuals could violate criminal laws with impunity simply by engaging in criminal activities which involve speech-related activity. The First Amendment does not countenance that kind of end run around criminal law.[147]

The DOJ recommends that prosecutors seek an *in limine* order precluding the introduction of "First Amendment defense" whenever possible.[148]

---

145. U.S. D.O.J., *Prosecution of I.P. Crime, supra* note 129. Although the DOJ indicates that employers and employees will not face criminal liability for taking with them general knowledge from one employer to another, an employee may nevertheless be enjoined from working for a new employer in the same field. Specifically, the "inevitable disclosure doctrine" serves as the basis for enjoining employees from working for new employers in the same field where disclosure of a former employer's trade secrets is inevitable due to the nature of the new employment. Unlike the EEA, the doctrine of inevitable disclosure does not focus on the means by which an employee comes to learn a trade secret, but is concerned with the inevitability of that secret's disclosure to the employee's new employer. *See, e.g.,* Pepsico, Inc. v. Redmond, 54 F.3d 1262 (7th Cir. 1995).

146. U.S. D.O.J., *Prosecution of I.P. Crime, supra* note 129.

147. U.S. v. Riggs, 743 F. Supp. 556, 560–61 (N.D. Ill. 1990).

148. *See* U.S. v. Martin, 228 F.3d 1, 10 (1st Cir. 2000).

b. Practical Considerations

Often the most important time to "defend" a cybercrime case is before indictment. Some practical strategies both in dealing with the prosecution and in actively defending an EEA case can be deduced from experience, the case law and the DOJ's guidance on the EEA. At the pretrial stage, the defense attorney must:

- Challenge the trade secret status of the information at issue.[149] If the defense can show a prosecutor that the defendant made an effort to determine whether the information was a trade secret, and reasonably determined that it was not, a responsible prosecutor would likely conclude the jury may reach the same conclusion.
- Show, when possible, that the information is not of significant economic value.
- Focus the prosecutor on the standard of showing criminal intent beyond a reasonable doubt. The prosecutor will be looking primarily to civil case law in developing his or her theories and definitions of the case and may therefore forget that this is not a civil trade secret case.
- Portray the information used by the client as "soft" business competitive information, as opposed to "hard" scientific data. The DOJ is more likely to prosecute theft of scientific information that is concrete and defined.
- Suggest that the DOJ should be reluctant to thrust itself into business disputes that are being addressed by civil litigation.

B. The Copyright Act

Copyright protection is as old as the constitution itself,[150] yet is significantly challenged by computer technology. Criminal penalties for copyright infringement first appeared in 1909.[151] In 1976, Congress preempted state law, making criminal copyright enforcement exclusively a federal func-

---

149. Note, this is not a defense to a charge of attempt or conspiracy to steal trade secrets. *See* U.S. v. Yang, 281 F.3d 534 (2002) (attempt and conspiracy only require the intent to steal trade secrets); U.S. v. Hsu, 155 F.3d 189 (1998).

150. U.S. Const. art. I, § 8, cl. 8.

151. *See* Copyright Act of 1909 § 104, 61 Stat. 652 (codifying the 1909 Act as amended), *repealed by* Copyright Act of 1976, 90 Stat. 2541.

tion.[152] And, in the last twenty-five years, Congress has consistently expanded the scope of the copyright laws and dramatically increased the corresponding penalties.[153] Criminal sanctions for copyright violations are found in both Titles 17 and 18 of the United States Code.[154] With increased use of computers and, more specifically, the Internet, copyright infringement has recently become an even greater focus of law enforcement.[155]

1. Criminal Copyright Infringement and the NET Act

Title 17 U.S.C. § 506(a) (2000) is the principle criminal statute protecting copyrighted works. It provides: "Any person who infringes a copyright willfully and for purposes of commercial advantage or private financial gain shall be punished as provided in section 2319 of title 18."[156] Section 2319 in turn provides for both imprisonment and a fine, both to be determined based on the amount and value of distribution in violation of section 506.[157] While the base guideline sentence level for infringement is zero to six months, the sentence automatically increases to ten to sixteen months if the offense involved uploading infringing items.[158]

---

152. See 17 U.S.C. § 301 (2000).

153. See id. § 506(a) (criminalizing copyright infringement); id. § 506(c)-(e) (criminalizing conduct that undermines the integrity of the copyright system); 18 U.S.C. § 2319 (2000)(outlawing unauthorized production of trafficking in sound recordings and musical videos of live performances, and computer theft of copyrighted works).

154. See 17 U.S.C. § 506(a) (2000) (criminalizing copyright infringement); id. § 506(c)-(e) (criminalizing conduct that undermines the integrity of the copyright system); 18 U.S.C. § 2319 (2000)(outlawing unauthorized production of trafficking in sound recordings and musical videos of live performances, and computer theft of copyrighted works).

155. MP3.com and Napster.com, both specializing in access to digital copies of CDs, made headlines when they were sued for copyright infringement by the Recording Industry Association of America (RIAA). Although civil disputes, the cases and the potential damages involved illustrate the need for companies to be aware of the reach of copyright laws in the age of computers. See UMG Recordings, Inc. v. MP3.Com, Inc., 109 F. Supp. 2d 223 (S.D.N.Y. 2000); A & M Record, Inc. v. Napster, Inc., 114 F. Supp. 2d 896 (N.D. Cal. 2000), aff'd in part & rev'd in part, 239 F.3d 1004 (9th Cir. 2001).

156. 17 U.S.C. § 506(a) (2000).

157. 18 U.S.C. § 2319(b) (2000); See U.S. Sentencing Guidelines Manual § 2B5.3 (1998). Criminal Infringement of Copyright or Trademark carries a base sentence of zero to six months and increases depending on the dollar amount of the infringement.

158. See U.S. Sentencing Guidelines Manual § 2B5.3(b)(2) (1998).

To prove copyright infringement after the enactment of the NET Act, the prosecution must show: (1) the existence of a valid copyright, (2) infringement of the copyright by the defendant, (3) that the defendant acted willfully, either (4) for purposes of commercial advantage or private financial gain, or by the reproduction or distribution, including by electronic means, during any 180-day period, of one or more copies or phonorecords of "1 or more copyrighted works, which have a total retail value of more than $1,000."[159]

2. Defenses to Criminal Copyright Infringement

a. Willfulness: The Use Was Authorized

Because the Copyright Act prohibits only unauthorized infringement, it is a defense to a claim of copyright infringement that the distribution, reproduction or other use of a copyright work was, in fact, "authorize[d]."[160] A clear-cut example of such a defense would be where the defendant possesses evidence of a license for distribution.

The Copyright Act does not define "authorization," however, and not all examples are so simple. Rather than asserting that the use at issue was actually authorized, a defendant may rely on "apparent authority." An example of apparent authority is a good faith belief that the reproduction or distribution at issue was within the scope of a license from the copyright holder. As revealed in the legislative history of the Copyright Act, Congress did not intend the criminal law to be the forum for resolving "the scope of licenses" or other private disputes between businesses.[161]

b. Invalidate the Copyright

A built-in defense to a claim of copyright infringement is that the copyright at issue is not valid. A defendant can attack the validity of a copyright

---

159. Additionally, the Sixth and Ninth Circuits require proof of absence of a "first sale". *See, e.g.,* U.S. v. Sachs, 801 F.2d 839 (6th Cir. 1986); U.S. v. Atherton, 561 F.2d 747, 749 (9th Cir. 1977).

160. *See* 17 U.S.C. § 106 (2000) (Both granting exclusive rights to the owner of the copyright and allowing the owner to authorize others to exercise these rights).

161. H.R. Rep. No. 102-997, at 5 (1992), *reprinted in* 1992 U.S.C.C.A.N. 3569, 3573. For a more complete discussion of authority as a defense to copyright infringement, *see* Robert C. Kain, Jr., *Independent Contractors and Computer Crimes—The Impossible Prosecution?,* 1 B.U. J. Sci. & Tech. L. 13 (1995).

in several ways. The copyright must first be registered; otherwise, infringement of an unregistered copyright is not generally criminally punishable.[162] The law does not require, however, that the copyright be registered at the time of infringement. A subsequent valid registration meeting the requirements of the Register of Copyrights is evidence of a valid copyright.[163]

A defendant can also invalidate a copyright by demonstrating fraud in obtaining the copyright. This requires proof that, but for the fraud, the copyright would not have been registered.[164] For example, the defendant could show that the entity that registered the copyright was not its author under the copyright act. When a defendant challenges a copyright's validity, the government must then independently prove validity.

c. No Infringement

The Copyright Act defines an infringer of a copyright as "[a]nyone who violates any of the exclusive rights" of the copyright as enumerated in the statute.[165] Sections 106 and 106A list the exclusive rights as: the right to prepare derivative works, the right to public display or performance of the work, and the right to reproduce and distribute copies of the work.[166] To prove the element of infringement, the government must demonstrate that the defendant exercised these exclusive rights of the owner.

Defendants may avail themselves of a number of statutory exceptions to infringement and limitations on exclusive rights including: reproduction of a limited number of copies by libraries and archives, certain exempted performances or displays, secondary transmissions of certain performances or displays to a controlled group, transmissions or distribution of ephemeral recordings, secondary transmissions of works by satellite carriers and networks for private home viewing, and reproduction and distribution of copies for blind and disabled people.[167] A further specific exemption allowing copying of computer programs for adaptation in order to use the program "in connection with a machine" or "for archival purposes" is codified at 17 U.S.C. § 117 (2000).

---

162. *See* 17 U.S.C. § 411(b) (2000).

163. A certificate of registration made within five years after the first publication of the work is prima facie evidence of the validity of the copyright under 17 U.S.C. § 410(c) (2000).

164. *See* 15 U.S.C. § 1115(b)(1) (2000).

165. *Id.* § 501(a) (2000).

166. *Id.* §§ 106, 106A (2000).

167. *See id.* §§ 108, 110-16, 118-19.

d. First Sale Doctrine

An affirmative defense (in most circuits) limiting the exclusive rights associated with copyright is the "first sale doctrine," which provides that a sale of a lawfully-made copy terminates the copyright owner's authority to restrict subsequent sales of distributions of that particular copy.[168] The doctrine, however, does not permit a purchaser of a lawful copy to reproduce or distribute additional copies of the work, and is unavailable to anyone who has acquired only possession of the copy at issue without also acquiring ownership of the copyrighted work.[169]

e. Fair Use Doctrine

Another defense to a claim of copyright infringement is the "fair use" doctrine,[170] which exempts from prosecution certain activities that actually further the purpose of copyright law, although they would otherwise constitute copyright infringement.[171] Fair use has been codified in Title 17:

> [T]he fair use of a copyrighted work ... for purposes such as criticism, comment, news reporting, teaching ... scholarship, or research, is not an infringement of copyright. In determining whether the use made of a work in any particular case is a fair use the factors to be considered shall include—
>
> (1) the purpose and character of the use, including whether such use is of a commercial nature or is for nonprofit educational purposes;
> (2) the nature of the copyrighted work;
> (3) the amount and substantiality of the portion used in relation to the copyrighted work as a whole; and
> (4) the effect of the use upon the potential market value for or value of the copyrighted work. The fact that a work is unpub-

---

168. *Id.* § 109(a) (2000). The Sixth and Ninth Circuits interpret the Copyright Act to require proof of the absence of a first sale, thereby viewing it as an element of the crime rather than an affirmative defense. *See, e.g.* U.S. v. Sachs, 801 F.2d 839 (6th Cir. 1986); U.S. v. Atherton, 561 F.2d 747, 749 (9th Cir. 1977).

169. *See* 17 U.S.C. § 109(d) (2000).

170. *See id.* § 107.

171. *See* Sony Corp. of America v. Universal City Studios, Inc., 464 U.S. 417, 477 (1984) ("There are situations ... in which strict enforcement of this monopoly would inhibit the very [goal] that copyright [was] intended to promote."). *See also* U.S. v. Morley, 348 F.3d 666, 668–69 (7th Cir. 2003).

lished shall not itself bar a finding of fair use if such finding is made upon consideration of all the above factors.[172]

The federal courts have considered these four factors in the context of alleged copyright infringement involving computers. The Ninth Circuit, for example, applied the fair use doctrine to a defendant copying of a video game object code through reverse engineering because the defendant company had a legitimate interest in determining how to make its game cartridges compatible with another video game console.[173] A First Circuit concurring opinion stated that defendant's use of Lotus' spreadsheet menu bar would constitute fair use even if such use otherwise constituted copyright infringement.[174]

However, the Seventh Circuit refused to apply the fair use doctrine in a case of Internet piracy.[175] In *U.S. v. Morley*, the defendant, along with other members of the group "Pirates with Attitude," unlawfully obtained and disseminated digital duplicates of commercially available software programs.[176] Morley alleged that the group committed such acts for educational and entertainment purposes, and did not charge members to download the software.[177] The Court found the transactions were not purely non-commercial because members had to offer their hacking or cracking services in order to obtain access to the software.[178] But even if the transaction was purely non-commercial, the remaining factors of the fair use test weigh against its application in cases of Internet piracy, commenting, "[i]t is preposterous to think that Internet piracy is authorized by virtue of the fair use doctrine."[179]

f. Copyright Misuse

A defendant may also raise the defense of copyright misuse to claims of copyright infringement involving computer software. When arguing copyright misuse, the defendant asserts that the owner is using the copyright in

---

172. 17 U.S.C. § 107 (2000).

173. *See* Sega Enterprises Ltd. v. Accolade, Inc., 977 F.2d 1510 (9th Cir. 1992).

174. *See* Lotus Dev. Corp. v. Borland Int., Inc., 49 F.3d 807, 821 (1st Cir. 1995) (Boudin, concurring), *aff'd*, 516 U.S. 233 (1996) (equally divided court).

175. *See* U.S. v. Morley, 348 F.3d 666, 668–69 (7th Cir. 2003).

176. *Id.* at 669.

177. *Id.*

178. *Id.* (the Court commented that Morley's arguments "barely pass the straight face test").

179. *Id.*

a manner violative of public policy.[180] The defense, if successful, renders the copyright unenforceable, but does not invalidate the copyright.[181] Originally applied in patent cases, the misuse defense is generally raised in cases where a copyright owner attempts to extend the scope of his or her exclusive rights beyond those granted under the Copyright Act.[182]

The copyright misuse defense was successfully raised in *Qad. Inc. v. ALN Assoc. Inc.*,[183] where the defendants had copied part of plaintiffs' software. Defendants raised the affirmative defense of misuse, arguing that plaintiffs improperly extended their ownership rights because in creating their software, plaintiffs had copied another company's software program.[184] Agreeing with the defendants, the court allowed the defense and found that plaintiffs had misused their copyright in trying to assert ownership rights over portions of their software that had been copied from someone else.[185] The court stressed that it " ... should not and will not offer its aid to a copyright holder whose actions run contrary to the purpose of the copyright itself."[186]

Generally, when applying the misuse defense, courts will analyze whether the copyright owner has in some way acted contrary to the public policy of copyright law or violated an anti-trust law. Where neither has occurred, courts will typically refuse to apply the misuse defense in cases involving computer software infringement. Further, since this defense only renders the copyright unenforceable rather than invalid, it is likely not useful as a defense but may be useful at sentencing to show the limited harm from the defendant's conduct.

3. Pseudo-Copyright Infringement

Congress has enacted statutes imposing copyright-like criminal penalties and creating offenses that may be charged along with copyright infringement.

---

180. *See* Lasercomb Am., Inc. v. Reynolds, 911 F.2d 970, 978 (4th Cir. 1990). *See generally*, Ralph D. Clifford, *Simultaneous Copyright and Trade Secret Claims: Can the Copyright Misuse Defense Prevent Constitutional Doublethink?*, 104 DICK. L.R. 247, 252–71 (2000).

181. *See* Morton Salt Co. v. G.S. Suppiger Co., 314 U.S. 488, 492–94 (1942).

182. *See* 4 MELVILLE B. NIMMER & DAVID NIMMER, NIMMER ON COPYRIGHT, § 13.09[A], at 13–284 (2000).

183. 770 F. Supp. 1261 (N.D. Ill. 1991), *aff'd*, 974 F.2d 834 (7th Cir. 1992).

184. *Id.* at 1265–66.

185. *Id.* at 1270.

186. *Id.*

a. Trafficking in Counterfeit Labels or Computer Program Documentation or Packaging

Section 2318 of Title 18 prohibits two distinct offenses: (1) trafficking in counterfeit labels affixed or designed to be affixed to a phonorecord, a copy of a computer program, or documentation or packaging of a computer program, a copy of a motion picture or other audiovisual work; and (2) trafficking in counterfeit documentation or packaging of a computer program.[187] Violators may be subject to a fine or imprisonment of no more than five years, or both.[188]

For purposes of the statute, "trafficking" means transferring, transporting or otherwise disposing of the materials.[189] The label, documentation or packaging must be shown to be counterfeit, meaning that it is created to appear genuine but is not, as opposed to a pirated copy, which is not made to look legitimate.[190]

b. Unauthorized Fixation of and Trafficking in Sound Recordings and Music Videos of Live Performance

If a live performance is not "fixed in any tangible medium of expression," the unauthorized recording of a live performance may not violate the performer's copyright in the performance.[191] Section 2319A protects live performances and criminalizes the making of unauthorized "bootleg" recordings of live performances.[192]

The statute criminalizes the recording of sounds or images of a performance, transmitting the sounds or images, or distributing or offering to

---

187. 18 U.S.C. § 2318(a) (2000) provides:
   Whoever, in any of the circumstances described in subsection (c) of this section, knowingly traffics in a counterfeit label affixed or designed to be affixed to a phonorecord, or a copy of a computer program or documentation or packaging for a computer program, or a copy of a motion picture or other audiovisual work, and whoever, in any of the circumstances described in subsection (c) of this section, knowingly traffics in counterfeit documentation or packaging for a computer program, shall be fined under this title or imprisoned for not more than five years, or both.

188. *Id.*

189. *Id.* § 2318(b)(2).

190. *See* U.S. v. Schultz, 482 F.2d 1179, 1180–81 (6th Cir. 1973).

191. An unauthorized recording would likely infringe a copyright on the underlying musical work. *Cf.* Broadcast Music, Inc. v. Claire Boutiques, Inc., 949 F.2d 1482, 1486 (7th Cir. 1991), *cert. denied*, 504 U.S. 911 (1992).

192. 18 U.S.C. § 2319A(a) (2000).

distribute or sell the sounds and images of a live musical performance.[193] The government must also show that the defendant acted knowingly, for purposes of commercial or financial gain, and without the consent of the performers.[194] Penalties under the statute for first time offenders include fines up to $250,000, five years imprisonment, or both and for repeat offenders include up to $250,000, ten years imprisonment, or both.[195]

4. Digital Millennium Copyright Act

The Digital Millennium Copyright Act[196] ["DMCA"] amended the Copyright Act to tackle copyright protection issues posed by digital information and the Internet. These amendments created two new criminal copyright offenses. Section 1201 protects against circumvention of technological measures used to protect copyright systems, which includes methods "to descramble a scrambled work, to decrypt an encrypted work, or otherwise to avoid, bypass, remove, deactivate, or impair a technological measure, without the authority of the copyright owner."[197] "Fair use" is a defense under section 1201.[198]

Section 1202 protects against the concealment of copyright infringement caused by tampering with copyright management information ["CMI"]. CMI includes: (1) identifying information about the work, author, owner or performer of the work; (2) the terms and conditions for the use of the work; (3) identifying numbers or symbols referring to such information, or links to such information; and (4) other information as prescribed by the Register of Copyrights by regulation.[199] First time offenders of Section 1201 or 1202 can be fined up to $500,000 and/or imprisoned for not more than five years.[200] A repeat offender may be fined up to $1,000,000 and/or imprisoned for not more than ten years.[201] Where nonprofit libraries, archives or educational institutions unknowingly commit violations, criminal penalties are not applied, but money damages may be awarded.[202]

---

193. *Id.*
194. *See id.*
195. *See id.*
196. Pub. L. No. 105-304 §§ 101–05, 112 Stat. 2872 (1998), *codified at* 17 U.S.C. §§ 1201–05 (2000).
197. 17 U.S.C. § 1201(a)(3)(A) (2000).
198. *Id.* § 1201(c)(1).
199. *Id.* § 1202(c).
200. *Id.* § 1204(a)(1).
201. *Id.* § 1204(a)(2).
202. *Id.* § 1203(b)(5)(B)(ii).

a. Constitutional Challenges to the DMCA

Challenges to the constitutionality of the DMCA have, thus far, failed. In *U.S. v. Elcom, Ltd.*,[203] defendant Elcomsoft sold a product called the eBook Processor that allowed users to remove the use restrictions from Adobe Acrobat PDF files and files formatted for the Adobe Acrobat eBook Reader. Elcomsoft moved to dismiss the indictment, challenging the DMCA's constitutionality on several grounds.

Elcomsoft argued that the DMCA violated the First Amendment as a content based restriction on speech that is over broad and unconstitutionally vague. The Court found that computer code is speech that is protected at some level by the First Amendment.[204] However, the Court rejected Elcomsoft's argument, finding that the DMCA prohibited certain code due to the function it performed rather than its content.[205] Additionally the Court held that there is no First Amendment right to fair use of a work, so any impact the DMCA may have on fair use does not render the DMCA unconstitutionally over broad.

5. *Fraudulent Copyright Notice and Removal of Such Notices*

Use of a notice of copyright informs the public of the copyright ownership and rights. Fraudulently using and/or removing such notices are distinct criminal offenses.[206] Violations of either section can lead to a fine of up to $2500.[207]

6. *False Representation in Application to Register Copyright*

In order to receive statutory damages for copyright infringement, a copyright owner must procure a registration of the copyright from the Library of Congress.[208] Section 506(e) prohibits the making of any false representations in an application to register a copyright.[209] The government must

---

203. 203 F. Supp. 2d 1111 (N.D. Cal. 2002).
204. *Id.* at 1126.
205. *Id.*
206. 17 U.S.C. § 506(c)-(d) (2000).
207. *Id.*
208. *Id.* § 411.
209. *Id.* § 506(e).

prove that the misstatement was material and that the defendant knowingly provided the erroneous information to the Copyright Office. Violations of this section can subject a defendant to a maximum fine of $2500.[210]

C. Child Pornography Prevention Act of 1996

In *Ashcroft v. Free Speech Coalition*,[211] the United States Supreme Court held certain provisions of the CPPA unconstitutional under the First Amendment. Specifically, the Supreme Court found that the section of the CPPA prohibiting "'any visual depiction, including any ... computer-generated image or picture' that 'is, or appears to be, of a minor engaging in sexually explicit conduct,'" to be over broad.[212] This decision implicitly found that the government cannot prohibit what has been termed "virtual child pornography" where computer generated images are used in place of actual children.

It remains unclear what type of showing the government must make with regards to the reality of the child in a computer image in order to convict a defendant under the CPPA.[213] The First Circuit confronted the issue in *U.S. v. Hilton*, holding first that the government must put on expert testimony to prove that the child involved was an actual child,[214] but quickly withdrew the opinion.[215] Upon rehearing the appeal, the Court found that since the trial court did not address the issue of whether the child was real, the defendant was entitled to habeas relief.[216] The Sixth Circuit also addressed this issue in *U.S. v. Farrelly*,[217] finding that the government was required to present the images to the jury and allow them to determine if the depictions were of actual children.[218] The defense never challenged the reality of the children, and the jury was instructed that they had to find the

---

210. *Id.*

211. Ashcroft v. Free Speech Coalition, 535 U.S. 234 (2002).

212. *Id.* at 234.

213. *See* U.S. v. Farrelly, 389 F.3d 649 (6th Cir. 2004); U.S. v. Hilton, 363 F.3d 58, 63–66 (1st Cir. 2004) (holding expert evidence required to show images are of real children), *withdrawn by* 2004 App. LEXIS 19528 (1st Cir. Sept. 20, 2004), *on rehearing*, 386 F.3d 13, 18–19 (1st Cir. Sept. 27, 2004) (affirming habeas relief because trial court did not make a finding of fact regarding the children involved).

214. U.S. v. Hilton, 363 F.3d 58 (1st Cir. 2004).

215. U.S. v. Hilton, 386 F.3d 13 (1st Cir. 2004).

216. *Id.* at 18–19.

217. U.S. v. Farrelly, 389 F.3d 649 (6th Cir. 2004).

218. *Id.*

images were of real children, therefore no additional evidence was necessary.

However, if the defendant raises the issue of the actuality of the children involved, the government may have to present expert witness testimony proving that the image in question is of a real child. The government indicates it intends to adopt that approach in *U.S. v. Frabizio*.[219] In *Frabizio*, the government intends to offer the testimony of Dr. Hany Farid who allegedly created a mathematical programming code that can supposedly determine whether electronic images of children are computer-generated or actual children.[220] As technology evolves, defendants may use this type of expert evidence to prove that images were computer generated and therefore not prohibited by law.

V. General Defenses to Cybercrime Allegations

A. Search and Seizure Issues[221]

1. Introduction

The advances in computer technology and emergence of computer-related crimes have presented some complex legal questions in the areas of personal privacy. With the rise of the computer as a primary tool in many criminal schemes, law enforcement officials have recognized that any search for incriminating evidence must now include a search of computer files and data, in addition to the areas traditionally searched. Additional concerns arise as an increasing number of people use computers to store private information and transmit personal messages. There is a growing risk that the government will invade private lives through electronic surveillance.

The legislature addressed some of these concerns with the enactment of statutes aimed at protecting the privacy of stored or transmitted computer data, such as the Electronic Communications Privacy Act ["ECPA"]. However, Congress amended ECPA through the USA PATRIOT Act of 2001[222]

---

219. U.S. v. Frabizio, 341 F. Supp. 2d 47 (D. Mass. 2004).

220. *Id.*

221. For further discussion of this topic *see generally* Raphael Winick, *Searches and Seizures of Computers and Computer Data*, 8 Harv. J.L. & Tech. 75 (1994) [hereinafter Winick, *Searches and Seizures*].

222. Uniting and Strengthening America by Providing Appropriate Tools Required to Intercept and Obstruct Terrorism Act of 2001 (USA PATRIOT Act), Pub. L. No. 107-56, 115 Stat. 272 (Oct. 26, 2001).

and the Homeland Security Act of 2002[223] to reduce restrictions on government access to electronic communications thereby removing some of the protections previously afforded electronic communications. The Fourth Amendment also provides constitutional protection by prohibiting unreasonable government searches and seizures. Each of these will be discussed in turn.

2. Federal Statutory Protection

a. ECPA — Interception of Electronic Communications[224]

ECPA protects wire and electronic communications affecting interstate commerce. In general, the government may intercept electronic communications within the meaning of ECPA only by obtaining prior judicial approval.[225] In order to obtain a judicial order, the government must show probable cause that certain communications linking defendant to an enumerated felony will be retrieved.[226] Additionally, statutory exceptions allow the government to intercept electronic communications in several specific instances, for example, where a party to the communication consents.[227]

ECPA allows for the suppression of unlawfully intercepted wire or oral communications, but does not make the same provision for the interception of electronic communications.[228] Although suppression of such evidence is not automatic, a criminal defendant may argue for a suppression order.[229] In addition, if the interception also violates the Fourth Amend-

---

223. Homeland Security Act, Pub. L. No. 109-296, 116 Stat. 2135 (Nov. 25, 2002).

224. See discussion of ECPA *supra* § II(B).

225. 18 U.S.C.A. § 2518 (2004). See discussion of what constitutes an interception of an electronic communication *supra* § II(B).

226. *Id.* § 2518(3). The USA PATRIOT Act added violations of the CFAA to the list of felonies for which the government may obtain an order allowing the interception of electronic communications.

227. The exceptions most often applied in computer cases are the (1) consent exception at § 2511(2)(c)-(d), (2) provider exception at § 2511(2)(a)(i), (3) the computer trespasser exception at § 2511(2)(I), (4) the extension telephone exception at § 2510(5)(a), (5) the inadvertently obtained criminal evidence exception at § 2511(3)(b)(iv), and (6) the accessible to the public exception at § 2511(2)(g)(i). For a discussion of these exceptions *see* C.C.I.P.S., *Searching and Seizing Computers and Obtaining Electronic Evidence in Criminal Investigations* IV(D) (2002), *available at* http://www.cybercrime.gov/s&smanual2002.htm#_IVD_.

228. 18 U.S.C.A. § 2518(10) (2004); *See* U.S. v. Steiger, 318 F.3d 1039 (11th Cir. 2003).

229. *Id.* § 2520(b)(1) (allowing "such preliminary and other equitable or declaratory relief as may be appropriate").

ment, a criminal defendant may still obtain exclusion of such evidence pursuant to the Fourth Amendment's exclusionary rule. ECPA also allows for money damages, which may include punitive damages and attorney's fees.[230]

b. Accessing Stored Electronic Communications

As previously discussed, the Stored Wire and Electronic Communications Act prohibits unauthorized access to stored electronic communications. The Act delineates specific procedures for the government to follow before stored electronic communications may be accessed. Where a communication is in electronic storage (unopened e-mail for example), a valid warrant is required before the government can access the content information.[231] Law enforcement officials may gain access to communications not in electronic storage through an administrative or grand jury subpoena, or through a court order, executed after notice has been given to the user.[232]

A government entity may obtain basic subscriber information from service providers through an administrative or grand jury subpoena.[233] The USA PATRIOT Act redefined basic subscriber information, which expanded the scope of information to which the government has access.[234] The USA PATRIOT Act also amended section 2702 to allow a service provider to voluntarily disclose basic subscriber or content information to a government entity without recourse if the provider reasonably believes that an emergency involving immediate danger of death or serious physical injury justifies disclosure.[235] The owner of a computer system may seek to quash an order to disclose by demonstrating that the communications demanded are too voluminous in nature or that compliance with the order is unduly burdensome.[236]

---

230. *Id.* § 2520.

231. *Id.* § 2703.

232. *Id.* § 2703(b)(1)(B).

233. *Id.* § 2703(c)(2).

234. Basic subscriber information includes, records of session times and durations, local or long distance telephone connection records, length and type of service, any temporarily assigned network address, and any means and source of payment including bank account and credit card numbers. *Id.* § 2703(c)(2); USA PATRIOT Act, Pub. L. No. 107-56, 115 Stat. 272, § 210 (Oct. 26, 2001).

235. 18 U.S.C.A. § 2702(c) (2004); USA PATRIOT Act, Pub. L. No. 107-56, 115 Stat. 272, § 210 (Oct. 26, 2001).

236. 18 U.S.C.A. § 2703(d) (2004).

Section 2709 permits the government to compel communications providers[237] to comply with a request for subscriber information or electronic communication transactional records made by the Director of the FBI in connection with an investigation "to protect against international terrorism or clandestine intelligence activities."[238] Section 2709(c) provides for penalties for the provider if the provider discloses the request to the subscriber or anyone else.[239] Recently, in *Doe v. Ashcroft*, Judge Marrero of the Southern District of New York held Section 2709 unconstitutional under the Fourth and First Amendments and enjoined the government from using the statute.[240] Judge Marrero found that the existence of the non-disclosure clause in effect authorized the government to conduct "coercive searches effectively immune from any judicial process, in violation of the Fourth Amendment."[241] Additionally, the Court found the non-disclosure clause constitutes an unconstitutional prior restraint and content-based restriction on speech.[242] Finally, the Court found that the non-disclosure clause could not be severed from the rest of section 2709, and so, the entire statute is invalid.[243] Currently, the extensive analysis by Judge Marrero provides defendants with powerful arguments that a search conducted under Section 2709 is unconstitutional.

c. Privacy Protection Act

The PPA limits the government ability to conduct intrusive searches of work product and documentary materials of those who disseminate public communications. The PPA restricts the government ability to carry out searches or seizures of materials connected to the media and others conducting First Amendment activities. The statute requires that government authorities use subpoenas, not warrants, when searching documents, and

---

237. Such as Internet service providers.

238. 18 U.S.C.A. § 2709(a)-(b) (2004); USA PATRIOT Act, Pub. L. No. 107-56, 115 Stat. 272, § 210 (Oct. 26, 2001). Prior to the USA PATRIOT Act amendments the government had to find that the information it seeks has a "nexus to a foreign power."

239. 18 U.S.C.A. § 2709(c) (2004).

240. Doe v. Ashcroft, 334 F. Supp. 2d 471 (S.D.N.Y. 2004).

241. *Id.* at 506.

242. *Id.* at 511–12. The government conceded that there are situations in which the need for secrecy does not exist or has become moot when the information is used publicly. The Court found that there could be less restrictive means to achieve the government's objective, such as requiring some sort of judicial review to determine the need for secrecy in individual cases.

243. *Id.* at 525–26. To date, no appeal has been filed.

computer systems of those who disseminate public communications. This prevents the government from conducting surprise searches of newspapers, broadcasters or other corporations who disseminate books or magazines to the public.[244] The PPA also prohibits government authorities from searching stand-alone computer systems that contain materials generated by the media or others disseminating public information, thereby eliminating a requirement under other privacy statutes that the computer be connected to a network affecting interstate commerce. Civil damages are the exclusive remedy for PPA violations, such that, evidence obtained in violation of the PPA will not be suppressed.

3. The Fourth Amendment

The Fourth Amendment protects citizens from unreasonable government searches and seizures. Most significantly, the Fourth Amendment requires that the government obtain a warrant before searching an area where an individual has a reasonable expectation of privacy. The warrant must be based on probable cause and particularly describe the place to be searched, and the persons or things to be seized.[245] Two exceptions to the warrant requirement that are particularly relevant to the area of computer searches and seizures are the "plain view" and "consent" exceptions.

The Fourth Amendment remains the principal basis of protection of stand-alone computers and the data or information stored on an individual computer from searches by the government. Individuals may generally assume a high expectation of privacy in their personal computers.[246] An individual's Fourth Amendment right is personal, however, and one can only claim an expectation of privacy in property he or she owns, possesses or controls.[247]

---

244. *See* 42 U.S.C. §§ 2000aa–2000aa-12 (2000).

245. U.S. Const. amend. IV.

246. Winick, *Searches and Seizures supra* note 221 at 103. (Home computers are exactly the sort of repositories of personal information that the Fourth Amendment protects most heavily).

247. *See* U.S. v. Taylor, No. 92 CR 322, 1992 WL 249969, at *19 (S.D.N.Y. Sept. 22, 1992) (One defendant attempted to challenge the search of a co-defendant computer. The court found that because the defendant did not present evidence of any ownership or possessory interest in the computer searched, she lacked standing to challenge the search.).

A search warrant must describe the place to be searched and the items to be seized with particularity.[248] The particularity requirement ensures the governments search is limited to suspected criminal activity and informs the defendant of the limits of the search.[249] The particularity requirement is important in cases of computer searches because such searches can turn into sweeping examinations of a wide array of information. Often, the government argues successfully that a computer search must be broad because files can be encrypted or mislabeled in order to evade detection.[250] However, the government has tools to limit the search to the scope of probable cause and should be made to use them.[251] "Given the wide variety of information stored on almost any computer network, it is highly unlikely if not impossible that the government can establish probable cause to believe the entire computer media is filled with evidence of criminal activity."[252] Despite the arguments made on both sides, courts differ in what they consider particularity when it comes to computer searches. While some courts have held that a search of hard disk space lacked particularity, others have found that warrants for seizure of all computer hardware and software were valid.[253]

The scope of a search may also be challenged for over breadth, where a defendant argues that the scope of the search exceeded the specific things and area for which there was probable cause to search.[254] Law enforcement

---

248. Groh v. Ramirez, 540 U.S. 551 (2004). *See* Andresen v. Maryland, 427 U.S. 463 (1976); Coolidge v. New Hampshire, 403 U.S. 443, 467 (1971); U.S. v. Carey, 172 F.3d 1268, 1271 (10th Cir. 1999) ("The Fourth Amendment requires that a search warrant describe the things to be seized with sufficient particularity to prevent a general exploratory rummaging in a person's belongings.").

249. U.S. v. Meek, 366 F.3d 705, 714 (9th Cir. 2004).

250. U.S. v. Carey, 172 F.3d 1268, 1272 (10th Cir. 1999); Amy Baron-Evans, *When the Government Seizes and Searches Your Client's Computer, available at* http://www.dwyercollora.com/articles/ACCAComputerArticleFINAL.pdf (last visited May 6, 2005) [hereinafter Baron-Evans, *Your Client's Computer*].

251. U.S. v. Carey, 172 F.3d at 1272. Law enforcement can limit searches by searching using filenames, directories, specific names, key words and phrases, file dates and times, and specific compartments of the hard drive.

252. *Id.*

253. *See* In re Grand Jury Subpoena Duces Tecum, 846 F. Supp. 11, 13–14 (S.D.N.Y. 1994). *See also* U.S. v. Hersch, CR-A-93-10339-2, 1994 WL 568728, at *1 (D. Mass. Sept. 27, 1994).

254. Maryland v. Garrison, 480 U.S. 79, 84 (1987).

officers must avoid searching files or data not identified in the warrant.[255] The over breadth analysis is applied to subpoenas as well as warrants. In *In re Grand Jury Subpoena Duces Tecum*, the defendants challenged a grand jury subpoena requiring the production of computer disks that contained relevant, as well as irrelevant information.[256] The court quashed the subpoena as over broad, noting that because a keyword search could have identified the relevant files, there was no need to subpoena all of the computer disks.[257]

Other courts have interpreted warrants as allowing authorities to search and seize *all* computers and data where the warrant did not specify which records were to be searched.[258] In *United States v. Sissler*, authorities acting pursuant to a warrant allowing for the search and seizure of records of drug transactions were allowed to seize a personal computer and a large number of disks.[259] The court also concluded that the search could be performed off-site because breaking through the computer's security devices would involve greater effort.[260] Additionally, a search can be performed by non-law enforcement entities. In *U.S. v. Bach*,[261] the Court upheld the seizure of the defendant's e-mail where officials simply sent the warrant to Yahoo! and had Yahoo! employees execute the warrant. If a search conducted is over broad, the defendant may move to suppress only the improperly seized evidence.[262] The defendant can move for suppression of all evidence only where the agent flagrantly disregarded the requirements of the warrant. In order to establish a flagrant disregard for the warrant the defendant must show the government "effected a widespread seizure of items not within the scope of the warrant and did not act in good faith."[263]

---

255. U.S. v. Walser, 275 F.3d 981, 986 (10th Cir. 2001).

256. 846 F. Supp. at 11.

257. *Id.* at 13.

258. *See* U.S. v. Musson, 650 F. Supp. 525, 531–32 (D. Colo. 1986) (allowing seizure of over 50 computer disks).

259. No. 90-CR-12, 1991 WL 239001 (W.D. Mich. Aug. 30, 1991), *aff'd*, 966 F.2d 1455, (6th Cir. 1992) (unpublished disposition), *cert. denied*, 506 U.S. 1079 (1993).

260. *Id.* at *4. *See* U.S. v. Campos, 221 F.3d 1143, 1147 (10th Cir. 2001). In *Campos*, the court quoted at length the FBI's explanation of why it is not usually feasible to search for computer files in a person home. The FBI stated that "[s]earching computer systems for criminal evidence is a highly technical process requiring expert skill and a properly controlled environment." 221 F.3d at 1147.

261. U.S. v. Bach, 310 F.3d 1063 (8th Cir. 2002).

262. U.S. v. George, 975 F.2d 72, 75 (2nd Cir. 1992).

263. U.S. v. Triumph Capital Group, Inc., 2002 U.S. Dist. LEXIS 21615 at *88 (D. Conn. 2002).

a. Intermingled Documents

The increasing focus of searches and seizures on computers and electronic data by authorities have increased the risk that a search will uncover not only information relevant to the investigation, but also personal information that is intermingled in the relevant documents. Preventing such widespread searches is precisely the purpose of the warrant requirement of the Fourth Amendment.

In *United States v. Tamura*, the Ninth Circuit announced a general rule to deal with the issues surrounding the search of intermingled documents.[264] The court held that when officers find relevant documents so intermingled with irrelevant documents, as they often are in computer directories, that they cannot reasonably be sorted at the site, they should seal off or hold the documents until a magistrate can either sort them out or authorize a broader search.[265]

The *Tamura* rule has been applied to computer searches involving intermingled documents.[266] This rule allows authorities to remove the computer hardware and data before evidence can be altered or destroyed. At the same time, it accounts for individual privacy interests because once the authorities have control over the information, the files to be searched must be specified, preventing a widespread search of all the data seized.[267] Once the computer data or hardware is lawfully seized, authorities may access password protected information and defeat other security devices or encryption methods without obtaining another warrant. The government must return the equipment when the search of computer hardware, data or software is complete.[268] An individual may petition the court for return of the property, and where the government destroys or loses seized property, an aggrieved party may be entitled to damages.[269]

b. Plain View Doctrine

The "plain view" doctrine was first announced in *Coolidge v. New Hampshire*, and allows for the warrantless seizure of evidence of a crime if the of-

---

264. 694 F.2d 591 (9th Cir. 1982).
265. *See id.* at 595–96.
266. *See* U.S. v. Carey, 172 F.3d 1268 (10th Cir. 1999) (applying the *Tamura* doctrine to computer search).
267. *See* U.S. v. Campos, 221 F.3d 1143, 1148 (10th Cir. 2000).
268. Fed. R. Crim. P. 41(d).
269. *Id.* 41(e).

ficer lawfully obtained a plain view of the object, if the object's incriminating character was immediately apparent, and if the officer had lawful access to the object itself.[270] The doctrine has been applied in cases where the search of a computer pursuant to a valid warrant led to the discovery of other computer files not specified in the warrant.

In *United States v. Carey*, the court concluded that the "plain view" exception to the warrant requirement did not authorize a detective to open computer files that were not clearly specified in the warrant itself.[271] The police obtained a warrant to search the defendant's computer files for "documentary evidence pertaining to the sale and distribution of controlled substances."[272] While searching, a detective noticed image files with sexually suggestive titles.[273] Unable to find drug-related files, the detective continued to look by opening one of the image files, saw that it contained child pornography, and proceeded to download the rest of the child pornography files.[274]

Convicted of possessing child pornography, the defendant appealed, claiming that the detective exceeded the scope of the search because the warrant provided for the search of drug-related materials only. The government claimed that the "plain view" exception applied and compared the computer search to looking for drug-related documents in a file cabinet and finding child pornography instead.[275] The court disagreed and stated that the plain view exception did not apply because the *contents* of the files were seized, not the files themselves.[276] The court added that because the detective had originally obtained a warrant, he knew he was acting without judicial authority when he abandoned the search for drug-related evidence.[277]

The court limited it's holding only to the image files opened *after* the inadvertent opening of the first file and stated that the image files in this case were closed and not in plain view. The court declined to answer the question as to what *would* constitute a plain view exception in the context of

---

270. 403 U.S. 443, 465 (1971).
271. 172 F.3d 1268, 1273 (10th Cir. 1999).
272. *Id.* at 1270.
273. *See id.* at 1270–71.
274. *See id.*
275. *Id.* at 1272.
276. *Id.* at 1273.
277. *Id.*

computer text files, where an officer might have to begin reading the files before determining their relevancy to the original search.

c. Consent Searches

A defendant may also challenge the validity of computer searches consented to by a business or an individual for exceeding the scope of the consent given. The scope of consent is measured by an objective reasonableness standard, and the court will look at what a reasonable person would have understood the consent to mean.[278] In *United States v. Turner*, the First Circuit held that a police search of the defendant's computer files exceeded the scope of the consent given, which objectively included only a search for incriminating objects in connection with the sexual assault of the defendant's neighbor.[279] In *Turner*, the defendant signed a consent authorizing police to search his apartment for evidence that the suspect of the assault had been inside the apartment.[280] While searching the apartment, the detective saw a photograph of a nude woman on the computer screen and, without obtaining a warrant, searched the computer hard drive and found evidence of child pornography.[281] Measuring the scope of consent by an "objective" reasonableness standard, the First Circuit affirmed the suppression of the computer files and held that the entire search was beyond the scope of the consent.[282]

The government in *Turner* also tried to argue that because the initial nude image was in "plain view," the rest of the files were "fair game" under the consensual search.[283] The court rejected this argument because the detectives did not tell the defendant the nature of the crime they were investigating. Therefore, the defendant could not have believed that his consent would include a search of evidence of a sexual nature.[284]

Additionally, giving consent to seize a computer does not give consent to search the files on the computer.[285] In *U.S. v. Carey*, the defendant con-

---

278. Florida v. Jimeno, 500 U.S. 248, 251 (1991).
279. 169 F.3d 84 (1st Cir. 1999).
280. *See id.* at 86.
281. *See id.*
282. *See id.* at 88.
283. *See id.*
284. *See id.*
285. Carey, 172 F.3d at 1274. *See* Baron-Evans, *Your Client's Computer, supra* note 250.

sented to the seizure of any property that may be evidence of his crime, however, officers needed to obtain a search warrant to search the seized items, including defendant's computer.[286] However, in *U.S. v. Al-Marri*,[287] a court interpreted the scope of the defendant's consent to the seizure of his laptop computer by the FBI very broadly.[288]

In *Al-Marri*, the FBI suspected the defendant of terrorist activity. In the course of a search of the defendant's home, FBI officials found a laptop computer and asked if they could take it back to their offices to "take a look at it," and the defendant consented. The FBI subsequently took the laptop, made several copies of the hard drive, analyzed the data on the computer to identify current and deleted files, and examined the Internet search engine's bookmarks.[289]

The defendant argued that this extensive search exceeded the scope of his consent to seize the computer. The court held that Al-Marri's consent to seize the computer extended to the search of his hard drive. The court found Al-Marri, a graduate student of computer science, should have realized the search would be "more than superficial" and he failed to object or place limits on the search at any time.[290] Additionally, after being interrogated at FBI offices, the defendant asked if he could have his computer back, to which the officials responded no. The court found that the defendant's acceptance of this answer without protest constituted more evidence that he consented to the FBI's search of the computer.[291]

The Court also found that the defendant's consent to search his home extended to his computer. Therefore, the search was constitutional regardless of whether the government's search exceeded the scope of consent or not with regard to the computer. The Court found that generally courts treat computers as closed containers, and therefore, government officials

---

286. Carey, 172 F.3d at 1274.

287. U.S. v. Al-Marri, 230 F. Supp. 2d 535 (S.D.N.Y. 2002).

288. *Id.*

289. *Id.* at 537.

290. *Id.* The court commented that Al-Marri was a graduate student in computer science and he was aware of the technology that could be used to search a computer. When the officers requested to take the computer with them, they stated that they did not personally have the expertise to search the computer, therefore, Al-Marri should have drawn the conclusion that they were going to conduct an extensive search.

291. *Id.* at 540 ("If Al-Marri had any need for use for use of the computer, or felt any reservation or objection about the FBI's prolonged retention of it, a reasonable person would have expected Al-Marri to ask for the computer to be restored to him within a specified time frame for whatever reason justified a prompt return.").

need not obtain separate consent to search closed containers within fixed premises.[292] Based on this analysis, the court found that the FBI was entitled to search Al-Marri's computer because he consented to a search of his apartment in which they found the computer.[293] However, the court's analysis focused on the law regarding the search of closed containers in automobile searches, which can and should be distinguished from searches involving computers and computer files.[294]

Another issue in consent cases, is whether the individual giving the consent had authority to do so. Generally, a third party may consent to the search of property he or she has joint access or control over.[295] Co-users of a computer may give consent for a search of the computer; however, there are limits to this authority. For example, a user of a shared computer does not have authority to consent to a search of password protected files of another user.[296]

d. Privilege

Searches of business premises, and particularly business computers, can lead to the seizure of attorney-client material that is privileged. Law enforcement agencies have also recognized the potential consequences in court of obtaining privileged material when executing a search warrant and have in many cases implemented "taint" procedures to minimize such a risk. Common "taint" procedures contemplate that agents executing a search

---

292. *Id.* at 541.

293. *Id.* Subsequently, Al-Marri was charged with violations of 18 U.S.C. § 1029 in connection with suspected credit card fraud. President Bush named Al-Marri an enemy combatant in December, 2003, and he is currently being held on a South Carolina naval base. Al-Marri is currently challenging his detention. The Seventh Circuit denied Al-Marri's request to pursue his case in Illinois, Al-Marri v. Rumsfeld, 360 F.3d 707 (7th Cir. 2004), and directed him to file in South Carolina where he is currently being detained. Al-Marri filed a petition for writ of habeas corpus and motion requesting immediate access to counsel in the South Carolina District Court. Al-Marri v. Hanfet, C.A. No. 2:04-2257, (D.S.C. 2004).

294. *Id;* Baron-Evans, *Your Client's Computer supra* note 250.

295. U.S. v. Matlock, 415 U.S. 164 (1974).

296. Trulock v. Freeh, 275 F.3d 391, 402–03 (4th Cir. 2001). *See* COMPUTER CRIME AND INTELLECTUAL PROPERTY SECTION, CRIMINAL DIVISION, UNITED STATES DEPARTMENT OF JUSTICE, SEARCHING AND SEIZING COMPUTERS AND OBTAINING ELECTRONIC EVIDENCE IN CRIMINAL INVESTIGATIONS § I(C)(1)(b) (2002), *available at* http://www.cybercrime.gov/s&smanual2002.htm. The DOJ states that a third party has authority to consent to search of password protected files if the user gave the password to the third party.

warrant should seize attorney-client materials, and then review those documents only to determine if they are potentially privileged. Potentially privileged documents are then to be segregated and delivered to an attorney (not involved in the investigation) who, in turn, reviews the contents of each potentially privileged document to determine if it is in fact protected by the attorney-client privilege.[297]

These "taint" procedures are often insufficient to protect privileged materials because during the search, case agents are still reviewing and handling the most sensitive communications between counsel and clients relating to the underlying investigation. Generally, defendants should move for an alternative procedure to protect privilege as soon as a warrant is issued.[298] In the alternative, defendants can challenge the search and demand the return of the documents or even disqualification of tainted case agents.

The court in *United States v. Lin Lyn Trading, Ltd.*,[299] supported the return of privileged documents and disqualification of tainted case agents. In that case, the government unlawfully seized a yellow notepad that contained privileged communications between the defendants and their attorney.[300] The notepad included incriminating statements and defenses relevant to the investigation. Defense counsel moved for a return of the notepad.[301] The district judge returned the notepad finding that it had been unlawfully seized and that the government's possession of it would cause irreparable injury.[302]

One month later, the defendants were indicted for various federal offenses and they moved to suppress the notepad and all evidence seized after that date claiming the illegally seized notepad provided a "roadmap" for the

---

297. *See* U.S. v. Triumph Capital Group, Inc., 2002 U.S. Dist. LEXIS 21615 *27–36 (D. Conn. Nov. 4, 2002) ("The use of a taint team is a proper, fair and acceptable method of protecting privileged communications when a search involves property of an attorney.").

298. Baron-Evans, *Your Client's Computer supra* note 250 at 15 (The "better option in a computer search is to have the defense team, with the aid of its own expert, screen all the data the computer specialist wishes to search before he searches it, and to have a judicial officer make the final determination as to anything in dispute."). Defendants may request a judicial officer or a special master to review the documents. *See* Black v. U.S., 172 F.R.D. 511 (S.D. Fla. 1997); U.S. v. Abbell, 914 F. Supp. 519 (S.D. Fla. 1995); U.S. v. Hunter, 13 F. Supp. 2d 574 (Vt. 1998).

299. 149 F.3d 1112 (10th Cir. 1998).

300. *See id.* at 1113

301. *See id.* at 1113–14.

302. *See id.* at 1114.

investigation.[303] The district court dismissed the indictment.[304] The Tenth Circuit recognized that the intentional seizure of privileged materials by government agents could violate the Fifth Amendment but adopted a remedy less drastic than dismissing the indictment.[305] That court held that there was "nothing to forbid the government from beginning a new investigation using the evidence legitimately acquired prior to [the seizure of the yellow notepad], and conducted by personnel—both investigatory and prosecutorial—untouched by the taint of the yellow notepad."[306]

e. Production of Seized Documents

Pursuant to Fed. R. Crim. P. 16(a)(1)(E) the defendant should request all evidence pertaining to the government's search in order to know the scope and methodology of the government's search. The defendant should move for all written records of the search as well as the physical evidence of the search, such as the mirror image of the hard drive and the working copy that the government searched. In the case the government created multiple working copies, the defendant should request that each one be preserved.[307]

In a child pornography case, the government has successfully argued that it would be unlawful to produce search results because production would constitute unlawful dissemination of child pornography.[308] Instead, courts have required the defendant to review the material at government offices, making meaningful review by a defense expert almost impossible.[309] However, recent decisions have rejected this argument finding that the defendant would be overly burdened by the government's refusal to produce the documents.[310] In U.S. v. Hill the Court found that the "defendant will be seriously prejudiced if his expert and counsel do not have copies of the materials."[311] In Hill, the defense presented evidence that the defense expert

---

303. See id.
304. See id. at 1115
305. See id. at 1117–18.
306. See id. at 1118.
307. See U.S. v. Triumph, 2002 U.S. Dist. LEXIS 21615 at *64–65 (D. Conn. Nov. 4, 2002) (court ordered government officials to preserve existing and future working copies of defendant's hard drive).
308. U.S. v. Kimbrough, 69 F.3d 723, 731 (5th Cir. 1995).
309. Id. See, Baron-Evans, Your Client's Computer supra note 250.
310. U.S. v. Hill, 322 F. Supp. 2d 1081, 1091 (C.D. Cal. 2004); U.S. v. Frabizio, 341 F. Supp. 2d 47 (D. Mass. 2004).
311. Hill, 322 F. Supp. 2d at 1091.

would have to make several out of state trips to view the information and would be precluded from using his own tools to review the information.[312] In these cases, any concern the court may have regarding the further dissemination of the materials can be satisfied with a protective order restricting access to the defense expert and defense counsel.[313]

B. Other Defenses

1. Anonymity

The degree of anonymity that computers and the Internet provide is unparalleled. A computer user's ability to be completely anonymous has significantly affected the criminal law, presenting challenges to law enforcement because computer users can attempt to hide behind false identities and screen names when carrying out illegal activity on a computer.[314] In fact, various services offered on the Internet "guarantee" anonymity.

Anonymous remailers are on-line systems designed to give a user an anonymous address to which people can send e-mail.[315] When the electronic mail is received at the anonymous address, it is then forwarded to the user's "real address." Anonymous remailers can also post or e-mail an individual's electronic messages without any trace of the sender's name or address.

A user's anonymity can be especially problematic in cases where a virus has been released on a system and law enforcement officials are looking for the author. In *United States v. Morris*,[316] the government faced this challenge with the investigation and prosecution of a Cornell University graduate student. In 1988, Morris released a "worm" from a computer at the Massachusetts Institute of Technology ["MIT"], intending to demonstrate the deficient security measures on the system and the ease with which the security could be bypassed.[317] The worm was released at MIT so as to disguise that

---

312. *Id.*

313. *Id*; Fabrizio, 341 F. Supp. 2d 47 (D. Mass. 2004).

314. *See* A. Michael Froomkin, *Flood Control on the Information Ocean: Living with Anonymity, Digital Cash, and Distributed Databases*, 15 J.L. & Com. 395, 398 (1996) ("the availability of anonymous electronic communication directly affects the ability of governments to regulate electronic transactions over the Internet (both licit and illicit).").

315. One of the most famous anonymous servers on the Internet is Anon.penet.fi with over 500 users in the database.

316. 928 F.2d 504 (2d Cir.), *cert. denied*, 502 U.S. 817 (1991).

317. *Id.* at 506.

it came from Morris at Cornell.[318] The worm spread quickly, causing severe damage to the computer networks.

The government's search for the author proved problematic because Morris had the advantage of anonymity. Once the defendant became a suspect, officials found copies of the worm that had been saved on the backup copies of his account. However, it was only when the defendant subsequently confessed, and the government was able to show that the defendant was logged on to his account at the time the worm was released, that the government was able to conclusively show that the defendant was the only author of the worm. In every case, "identity" thus becomes a crucial issue to pursue in the defense of an alleged cybercrime.

2. *First Amendment As a Defense to Computer Crime*[319]

Computer use, including the Internet, has presented new challenges to the protections of the First Amendment. An attempt can be made to cast certain activities on the computer as constitutionally protected speech, not crime. "At the heart of the First Amendment lies the principle that each person should decide for him or herself the ideas and beliefs deserving of expression, consideration, and adherence. Our political system and cultural life rest upon this idea."[320]

Computer programs and encryption codes do not fit neatly under the traditional definition of protected speech, but those definitions are being expanded. The U.S. District Court for the Northern District of California, for example, held that the source code for a computer cryptography program was protectable speech under the First Amendment.[321] The State Department argued that the code was not entitled to protection because it was not intended to convey a particular message and was functional, not communicative.[322] The court nevertheless found the code to be language, which "is by definition speech, and the regulation of any language is the regulation of speech."[323]

---

318. *Id.*

319. See prior discussion of First Amendment defenses in specific context *supra* §§ IV(A)(3)(a)(4), & IV(B)(4)(a).

320. Turner Broadcasting Sys. v. F.C.C., 512 U.S. 622, 641 (1994).

321. *See* Bernstein v. U.S. Dept. of State, 922 F. Supp. 1426 (N.D. Cal. 1996), *aff'd,* 176 F.3d 1132 (9th Cir.), *opinion withdrawn & hearing en banc ordered,* 192 F.3d 1308 (9th Cir. 1999), *decided,* No. C. 95-0582, (N.D. Cal. July 28, 2003). *See also* Junger v. Daley, 209 F.3d 481 (6th Cir. 2000).

322. *See* Bernstein, 922 F. Supp. at 1434.

323. *See id.* at 1435.

Simply falling under the definition of speech, however, is not enough to warrant First Amendment protection. Although not disputing that a computer program *may* constitute speech, in a criminal case, the Ninth Circuit denied First Amendment protection to a program because it was not *protected* speech.[324] For speech to be protected there must be "some evidence that the defendants' speech was information in a manner removed from immediate connection to the commission of a specific criminal act."[325] Because the computer program in question was not directed to any ideas or consequences other than committing a crime, the defendants' First Amendment claim was denied.[326] When appropriate, a defendant's conduct may be characterized as protected expression rather than criminal activity.

3. Entrapment

While the opportunity for anonymity on the Internet gives criminals the advantage of hiding behind pseudonyms, it also provides undercover officers with the same advantage in tracking criminals on the Internet.

Law enforcement officials are increasingly using undercover officers to "patrol" the Internet, especially in child pornography cases. Undercover officers have entered chat rooms and posted messages feigning interest in child pornography with the intent to catch child molesters and other sexual offenders. But such tactics may provide the basis for a claim of entrapment, at which point it is up to the government to show that the defendant was predisposed to commit the crime before the undercover agent entered the picture.

The Supreme Court has stated that "[i]n their zeal to enforce the law ... Government agents may not originate a criminal design, implant in an innocent person's mind the disposition to commit a criminal act, and then induce commission of the crime so that the Government may prosecute."[327] On the other hand, "the fact that officers or employees of the Government merely afford opportunity or facilities for the commission of the offense does not defeat the prosecution."[328] The Ninth Circuit has applied this analysis to solicitation by the government through a computer.[329]

---

324. *See* U.S. v. Mendelsohn, 896 F.2d 1183, 1185 (9th Cir. 1990).
325. *See id.*
326. *See id.* at 1185–86.
327. Jacobson v. U.S., 503 U.S. 540, 548 (1992).
328. *See id.* (quoting Sorrells v. U.S., 287 U.S. 435, 441 (1932)).
329. *See* U.S. v. Poehlman, 217 F.3d 692 (9th Cir. 2000).

In *United States v. Poehlman*, the defendant, while searching "alternative lifestyle" Internet sites for adult companions, encountered a government agent posing as a mother seeking a "sexual mentor" for her three daughters. He was convicted of crossing state lines to engage in sex acts with a minor.[330] The defendant appealed, claiming that he was induced by the government to commit the crime and that he was not otherwise predisposed to do so.[331] Looking at the defendant's state of mind prior to his contact with the government agent, the Ninth Circuit found no evidence that the defendant was predisposed to engage in sexual relations with minors and reversed the conviction.[332] Thus, keeping courts focused on the outer limits of acceptable Government conduct provides opportunities to defend cybercrime cases.

VI. Conclusion

Defense of cybercrime cases continues to evolve as the Government enacts more statutes, increases the penalties and becomes more aggressive in its investigative techniques. In every situation, counsel and the court is faced with analyzing long established protections for individual rights—free speech, freedom from search, no entrapment—in the context of new technologies, putting a premium on effective and creative advocacy.

---

330. *See id.* at 697.
331. *See id.* at 698.
332. *See id.* at 705.

CHAPTER FIVE

INTERNATIONAL CYBERCRIME: RECENT DEVELOPMENTS IN THE LAW

MIRIAM F. MIQUELON WEISMANN[*]

The Internet is fast, whereas criminal law systems are slow and formal. The Internet offers anonymity, whereas criminal law systems require identification of perpetrators.... The Internet is global, whereas criminal law systems are generally limited to a specific territory. Effective prosecution with national remedies is all but impossible in a global space.[1]

Ensuring the safety and security of networked information systems—what we call cybersecurity—is very important to the United States ... cybersecurity is very different from traditional national security issues. The government alone cannot ensure secu-

* Associate Professor, Southern New England School of Law, formerly United States Attorney Southern District of Illinois. Served as Assistant Special Counsel to the Office of Special Counsel, John C. Danforth, WACO Investigation. Has authored and taught for the U.S. Department of Justice. A very special thanks to Cathryn O'Neill,(JD, MLIS), Reference Librarian, Southern New England School of Law, for her research assistance and commentary.

1. Interview with Ulrich Sieber, Head of the Max Planck Institute for Foreign and International Criminal Law, Freiburg, Germany (Sept. 9, 2004), *available at* http://www.coe.int/t/e/com/files/interviews/20040910_interv_sieber.asp (last visited Nov. 10, 2004).

rity—we must have partnerships within our societies and around
the world.[2]

I. Introduction

Both international cybercrime and domestic cybercrime embrace the
same offense conduct, namely, computer related crimes and traditional offense conduct committed through the use of a computer.[3] The distin-
guishing, and most complicating, feature in the international arena is the
commission of the offense conduct across the territorial borders of sovereign nations, often by the mere click of a button. The resulting transfor-
mation from local to global crime raises numerous jurisdictional problems
and can create barriers to investigation and enforcement.

This chapter examines the current state of international law and the existing tools available for mutual cooperation; the workings of the proposed
treaty provisions of the Council of Europe Convention on Cybercrime, the
only existing treaty governing international enforcement and cooperation;
mutual legal assistance agreements; proposed recommendations by the
United Nations; the emergence of organized crime; and the application of
constitutional protections by U.S. courts.

II. In Search of a Definition

The ongoing debate among experts about what precisely constitutes a
"computer crime" or a "computer related crime" remains unresolved.[4]
There is no internationally recognized legal definition of these terms.[5] Instead, functional definitions identifying general offense categories are the

---

2. Lincoln Bloomfield, *U.S. Says Cybersecurity is a Global Responsibility*, Address to
the Southeastern European Cybersecurity Conference in Sophia, Bulgaria (Sept. 8, 2003),
available at http://usinfo.org/wf-archive/2003/030909/epf213.htm (last visited Nov. 8,
2004).

3. *See* Chapter Two, *infra.*

4. *See* Chapter Two, § II, *infra.*

5. International Review of Criminal Policy-United Nations Manual on the
Prevention and Control of Computer Related Crime ¶ 7 (1995), [hereinafter U.N.
Manual], *available at* http://www.uncjin.org/Documents/EighthCongress.html (last
visited Nov. 8, 2004).

accepted norms.[6] Thus, the focus shifts away from reaching global consensus over particular legal definitions to identifying general categories of offense conduct to be enacted as penal legislation by each participating country.

The offense conduct characterizing international cybercrime includes not only specific computer related crimes but also the use of the computer to commit a wide variety of traditional crimes that may also be committed through means other than by the use of a computer. Regardless of the particular label assigned by any one country to its penal legislation, the targeted unlawful conduct falls into several generally recognized categories. These categories were identified by the United Nations[7] as part of its study of cybercrime and include: fraud by computer manipulation,[8] computer forgery,[9] damage to or modifications of computer data or programs,[10] unauthorized

---

6. *Id.*

7. *See id.* ¶ 13. Interestingly, the categories of computer crime identified in the U.N. MANUAL in 1995 appear to serve as the model for the same offense conduct targeted by the Council of Europe Convention on Cybercrime. This treaty is discussed at point V, *infra.*

8. *See id.* ¶¶ 13–14. Intangible assets represented in data format, such as money on deposit and confidential consumer information, are the most common targets. Improved remote access to databases allows the criminal the opportunity to commit various types of fraud without ever physically entering the victim's premises. The U.N. MANUAL underscores the fact that computer fraud by input manipulation is the most common computer crime, as it is easily perpetrated and difficult to detect. Often referred to as "data diddling" it can be committed by anyone having access to normal data processing functions at the input stage. The U.N. MANUAL also identifies "program manipulation" through the use of a "Trojan Horse" covertly placed in a computer program to allow unauthorized functions and "output manipulation" targeting the output of computer information as other examples of unlawful manipulation.

9. *See id.* ¶ 14. Computer forgery can occur in at least two ways:1) altering data in documents stored in a computerized form; and, 2) using the computer as a tool to commit forgery through the creation of false documents indistinguishable from the authentic original.

10. *See id.* ¶ 15. This is a form of "computer sabotage" perpetrated by either direct or covert unauthorized access to a computer system by the introduction of new programs known as viruses, worms or logic bombs. A "virus" is a program segment that has the ability to attach itself to legitimate programs, to alter or destroy data or other programs, and to spread itself to other computer programs. A "worm" is similarly constructed to infiltrate and harm data processing systems, but it differs from a virus in that it does not replicate itself. A "logic bomb" is normally installed by an insider based on

access to computer systems and service,[11] and the unauthorized reproduction of legally protected computer programs.[12] Added to this list are child pornography[13] and the use of computers by members of organized crime and terrorist groups to commit computer related crimes and/or a wide variety of crimes involving traditional offense conduct.[14]

---

a specialized knowledge of the system and programs the destruction or modification of data at a specific time in the future. All three can be used as an ancillary part of a larger extortionate scheme that can involve financial gain or terrorism.

11. *See id.* ¶ 16. The motives of the "cracker" or "hacker" may include sabotage or espionage. Access is often accomplished from a remote location along a telecommunication network. Access can be accomplished through several means including insufficiently secure operating system software, lax security, "cracker programs" used to bypass passwords or obtain access through the misuse of legitimate maintenance entry points in the system, or activating illicitly installed "trap doors on the system."

12. *See id.* The problem has reached transnational dimensions through the trafficking of unauthorized reproductions over modern telecommunication networks at a substantial economic loss to the owners.

13. In 1996, the Stockholm World Congress Against the Commercial Exploitation of Children examined the recommendations and proposed initiatives in many countries and regions. In September 1999, the Austria International Child Pornography Conference drafted the Convention on the Rights of the Child, building on the Stockholm World Congress initiatives, to combat child pornography and exploitation on the Internet. U.S. Department of Justice, Computer Crime and Intellectual Property Section (CCIPS), *International Aspects of Computer Crime* § C(6) (2003), *available at* http://www.cybercrime.gov/intl.html (last visited Dec. 6, 2004).

14. The United Nations International Narcotics Control Board issued a report in 2002 stating that narcotics traffickers are using computers and the Internet to conduct surveillance of law enforcement, to communicate, and to arrange the sale of illegal drugs. *See* International Narcotics Control Board, Report of the International Narcotics Control Board for 2002 at Ch 2, ¶ 121 (2002), *available at* http://www.incb.org/e/ind_ar.htm (last visited Oct. 19, 2004). The Deputy Assistant Attorney General Bruce Schwartz, in remarks to the Senate Foreign Relations Committee, stated:

> ... criminals around the world are using computers to commit or assist a great variety of traditional crimes, including kidnaping, child pornography, child sexual exploitation identity theft, fraud, extortion and copyright piracy. Computer networks also provide terrorist organizations and organized crime groups the means with which to plan, coordinate and commit their crimes.

The Council of Europe on Cybercrime; Hearing Before the Senate Comm. on Foreign Relations § C (Jun. 17, 2004) (statement of Bruce Schwartz, Deputy Assistant Attorney General, Criminal Division), *available at* http://www.cybercrime.gov/swartzTestimony061704.htm (last visited Nov. 8, 2004).

III. Historical Development of International Law

United States Senator Ribikoff introduced the first piece of cybercrime legislation in the U.S. Congress in 1977.[15] While the legislation did not pass, it is credited for stimulating serious policy making activity in the international community.[16] In 1983, the Organisation for Economic Co-operation and Development (OECD)[17] conducted a study of existing cybercrime legislation in international states and considered the possibility of unifying these divers systems into a unitary international response.[18] On September 18, 1986, the OECD published *Computer-Related Crime: An Analysis of Legal Policy*.[19] The report surveyed existing laws in several countries and recommended a minimum list of offense conduct requiring the enactment of penal legislation by participating international states.[20] The recommendations included fraud and forgery, the alteration of computer programs and data, the copyright and interception of the communications or other functions of a computer or telecommunication system, theft of trade secrets, and the unauthorized access to, or use of, computer systems.[21] The OECD envisioned this list as a "common denominator" of acts to be addressed through legislative enactment by each member country.[22]

---

15. S.R. 1766, 95th Cong., vol. 123, part 17, p. 21,023.

16. Stein Schjolberg, *The Legal Framework — Unauthorized Access to Computer Systems: Penal Legislation in 44 Countries* (2003), *available at* http://www.mosstingrett. no/info/legal.html (last visited Nov. 8, 2004). Judge Schjolberg is the Chief Judge, Moss District Court, Norway.

17. The OECD is an intergovernmental organization that promotes multilateral dialogue and international cooperation on political, social and economic issues. While it does not have legal authority, it has been a significant influence in policy making among member and non-member states and the United Nations. It is comprised of 29 countries, including the United States. *See generally* Organization of Economic Development, OECD Online, *available at* http://www.oecd.org (last visited Oct. 19, 2004).

18. Schjolberg, *supra* note 16, at n.1. A group of experts met in Paris on May 30, 1983 representing France, the United Kingdom, Belgium, Norway and Germany.

19. U.N. Manual, *supra* note 5, ¶ 9.

20. OECD Report, ICCP No. 10, *Computer Related Analysis of Legal Policy* 1986

21. *Id.*

22. Schjolberg, *supra* note 16, ¶ 118.

Following the completion of the OECD report, the Council of Europe (CoE)[23] initiated its own study to develop categories of proposed offense conduct and guidelines for enacting penal legislation, taking into account the immediate and critical need for enforcement without affronting due process and abrogating individual civil liberties.[24] The CoE issued Recommendation No. R(89)9 on September 13, 1989.[25] That Recommendation expanded the earlier list of offense conduct proposed by the OECD to include matters involving privacy protection, victim identification, prevention, international search and seizure of data banks, and international cooperation in the investigation and prosecution of international crime.[26]

On September 11, 1995, the CoE adopted Recommendation No. R(95)13.[27] Significantly, this Recommendation goes beyond the identification of substantive offense categories and explores procedural issues concerning the need to obtain information through conventional criminal procedure methods, including search and seizure, technical surveillance, obligations to cooperate with investing authorities, electronic evidence, and the use of encryption. At the same time, the Recommendation emphasizes the need to protect civil rights by minimizing intrusions into the privacy rights of individuals during the investigatory phase. This concern with individual privacy rights would shape the development of the first proposed international treaty on cybercrime authored by the CoE.

The next important development in international law came in 1997, when the Committee of Experts on Crime in Cyberspace (PC-CY) was ap-

---

23. *See* U.S. Department of Justice, *Frequently Asked Questions and Answers about the Council of Europe Convention on Cybercrime* (2001), *available at* http://www. usdoj.gov/criminal/cybercrime/newCOEFAQs.html (last visited Oct. 19, 2004). The Council of Europe (CoE) was established in 1949 to strengthen human rights, promote democracy and the rule of law in Europe. The organization consists of 44 member states, including all of the members of the European Union. The United States is not a member state. *See* http://www.coe.int/DefaultEN.asp (last visited Nov. 8, 2004).

24. U.N. MANUAL, *supra* note 5, ¶¶ 144–45.

25. *Computer Related Crime: Recommendation No. R(89)9*, adopted by the Committee of Ministers of the Council of Europe(1989) and *Report by the European Committee on Crime Problems* (1990), *available at* http://www.oas.org/juridico/english/89-9&Final%20Report.pdf (last visited Oct. 19, 2004).

26. U.N. MANUAL, *supra* note 5, ¶¶ 119–22.

27. *Recommendation No. R(95)13 of the Committee of Ministers to Member States Concerning Problems of Criminal Procedural Law Connected With Information Technology*, (1995), *available at* http://www.usdoj.gov/criminal/cybercrime/crycoe.htm (last visited Oct. 19, 2004).

pointed by the CoE to identify new crimes, jurisdictional rights and criminal liability due to communication on the Internet.[28] Canada, Japan, South Africa, and the United States were invited to meet with the PC-CY and participate in the negotiations.[29] In 2001, the PC-CY issued its Final Activity Report styled as the Draft Convention on Cyber-crime and Explanatory Memorandum Related Thereto,[30] that was to serve as the master blueprint for the first international treaty. Finally, after several years of intense effort, the proposed international treaty was adopted by the Ministers of Foreign Affairs on November 8, 2001.[31] Representatives from 26 member countries together with Canada, Japan, South Africa and the United States signed the treaty known as the Council of Europe, Convention on Cybercrime (CoE Convention).[32] The number of signatories has recently increased to 38 countries. The CoE Convention remains to be ratified by the United States Congress.[33]

---

28. Schjolberg, *supra* note 16, § I.

29. The G-8 (United States, Japan, Germany, Britain, France, Italy, Canada and Russia) also convened in 1997 to discuss and recommend international cooperation in the enforcement of laws prohibiting computer crimes. United States Department of Justice, Meeting of the Justice and Interior Ministers of the Eight, Communique (1997), *available at* http://www.cybercrime.gov/communique.htm (last visited Oct. 19, 2004).

30. *Available at* www.privacyinternational.org/issues/cybercrime/coe/cybercrime-final.html (last visited Dec. 13, 2004).

31. *Available at* http://conventions.coe.int/Treaty/en/Treaties/Html/185.htm (last visited Oct. 19, 2004)

32. *Message from the President of the United States,* 108th Congress, 1st Session, Treaty Doc. 108-11 (2003), *available at* http://www.whitehouse.gov/news/releases/2003/11/20031117-11.html (last visited Dec. 13, 2004). The treaty was transmitted to the Congress by the president, recommending ratification, on November 17, 2003.

33. Other developments in the closely related fields of information security and information infrastructures overlap with CoE efforts. The Commission of European Communities (EC) issued the Communication from the Commission to the Council, the European Parliament, the European Economic and Social Committee and the Committee of the Regions: Network and Information Security: Proposal for a European Policy Approach, COM(2001)298 final (2001), *available at* http://europa.eu.int/eur-lex/en/com/cnc/2001/com2001_0298en01.pdf (last visited Oct. 19, 2004). The United States responded to the EC with formal comments on the proposal to protect information infrastructure on November 21, 2001. Comments of the U.S. Government, Communication from the European Commission: "Network and Information Security: Proposal for a European Policy Approach" (2001), *available at* http://www.usdoj.gov/criminal/cybercrime/intl/netsec_USComm_Nov_final.pdf. (last visited Oct. 19, 2004).

IV. Practical Impediments to International Investigation and Enforcement

Unquestionably, the slow response of the international community to act on the cybercrime problem seriously impedes meaningful international enforcement. At the CoE 2004 International Conference on Cybercrime, the forty-five nation participants agreed that governments are "dragging their heels" in implementing needed international reform through the final ratification of the treaty.[34] Simply put, the laws, criminal justice systems and levels of international cooperation have not kept pace with the lightening fast speed of technological development, despite the concerted efforts of the United Nations and the CoE.[35] The explanation lies in part in the magnitude and complexity of the problem when elevated from the national arena to the international venue,[36] particularly where many countries have yet to enact domestic legislation prohibiting the targeted offense conduct.

Historically, the practical impediments to enforcement and prosecution[37] include:[38]

1. the absence of a global consensus on the types of conduct that constitute a cybercrime;
2. the absence of a global consensus on the legal definition of criminal conduct;

---

34. *Cybercrime A Worldwide Headache*, CBS News.com, Sept. 16, 2004, *available at* http://www.cbsnews.com/stories/2004/09/16/tech/main643897.shtml (last visited Oct. 19, 2004) [hereinafter CBS News, *Worldwide Headache*]

35. U.N. Manual, *supra* note 5, ¶ 5

36. According to INSEAD/World Economic Forum: The Network Readiness Index (2003–2004) by 2002, the number of Internet users worldwide increased to 600 million from only 300 million in 1999. A 2004 survey of 494 U.S. corporations found 20% had been subject to "attempts of computer sabotage and extortion among others through denial of service attacks." CBS News, *Worldwide Headache, supra,* note 34.

37. For an interesting discussion of the investigative and enforcement hurdles faced in the prosecution of two high profile cybercrime cases, the "Rome Labs" and "Invita" cases, *see* Susan Brenner and Joseph Schwerha, *Transnational Evidence Gathering and Local Prosecution of International Cybercrime*, 20 J. Marshall J. Computer & Info. L. 347 (2002).

38. These impediments to investigation and enforcement were identified by the United Nations as a result of its in-depth study and analysis in 1995. U.N. Manual, *supra* note 5, ¶ 7.

3. the lack of expertise on the part of police, prosecutors and courts in the field;

4. the inadequacy of legal powers for investigation and access to computer systems, including the inapplicability of seizure powers to computerized data;

5. the lack of uniformity between the different national procedural laws concerning the investigation of cybercrimes;

6. the transnational character of many cybercrimes; and,

7. the lack of extradition and mutual legal assistance treaties,[39] synchronized law enforcement mechanisms that would permit international cooperation in cybercrime investigations, and existing treaties that take into account the dynamics and special requirements of these investigations.

The following discussion addresses the development of the international tools aimed at resolving these logistical and jurisdictional complications attendant to global investigation and enforcement in international cybercrime cases. However, the implementation of meaningful international cooperation, facilitated by these international tools, remains plagued by another inherent limitation. There is no singular global consensus supported by the unanimous participation of all foreign governments.

The United States, in its response to the "Cybercrime Communication Issued by the European Commission," emphasized the problem: "[w]ith the globalization of communications networks, public safety is increasingly dependent on effective law enforcement cooperation with foreign governments. That cooperation may not be possible, however, if a country does not have substantive laws in place to prosecute or extradite a perpetrator."[40] Thus, in a very real sense, international cooperation is limited to the particular participants and/or treaty signatories who have affirmatively enacted implementing domestic cybercrime legislation. Inadequate domestic legislation, combined with the failure of unanimous global cooperation, creates a gap in enforcement that provides safe havens for targeted conduct. Meaningful international prosecutive efforts will remain arduous at best without global commitment and global participation.

---

39. *See*, section VI, *infra*, for a discussion regarding the availability and practical uses of MLATs.

40. *Available at* http://www.cybercrime.gov/intl/USComments_CyberCom_final.pdf (last visited Dec. 17, 2004).

V. The Council of Europe Convention on Cybercrime

A. General Principles

The Council of Europe Cybercrime Convention (the "CoE Convention")[41] is the first and only multilateral treaty to address computer-related crime and evidence gathering.[42] The United States signed the CoE Convention on November 23, 2001.[43] The President of the United States transmitted the CoE Convention to the Senate for ratification on November 17, 2003.[44] As of June, 2004, thirty-eight countries have signed the CoE Convention with eight countries later ratifying it.[45] The Convention entered into force on July 1, 2004.[46]

The Official Explanatory Report, accompanying the CoE Convention, was formally adopted by the CoE's Committee of Ministers on November 8, 2001 (the "CoE Explanatory Report").[47] The CoE Explanatory Report provides an analysis of the CoE Convention. Under established CoE practice, such reports reflect the understanding of the parties in drafting treaty

---

41. Council of Europe, Convention On Cybercrime, ETS 185, U.S.-CoE, Treaty Doc. 108–11 (2001) [hereinafter CoE Convention], *available at* http://conventions.coe.int/Treaty/en/Treaties/Html/185.htm. (last visited Oct. 19, 2004).

42. *The Council of Europe on Cybercrime; Hearing Before the Senate Comm. On Foreign Relations* (2004) (statement of Bruce Schwartz, Deputy Assistant Attorney General, Criminal Division), *available at* http://www.cybercrime.gov/swartzTestimony061704.htm (last visited Oct. 19, 2004).

43. *Available at* http://conventions.coe.int/Treaty/Commun/ChercheSig.asp?NT=185 &CM=8&DF=24/12/04&CL =ENG (last visited Dec. 29, 2004).

44. *Available at* www.whitehouse.gov/news/releases/2003/11/20031117-11.html (last visited Dec. 6, 2004).

45. Council Of Europe, Chart Of Signatures and Ratifications, *available at* http://conventions.coe.int/treaty/en/searchsig.asp?NT (last visited Nov. 8, 2004). The eight ratifying countries include: Albania, Croatia, Estonia, Hungary Lithuania, Romania, Slovenia, and Macedonia. The 45 nation Council of Europe recently agreed at the CoE conference in Strasbourg, France that "governments are dragging their heels" on ratification. CBS News, *Worldwide Headache, supra* note 34.

46. *The Council of Europe on Cybercrime; Hearing Before the Senate Comm. On Foreign Relations,* (2004) (statement of Samuel M. Witten, Deputy Legal Advisor, U.S. Department of State), *available at* http://foreign.senate.gov/testimony/2004/WittenTestimony040617.pdf, at 9 (last visited Oct. 19, 2004).

47. *See* CoE Convention, *supra* note 41, at (v).

provisions and are accepted as fundamental bases for interpretation of CoE conventions.[48] Explanatory Reports are analogous to the legislative history that typically accompanies legislation in the United States.

The CoE Convention provides a treaty-based framework that imposes three necessary obligations on the participating nations to:

1. enact legislation criminalizing certain conduct related to computer systems;
2. create investigative procedures and ensure their availability to domestic law enforcement authorities to investigate cybercrime offenses, including procedures to obtain electronic evidence in all of its forms; and,
3. create a regime of broad international cooperation, including assistance in extradition of fugitives sought for crimes identified under the CoE Convention.[49]

The United States does not require implementing legislation once the treaty is ratified.[50] Existing federal law is adequate to meet the requirements of the treaty.

As a caveat, the CoE Convention contains significant restrictive language in the areas of transborder search and seizure and data interception, deferring authority to domestic laws and territorial considerations. Additionally, the CoE Convention does not supercede pre-existing mutual legal assistance or other reciprocal agreements between parties. These restrictions are considered in the "Application and Analysis of Significant Treaty Provisions" in section V(C) below.

B. Summary of Treaty Provisions

The CoE Convention consists of forty-eight articles divided among four chapters: (I) "Use of terms"; (II) "Measures to be taken at the national level"; (III) "International cooperation"; and, (IV) "Final provisions."[51]

Chapter II, Section 1. Articles two through thirteen addresses substantive law issues and includes criminalization provisions and other related provi-

---

48. *Id.*

49. *Letter Of Submittal To President Bush From Secretary Of State Colin Powell,* United States Department of State, reprinted in Convention on Cybercrime, 108th Congress, 1st Session, Treaty Doc. 108–11 (2003) at vi, *available at* http://conventions. coe.int/Treaty/en/Treaties/Html/185.htm. (last visited Oct. 20, 2004).

50. *Id.*

51. *See* CoE Convention, *supra* note 41.

sions in the area of computer or computer-related crime. Specifically, it defines nine offenses grouped into four different categories. The offenses include: illegal access, illegal interception, data interference, system interference, misuse of devices, computer-related forgery, computer-related fraud, offenses related to child pornography and offenses related to copyright.[52] The section also addresses ancillary crimes and penalties.

Chapter II, Section 2. Articles fourteen through twenty-one addresses procedural law issues. The section applies to a broader range of offenses than those defined in Section 1, including any offense committed *by means of* a computer system or evidence of which is in electronic form.[53] As a threshold matter, it provides for the common conditions and safeguards applicable to all procedural powers in the chapter.[54] Specifically, Article 15 requires the parties to provide for safeguards that are adequate for the protection of human rights and liberties. According to the CoE Explanatory Report, the substantive criteria and procedure authorizing an investigative power may vary according to the sensitivity of the data being sought in the investigation.[55]

The procedural powers include: expedited preservation of stored data, expedited preservation and partial disclosure of traffic data, and interception of content data.[56] Traditional application of search and seizure methodology is provided for within a party's territory along with other procedural options, including real-time interception of content data (Articles 20–21).[57]

Chapter II, Section 3. The second chapter ends in Article twenty-two with an explanation of the jurisdictional provisions.[58]

---

52. Council of Europe, Convention On Cybercrime, ETS 185, Explanatory Report, at 28, para. 18 (Nov. 2001) [hereinafter COE Explanatory Report], *available at* http://conventions.coe.int/Treaty/en/Treaties/Html/185.htm. (last visited Oct. 19, 2004).

53. *Id.* at 29, para. 19.

54. The issue of providing adequate procedural safeguards to protect the civil rights and privacy of putative defendants was a major discussion point during treaty negotiations. Based on those discussions, the United States asserted "six reservations and four declarations" that qualify its participation as a party. *See,* Powell, *supra* note 49, at vi. Procedural safeguards built into the CoE Convention are discussed in Section V(C)(2) of this chapter, *infra.*

55. CoE Explanatory Report, *supra* note 52, at 31, para. 31.

56. *Id.* at 29, para. 19.

57. *Id.* at 48, para. 143.

58. *Id.* at 29, para. 19.

Chapter III. This chapter addresses traditional and cybercrime related mutual assistance obligations as well as extradition rules.[59] Traditional mutual assistance is covered in two situations:

1. where no legal treaty, reciprocal legislation or other such agreement exists between the parties, and
2. where such pre-existing legal relationship exists between the parties.

In the former situation, the provisions of the CoE Convention apply. In the latter situation, however, pre-existing legal relationships apply "to provide further assistance" under the CoE Convention.[60] It bears emphasizing that the three general principles of international cooperation in Chapter III do *not* supercede the provisions on international agreements on mutual legal assistance and extradition, reciprocal agreements between parties, or relevant provisions of domestic law applying to international cooperation.[61]

Finally, Chapter III provides transborder access to stored computer data not requiring mutual assistance because there is either consent or the information is otherwise publicly available.[62] There is also provision for the establishment of a "24/7 network" for ensuring speedy assistance between the parties.[63]

C. Application and Analysis of Significant Treaty Provisions

1. Four Basic Definitions

The drafters of the CoE Convention agreed that parties would not be obliged to copy verbatim into their domestic laws the particular definitions

---

59. The provisions addressing computer or computer related crime assistance provide the same range of procedural powers as defined in Chapter II.

60. CoE Explanatory Report, *supra* note 52, at 29, para. 20.

61. *Id.* at 69, paras. 233–34. This basic principle of international cooperation is explicitly reinforced in Articles 24 (extradition), 25 (general principles applying to mutual assistance), 26 (spontaneous information), 27 (procedures pertaining to mutual legal assistance in the absence of applicable international agreements), 28 (confidentiality and limitations on use), 31(mutual assistance regarding accessing of stored computer data), 33 (mutual assistance regarding the real-time collection of traffic data) and 34 (mutual assistance regarding the interception of content data).

62. *Id.*

63. *Id.*

contained in the CoE Convention, provided that such domestic laws cover these concepts in a manner "consistent with the principles of the convention and offer an equivalent framework for its implementation."[64] The United Nations identified uniformity in law and consensus over definitional terms as two of the impediments that had to be overcome in order to achieve meaningful cooperation and successful enforcement.[65] The CoE Convention accomplishes this goal using four principle definitions.

A "computer system" is defined[66] as a device consisting of hardware and software developed for automatic processing of digital data.[67] It may include input, output, and storage facilities. It may stand alone or be connected in a network. A "network" is an interconnection of two or more computer systems.[68] The Internet is a global network consisting of many interconnected networks, all using the same protocols. It is essential that data is exchanged over the network.[69]

"Computer data" means any representation of facts, information or concepts in a form suitable for processing in a computer system including a program suitable to cause a computer system to perform a function.[70] Computer data that is automatically processed may be the target of one of the criminal offenses defined in the CoE Convention as well as subject to the application of one of the investigative measures defined by the CoE Convention.[71]

The term "service provider" encompasses a very broad category of persons and /or entities that provide to users of its services the ability to communicate by means of a computer system. Both public and private entities that provide the ability to communicate with one another is covered.[72] It also includes persons or entities that process or store computer data on behalf of such communication services or users of communication services.[73]

---

64. *Id.* at 29, para. 22.

65. *See* discussion Point IV, *supra.*

66. CoE Convention, *supra* note 41, at ch. 1, art. 1(a).

67. "[P]rocessing of data" means that data in the computer system is operated by executing a computer program. A "computer program" is a set of instructions that can be executed by the computer to achieve the intended result. CoE Explanatory Report, *supra* note 52, at 29, para. 23.

68. CoE Convention, *supra* note 41, at ch. 1, art. 1(a).

69. CoE Explanatory Report, *supra* note 52 at 30, para. 24.

70. CoE Convention, *supra* note 41, art. 1(b).

71. CoE Explanatory Report, *supra* note 52 at 30, para. 25.

72. *Id.* at 30, para. 26.

73. CoE Convention, *supra* note 41, art. 1(c).

However, a mere provider of content, such as a person who contracts with a web hosting company to host his web site, is not included in the definition if the content provider does not also offer communication or related data processing services.[74]

Finally, "traffic data" means *any* computer data relating to a communication by means of a computer system, generated by a computer system that formed a part of the chain of communication, indicating the communication's origin, destination, route, time, date, size, duration or type of underlying service.[75] Collecting traffic data in the investigation of a criminal offense committed in relation to a computer system is critical.[76] The traffic data is needed to trace the source of the communication as a starting point for the collection of further evidence or as evidence of part of the offense.[77] Because of the short lifespan of traffic data, it is necessary to order its expeditious preservation and to provide rapid disclosure of the information to law enforcement to facilitate quick discovery of the communication's route before other evidence is deleted or to identify a suspect.[78] The collection of this data is legally regarded to be less intrusive because it does not reveal the content of communication that is viewed as more privacy sensitive.[79]

2. Procedural Safeguards

The CoE Convention addresses the complicated problem of guaranteeing the protection of the civil rights of citizens living in different cultures and political systems.[80] Recognizing that it was not possible to specify in detail all of the conditions and safeguards necessary to circumscribe each

---

74. CoE Explanatory Report, *supra* note 52, at 30, para. 27.

75. CoE Convention, *supra* note 41, art. 1(d).

76. CoE Explanatory Report, *supra* note 52, at 30, para. 29. Specifically, the evidence that may be obtained from traffic data can include a telephone number, Internet Protocol address (IP) or similar identification of a communication facility to which a service provider renders service, the destination of the communication, and type of underlying service being provided (ie, file transfer, electronic mail, or instant messaging).

77. *Id.*

78. *Id.*

79. *Id.*

80. *Id.* at 49, para. 145. This sensitivity to the differences in legal responses to criminality based upon different legal cultures and traditions was emphasized in the recommendations of the Association Internationale de Droit Penal (AIDP) in the Draft Resolution of the AIDP Colloquium held at Wurrzburg on October 5–8, 1992. The CoE Convention implements this sentiment by proscribing minimum standards to be implemented by domestic legislation. *See,* U.N. Manual, *supra* note 5, at ¶¶270–3.

power and procedure provided for in the CoE Convention, Article 15 was drafted to provide "the common standards or minimum safeguards to which Parties to the Convention must adhere."[81] These standards or minimum safeguards arise pursuant to the obligations that a party has undertaken under applicable human rights instruments. These instruments include the 1950 European Convention for the Protection of Human Rights and Fundamental Freedoms and its additional Protocols Nos. 1, 4, 6, 7 and 12;[82] the 1966 United Nations International Covenant on Civil and Political Rights; and "other international human rights instruments, and which shall incorporate the principle of mandates that a power or procedure implemented under the Convention shall be proportional to the nature and circumstances of the offense."[83] Thus, domestic law must limit the overbreadth of protection orders authorized, provide reasonableness requirements for searches and seizures, and minimize intrusion regarding interception measures taken with respect to the wide variety of offenses.[84] The CoE Explanatory Report specifies the mandatory procedural safeguards "as [those] appropriate in view of the nature of the power or procedure, judicial or independent supervision, ground justifying the application of the power or procedure and the limitation on the scope or duration thereof."[85] The bottom line is that "[n]ational legislatures will have to determine, in applying binding international obligations and established domestic principles, which of the powers and procedures are sufficiently intrusive in nature to require implementation of particular conditions and safeguards."[86]

3. Methods of Collecting Evidence

The four methods for securing evidence are found in Article 18 ("Production Order"), Article 19 ("Search and Seizure of Stored Computer Data"), Article 20 ("Real time collection of traffic data"), and Article 21 ("Interception of Collection Data").[87] While attempting to overcome the

---

81. CoE Explanatory Report, *supra* note 52, at 49, para. 145.
82. *Id.* at 49, para. 145, ETS Nos. 005, (4), 009, 046, 114, 117,& 117.
83. *Id.* at 50, para. 146.
84. *Id.*
85. *Id.*
86. *Id.*
87. Notably, Articles 16 and 17 of the CoE Convention refer only to data preservation and not data retention. The CoE Explanatory Report observes that data preservation for most countries is an entirely new legal power or procedure in domestic law. Likewise, it is an important new investigative tool in addressing computer crime, especially committed through the Internet. Because of the volatility of computer evidence,

territorial sensitivity of each nation to transborder evidence collection, the CoE Convention carefully limits the scope of these powers by deferring to domestic legislative requirements as mandated by the CoE Convention, qualified by a strong admonition encouraging mutual cooperation between the parties as provided for in Article 23.[88] In short, transborder access to evidence will be whatever the participating nation decides is appropriate in conformity with the parameters of the treaty. Uniformity in the process among participating nations remains an open and unresolved issue. However, the CoE Convention does require the enactment of certain minimal procedures by a party.

Article 18 provides for the use of Production Orders. Under this Article, a party must have the legal authority to order a person within its territory, including a third party custodian of data, such as an ISP, to produce data, including subscriber information, that is in the person's possession or control.[89] Production orders are viewed as a less intrusive measure than search and seizure for requiring a third party to produce information. A production order is similar to subpoena powers in the United States.[90] However, Article 18 does not impose an obligation on the service provider to compile and maintain such subscriber information in the ordinary course of their business. Instead, a service provider needs only produce subscriber information that it does in fact keep, and is not obliged to guarantee the correctness of the information.[91] The application of the "proportionality principle," that is, the scope of the intrusion being limited to its purpose, is reemphasized in the CoE Explanatory Report.[92]

Significantly, the provision does not contain any minimal requirements concerning confidentiality of materials obtained through a production order. Except in the area of real-time interception of communications and

it is easily subject to manipulation or change. Thus, valuable evidence of a crime can be easily lost through careless handling or storage practices, intentional manipulation, or deletion designed to destroy evidence or routine deletion of data that is no longer required to be maintained. See CoE Explanatory Report, *supra* note 52 at 51, para. 155.

88. Article 23 of the CoE Convention sets forth three general principles with respect to international co-operation. First, international co-operation is to be extended between the parties "to the widest extent possible." Second, co-operation is to be extended to all criminal offenses described in paragraph 14. Finally, co-operation is to be carried out through the provisions of the CoE Convention along with all pre-existing international mutual assistance and reciprocal agreements.

89. CoE Explanatory Report, *supra* note 52, at 56–57, para. 177.

90. *Id.* at 55, para. 170.

91. *Id.* at 57, paras. 181 & 188.

92. *Id.* at 56, para. 174.

the other general admonitions of the CoE Convention to protect the due process and privacy rights of citizens in accordance with existing conventions of international law, there are no confidentiality provisions attendant to any of the evidence gathering tools provided for in the CoE Convention nor are there any proposed minimal requirements.[93] Again, this is an area left to the domestic legislative discretion of the parties leaving the issue of uniformity in the method of handling confidential information between nations unresolved. Issues of privacy and standards of protection in one nation may differ materially from those in another nation and may impact dissemination of seized evidence. The legal contours of information dissemination remains unresolved by the treaty and will have to be resolved on a case-by-case basis.

Article 19 is intended to enable investigating authorities, within their own territory, to search and seize a computer system, data stored in a computer system and data stored in storage mediums, such as diskettes.[94] Two significant limitations curb the powers to search and seize, however. First, and most important, Article 19 does not address "transborder search and seizure" whereby one country could search and seize data in the territory of other countries without first having to go through usual channels of mutual legal assistance.[95] Second, the measures contained in Article 19 are qualified by reference to the wording "in its territory," as a "reminder" that this provision — as well as all of the articles in this section — concerns only measures that are required to be taken at the national level.[96] Again, these measures operate between parties either through the tool of international cooperation, also explained in the CoE Convention, or through channels of pre-existing mutual legal assistance arrangements.

Article 19 addresses the hugely problematic absence in many jurisdictions of laws permitting the seizure of intangible objects, such as stored computer data, which is generally secured by seizing the data medium on which it is stored. Such national domestic legislation is necessary, not only to protect the preservation of easily destroyed data, but also to provide available enforcement tools to assist other countries. Without these laws, a nation investigating a transborder crime is effectively prevented from seeking international cooperation under the CoE Convention or through mu-

---

93. *Id.* at 56, para. 175.
94. *Id.* at 58, paras. 187–89.
95. *Id.* at 60, para. 195.
96. *Id.* at 59, para. 192.

tual legal assistance to investigate in a country that fails to authorize lawful search and seizure within its territory.

Accordingly, paragraph 1 requires the parties to empower law enforcement authorities to access and search computer data, which is contained either within a computer system or part of it or on an independent data storage medium (such as a CD-ROM or diskette).[97] Paragraph 2 allows investigating authorities to extend their search or similar access to another computer system if they have grounds to believe that the data required is stored in the other system. However, this system must also be within the party's own territory.[98] Paragraph 3 authorizes the seizure[99] of computer data that has been accessed under the authority of paragraphs 1 and 2.[100] Paragraph 4 is a "coercive measure" that allows law enforcement authorities to compel systems administrators to assist during the search and seizure as may reasonably be required.[101]

While Article 19 applies to "stored computer data,"[102] Articles 20 and 21 provide for the real-time collection of traffic data and the real-time interception of content data associated with specified communications transmitted by a computer system.[103] Additionally, confidentiality considerations are addressed here.[104]

Specifically, Articles 20 and 21 require parties to establish measures to enable their competent authorities to collect data associated with specified communications in their territory at the time of the data's communication, meaning in "real time." However, Article 20 contains a provision allowing a party to make a "reservation" to the CoE Convention limiting the types of crimes to which Article 20 applies.[105]

---

97. *Id.* at 59, para. 190.

98. *Id.* at 59, para. 193.

99. In the Convention, seizure means "to take away the physical medium upon which data or information is recorded, or to make and retain a copy of such data or information." Seize also mean in this context the right to secure data. *Id.* at 59, para. 197.

100. *Id.* at 59, para. 196.

101. *Id.* at 61, para. 200.

102. *Id.*

103. *Id.* at 61–62, para. 205.

104. *Id.*

105. Greater limitations may be employed with respect to the real-time collection of content data than traffic data. *Id.* at 62–63, para. 210. The United States has taken the position that a formal reservation is not needed because federal law already makes the mechanism generally available for criminal investigations and prosecutions. *See* Powell, *supra,* note 49, at xv.

Under Articles 20 and 21, subject to the party's actual technical capabilities,[106] a party is generally required to adopt measures enabling its competent authorities to:

1. collect or record data themselves through application of technical means in the territory of that party; and,

2. compel a service provider, to either collect or record data through the application of technical means or cooperate and assist competent authorities in the collection or recording of such data.[107]

The CoE Explanatory Report recognizes a critical distinction in the nature and extent of the possible intrusions into privacy between traffic data and content data.[108] With respect to the real-time interception of content data, laws often limit interception to investigations of serious offenses or serious offense categories, usually defined by certain maximum periods of incarceration.[109] Whereas, the interception of traffic data, viewed as less intrusive, is not so limited and in principle applies to every offense described by the CoE Convention.[110] In both cases, the conditions and procedural safeguards specified in Articles 14 and 15 apply to qualify the use of these interception provisions.[111]

4. Crimes

Section 1, Articles 2–13 of the CoE Convention establish a "common minimum standard of relevant offenses."[112] The Convention requires that all of the offenses must be committed "intentionally,"[113] although the exact meaning of the word is left to national interpretation.[114] Laws should be drafted with as much clarity and specificity as possible in order to guaran-

---

106. CoE Explanatory Report, *supra* note 52, at 65, para. 221. There is no obligation to impose a duty on service providers to obtain or deploy new equipment or engage in costly reconfiguration of their systems in order to assist law enforcement.

107. Id.

108. *Id.* at 66, para. 227.

109. *Id.* at 63, para. 212.

110. *Id.* at 63, para. 214.

111. *Id.* at 63–64, para. 215.

112. *Id.* at 31, paras. 33–34. Notably the list is based on the guidelines developed earlier by the CoE in Recommendation No. R(89)9. *See infra,* note 25.

113. CoE Explanatory Report, *supra* note 52, at 32, para. 39.

114. *Id.*

tee adequate forseeability with regard to the type of conduct that will result in a criminal sanction.[115] As noted above, the United States maintains
that its legislative structure adequately covers the offenses described in the
CoE Convention and that no further implementing legislation will be required in order to ratify the treaty.[116]

The offenses described in Chapter II, Section I of the CoE Convention
include:

Title 1, Articles 2–6, *Offenses against the confidentiality, integrity
and availability of computer data and systems:* illegal access, illegal
interception, data interference, system interference, misuse of devices;

---

115. *Id.* at 33, para. 41.

116. The Computer Fraud and Abuse Act [CFAA] was originally enacted in 1984 as
the "Counterfeit Access Device and Computer Fraud and Abuse Act." Pub. L. No. 98-
473, 2101(a), 98 Stat. 2190 (1984) (codified at 18 U.S.C. § 1030). In 1986 the statute was
substantially revised and the title was changed to CFAA. The Act was revised and the
scope of the law was expanded in 1988, Pub. L. No. 100-690, 102 Stat. 4404 (1988); 1989,
Pub. L. No. 101-73, 103 Stat. 502 (1989); 1990, Pub. L. No. 101-647, 104 Stat. 4831, 4910,
4925 (1990); and 1994, Pub. L. No. 103-322, 108 Stat. 2097-99 (1994). In 1996, the CFAA
was amended by the National Information Infrastructure Protection Act of 1996
[NIIPA], Pub. L. No. 104-294, tit. II, § 201, 110 Stat. 3488, 3491-96 (1996) (Economic
Espionage Act of 1996, Title II). The CFAA proscribes 7 areas of offense conduct: (a)(1)
knowing and willful theft of protected government information, (a)(2) intentional theft
of protected information, (a)(3) intentional gaining of access to government information, (a)(4) fraud through a protected computer, (a)(5)(A) intentionally causing damage through a computer transmission, (a)(5)(B) recklessly causing damage through
unauthorized access, (a)(5)(c)) causing damage through unauthorized access, (a)(6)
fraudulent trafficking in passwords, and (a)(7) extortion. Portions of § 1030 were
amended and expanded by provisions of the antiterrorism legislation entitled Uniting
and Strengthening America by Providing Appropriate Tools Required to Intercept and
Obstruct Terrorism Act of 2001, Pub. L. No. 107-56, § 814 (d)(1), 115 Stat. 272 (2001)
(also referred to as the USA PATRIOT Act of 2001). Congress also enacted the Cybersecurity Enhancement Act of 2002, Pub. L. No. 107-296, § 225, 116 Stat. 2135, 2156
(2002). These provisions are discussed in more detail in section VII of this chapter, *infra.*
Additionally, other traditional federal criminal laws may be used to prosecute computer
related crimes, such as charges of copyright infringement, 17 U.S.C. § 506 (1997); conspiracy, 18 U.S.C. § 371 (1994); wire fraud, 18 U.S.C. § 1343 (2002); illegal transportation of stolen property, 18 U.S.C. § 2314 (1994); Electronic Communications Privacy
Act, 18 U.S.C. §§ 2510-21, 2701-10 (2002); illegal interception devices and equipment,
18 U.S.C. § 2512 (2002); and unlawful access to stored communications, 18 U.S.C.
§§ 2701 et. seq. (2002).

Title 2, Articles 7–8, *Computer-related offenses*: computer-related forgery and computer-related fraud;

Title 3, Article 9, *Content-related offenses*: offenses related to child pornography;

Title 4, Article 10, *Offenses related to infringements and related rights*: offenses related to infringements of copyright and related rights; and,

Title 5, Articles 11–13, *Ancillary Liability and sanctions*: attempt and aiding or abetting, corporate liability, and sanctions and measures.

The CoE Explanatory Report includes several caveats regarding the intent and application of these provisions. For example, criminal offenses defined under Articles 2–6 are intended to protect the confidentiality, integrity and availability of computer systems or data and are not intended to criminalize legitimate and common activities inherent in the design of networks, or legitimate and common operating and commercial practices.[117] Each section is also subject to Article 8 of European Convention on Human Rights guaranteeing the right to privacy where applicable.[118]

To summarize, these provisions are the minimum offense descriptions mandated by the CoE Convention. Each party is to implement them through domestic legislation.

5. Jurisdiction and Extradition

Article 22 undertakes the seemingly monumental task of resolving the question of "who has jurisdiction" over the commission of computer related offenses committed across sovereign borders. A series of criteria, grounded in international law principles,[119] is applied under which the parties are obligated to establish jurisdiction over the criminal offenses enumerated in Articles 2–11.[120]

Article 22(1)(a) provides that each party "shall adopt" legislative measures to establish jurisdiction to prosecute the offenses listed in Articles

---

117. CoE Explanatory Report, *supra* note 52, at 33, para. 43.

118. *Id.* at 34, para. 51.

119. For an in depth discussion of international jurisdictional principles, *see* JULIE O'SULLIVAN, FEDERAL WHITE COLLAR CRIME, 735–50 (2d ed. 2003).

120. CoE Explanatory Report, *supra* note 52, at 67, para. 232.

2–11 where committed "in its territory."[121] This provision is grounded upon the principle of territoriality[122] which is based on mutual respect of sovereign equality between States and is linked with the principle of nonintervention in the affairs and exclusive domain of other States.[123]

The "ubiquity doctrine" may also apply to determine the "place of commission of the offense."[124] Under this doctrine, a crime is deemed to occur "in its entirety" within a country's jurisdiction if one of the constituent elements of the offense, or the ultimate result, occurred with that country's borders. Jurisdiction applies to co-defendants and accomplices as well.[125]

Article 22(d) requires the parties to establish jurisdictional principles when the offense is committed by one of a party's nationals, if the offense is punishable under criminal law where it was committed or if the offense is committed outside the territorial jurisdiction of any state. This provision is based on the principle of nationality, a different jurisdictional principle from the other subsections of the article.[126] It provides that nationals are required to abide by a party's domestic laws even when they are outside its territory. Under subsection (d), if a national commits an offense abroad, the party must have the ability to prosecute even if the conduct is also an offense under the law of the country in which it was committed.[127]

However, the treaty does not resolve the central jurisdictional dilemma when more than one country has a "jurisdictional claim" to the case. The CoE Explanatory Report, interpreting Article 22(5) addresses this situation as follows:

> In the case of crimes committed by use of computer systems, there will be occasions when more than one Party has jurisdiction over some or all of the participants in the crime ... the affected parties are to consult in order to determine the proper venue for prosecution. In some cases, it will be most effective for the States con-

---

121. CoE Convention, *supra* note 41, art. 22(1)(a).

122. CoE Explanatory Report, *supra* note 52, at 67, para. 233. Note that subparagraph (b) and (c) are based upon a "variant of the principle of territoriality" where the crime is committed aboard a ship or aircraft registered under the laws of the State. *Id.* at 68, para. 235.

123. U.N. MANUAL, *supra* note 5, ¶ 249.

124. CoE Explanatory Report, *supra* note 52, at 70–71, para. 250.

125. *Id.*

126. *Id* at 67, para. 236.

127. *Id.*

cerned to choose a single venue for prosecution; in others, it may be best for one State to prosecute some participants, while one or more other States pursue others ... Finally, the obligation to consult is not absolute, but is to take place "where appropriate."[128]

Additionally, in those instances where a party refuses a request to extradite on the basis of the offender's nationality[129] and the offender's presence in the territory of a party, (where the request is made under Article 24), paragraph 3 of Article 22 mandates the party to enact jurisdictional provisions enabling the prosecution domestically.[130] Ostensibly, this provision should avoid the possibility of offenders seeking safe havens from prosecution by fleeing to another country. The bottom line is that a party must either extradite or prosecute.[131]

Article 24, entitled "Extradition," does not provide any mechanism to implement or expedite extradition when a request is made by a party. Instead, subparagraph 5 merely provides that "[e]xtradition shall be subject to the conditions provided for by the law of the requested Party or by applicable extradition treaties, including the grounds on which the Party may refuse extradition."[132] However, the treaty does require each party to include as extraditable offenses those contained in Articles 2–11 of the CoE Convention.[133]

Finally, Article 35 requires each party to designate a point of contact available on a 24 hours, 7 days per week basis. This ensures co-operation in the investigation of crimes, collection of evidence or other such assistance.

---

128. *Id.* at 68, para. 239.

129. *See* Powell, *supra* note 49, at xvii. United States law permits extradition of nationals, accordingly no implementing legislation is required.

130. CoE Explanatory Report, *supra* note 52, at 68, para. 237.

131. This article resembles the text of Articles 15(3) and 16 (10) of the UN CONVENTION ON TRANSNATIONAL ORGANIZED CRIME, which is incorporated by reference into the PROTOCOL TO PREVENT, SUPPRESS, AND PUNISH TRAFFICKING IN PERSONS, ESPECIALLY WOMEN AND CHILDREN SUPPLEMENTING THE UNITED NATIONS CONVENTION AGAINST TRANSNATIONAL ORGANIZED CRIME, *available at* http://untreaty.un.org/English/notpubl/18-12E.doc and http://untreaty.un.org/English/notpubl/18-12-a.E.doc (last visited Oct. 20, 2004). Those provisions require the views of the requesting nation to be taken into account and require the prosecuting nation to act diligently.

132. CoE Convention, *supra* note 41, art. 24(5).

133. *Id.*, art. 24(2).

VI. Mutual Legal Assistance Treaties (Mlats) and Other International Cooperation Agreements

As explained above, the CoE Convention addresses both the situation where a traditional pre-existing legal relationship either in the form of a treaty, reciprocal legislation, memorandum of understanding ["MOU"][134] or other such agreement exists between the parties and the situation where there is no such pre-existing relationship. Where there is a pre-existing relationship, that legal relationship applies "to provide further assistance" under the CoE Convention.[135] Traditional pre-existing legal relationships are not superceded by the CoE Convention.

Additionally, the three general principles of international cooperation in Chapter III of the Convention do not supercede the provisions of international agreements on mutual legal assistance and extradition, reciprocal agreements between parties, or relevant provisions of domestic law applying to international cooperation.[136] Because these traditional means remain useful in cybercrime cases, each will be briefly explained.

The U.S. Department of State describes Mutual Legal Assistance Treaties or "MLATs" as a means of "impro[ving] the effectiveness of judicial assistance and to regularize and facilitate procedures" with foreign nations.[137] The treaties typically include agreed upon procedures for summoning wit-

---

134. For example, the Securities and Exchange Commission has "case-by-case" informal MOUs to facilitate production with Switzerland, Japan, Canada, Brazil, Netherlands, France, Mexico, Norway, Argentina, Spain, Chile, Italy, Australia, the United Kingdom, Sweden, South Africa, Germany, Luxembourg and Hungary, as well as Joint Statements of Cooperation with the European Union (EU). *See* United States Department of State, *Mutual Legal Assistance in Criminal Matters Treaties (MLATs) and Other Agreements,* available at http://travel.state.gov/law/mlat.html (last visited Oct. 20, 2004).

135. CoE Explanatory Report, *supra* note 52, at 29, para. 20.

136. *Id.* at 69, paras. 233–34. This basic principle of international cooperation is explicitly reinforced in Articles 24 (extradition), 25 (general principles applying to mutual assistance), 26 (spontaneous information), 27 (procedures pertaining to mutual legal assistance in the absence of applicable international agreements), 28 (confidentiality and limitations on use), 31(mutual assistance regarding accessing of stored computer data), 33 (mutual assistance regarding the real-time collection of traffic data) and 34 (mutual assistance regarding the interception of content data).

137. MLAT, *supra* note 134.

nesses, compelling the production of documents and other evidence, issuing search warrants and serving process.[138]

Notably, these remedies are available only to prosecutors. The Office of International Affairs (OIA), Criminal Division, United States Department of Justice, is responsible for administering procedures under the MLATs and assisting domestic prosecutions by the respective United States Attorneys Offices. Thus, to the extent that the MLATs "supercede" the CoE Convention,[139] defense attorneys are effectively excluded from participating in that part of the process of international enforcement activity.

The operative provisions of MLATs often have the effect, whether intended or not, of limiting international enforcement efforts. Many such agreements require "dual criminality," that the crime for which information is being sought by a requesting country also be offense conduct in the nation possessing the needed information. Where the nation has not criminalized targeted conduct, the investigation cannot proceed. For example in 1992, the United States requested information from Switzerland in connection with its investigation of a Swiss-based hacker who attacked the San Diego Supercomputer Center. Switzerland had not criminalized hacking and was, therefore, unable to assist in the investigation.[140]

In any event, the CoE Convention does not refer to the role or participation of defense counsel in the process at all, except to the extent that the privacy rights of citizens are addressed. Defense attorneys must obtain evidence in criminal cases from foreign or "host" countries, pursuant to the laws of the host nation, through a procedure known as "Letters Rogatory."[141]

---

138. *Id.* The United States has bilateral Mutual Legal Assistance Treaties with Anguilla, Antigua/Barbuda, Argentina, Austria, Bahamas, Barbados, Belgium, Brazil, British Virgin Islands, Canada, Cayman Islands, Cyprus, Czech Republic, Dominica, Egypt, Estonia, Greece, Grenada, Hong Kong, Hungary, Israel, Italy, Jamaica, South Korea, Latvia, Lithuania, Luxembourg, Mexico, Montserrat, Morocco, Netherlands, Panama, Philippines, Poland, Romania, St. Kitts-Nevis, St. Lucia, St. Vincent, Spain, Switzerland, Thailand, Trinidad, Turkey, Turks and Caicos Islands, Ukraine, United Kingdom and Uruguay.

139. CoE Explanatory Report, *supra* note 52, at 29, para. 20 & 67, paras. 233–34. The three general principles of international co-operation in Chapter III of the CoE Convention do *not* supercede the provisions on international agreements on mutual legal assistance and extradition, reciprocal agreements between parties, or relevant provisions of domestic law applying to international co-operation.

140. ABA Privacy and Computer Crime Committee, *International Cybercrime Project* (2001), *available at* http://www.abanet.org/scitech/computercrime/cybercrimeproject.html (last visited Oct. 20, 2004).

141. MLAT, *supra* note 134.

To the extent that the United States maintains agreements with the various host nations, the State Department publishes "country specific information" to enable a litigant to avail himself of extraterritorial discovery.[142] There are strict requirements for the form of the request submission[143] and the requesting party must pay all expenses associated with the process.[144] It is unclear if and to what extent the CoE Convention affects the rules with respect to treaties governing Letters Rogatory.

Rogatory usually requires pre-authorization by a judicial or administrative body and requires transmission by a designated "central authority."[145] The process may be "cumbersome and time consuming"[146] and the treaties generally do not provide time lines for production of the requested information.[147] The Letters Rogatory was codified under 28 U.S.C. § 1781 (2000).[148] Under this section, the State Department is vested with the power in both civil and criminal cases to transmit the request for evidence to "a foreign or international tribunal, officer or agency to whom it is addressed."[149] The request may be used for providing notice, serving sum-

---

142. *See* United States Department of State, International Judicial Assistance, *Notarial Services and Authentication of Documents, available at* http://travel.state.gov/law/judicial_assistance.html (last visited Oct. 20, 2004) [hereinafter *Notarial Services*].

143. Additional Protocol to the Inter American Convention on Letters Rogatory, art. 3 (2003), *available at* http://www.oas.org/juridico/english/treaties/b-46.html (last visited Oct. 20, 2004).

144. *Id.* at art. 5.

145. *E.g., Id.* at art. 1 & 2.

146. MLAT, *supra* note 134.

147. *Notarial Services, supra* note 142.

148. The section provides in pertinent part:

(a) The Department of State has power, directly, or through suitable channels—

...

(2) to receive a letter rogatory issued, or request made, by a tribunal in the United States, to transmit it to the foreign or international tribunal, officer, or agency to whom it is addressed, and to receive and return it after execution ...

(b) This section does not preclude—

...

(2) the transmittal of a letter rogatory or request directly from a tribunal in the United States to the foreign or international tribunal, officer, or agency to whom it is addressed and its return in the same manner.

28 U.S.C. § 1781 (2000).

149. *Id.* § 1781(a)(2).

mons, locating individuals, witness examination, document inspection and other evidence production. The foreign tribunal can only honor requests that fall within its procedures and jurisdiction. Again, if criminal activity does not fall within the domestic legislation of the foreign country, then the Letters Rogatory request cannot be honored.

There are some limited international tools available to side step time consuming and complicated procedures for obtaining information where the charge involves drug trafficking. For example, Article 7 of the UNITED NATIONS CONVENTION AGAINST ILLICIT TRAFFIC IN NARCOTIC DRUGS AND PSYCHOTROPIC SUBSTANCES,[150] provides a procedure to obtain evidence from other participating nations without Letters Rogatory.[151]

Additionally, those international organizations, such as the Organization of American States (OAS), which do provide protocols for Letter Rogatory, have taken steps to encourage participating OAS nations to incorporate the CoE Convention into existing protocols. Specifically, the Ministers of Justice of the OAS in April 2004 called upon OAS members to accede to the CoE Convention and incorporate its principles into their national legislation.[152] Arguably, accession to CoE Convention principles may be read into existing Letters Rogatory protocols possibly extending at least some of the procedures to defense counsel. Whether this argument, if asserted, would be successful remains to be seen in future application if the OAS members follow the recommendation.

In short, the defense is relegated in a very real sense to relying upon the limited discovery obligations of the prosecutor to obtain access to evidence.[153] The limitations are obvious in that the defendant's desire for specific information in the possession of the host country may materially differ from the information sought and obtained by the prosecution. Arguably, the paradigm of international enforcement may be lopsided in an effort to facilitate international cooperation to regulate a serious crime problem, the

---

150. The 1988 Convention is available at http://www.incb.org/e/conv/1988/index.htm (last visited Nov. 16, 2004).

151. MLAT, *supra* note 134. This convention entered into force on November 11, 1990.

152. Guy De Vel, Director General of the Legal Affairs of the Council of Europe, Remarks at the Council of Europe, Conference on the Challenge of Cybercrime (Sept. 15–17, 2004), *available at* http://www.coe.int/T/E/Com/Files/Events/2004-09-cyber-crime/disc_deVel.asp (last visited Oct. 20, 2004). Mr. De Vel also recognizes the decision of APEC leaders in 2002 to recommend to their members to adopt laws against cybercrime in conformity with the CoE Convention.

153. FED. R. CRIM. P. 16(a)(1)(E)(i)-(iii).

prosecution of which requires international cooperation. The burden of providing procedural due process is for the most part left to domestic legislation and, therefore, the scope and protection will necessarily vary from nation to nation.

VII. The PATRIOT Act and Other Federal Legislation

The Computer Fraud and Abuse Act (CFAA)[154] was originally enacted in 1984 as the "Counterfeit Access Device and Computer Fraud and Abuse Act."[155] In 1986 the statute was substantially revised and the title was changed to CFAA. The Act was revised again in 1988, 1989, 1990, and 1994.[156] In 1996, the CFAA was amended by the National Information Infrastructure Protection Act of 1996.[157]

Section 1030 proscribes nine areas of offense conduct:

1. knowing and willful theft of protected government information,[158]
2. intentional theft of other protected information,[159]
3. intentional gaining of access to government information,[160]
4. perpetrating fraud by using a protected computer,[161]
5. intentionally causing damage to a protected computer through a transmission, e.g., a virus,[162]
6. recklessly causing damage through unauthorized access,[163]
7. causing damage through unauthorized access,[164]
8. fraudulent trafficking in passwords,[165] and

---

154. 18 U.S.C. § 1030 (2002).
155. Pub. L. No. 98-473, 2101(a), 98 Stat. 2190 (1984).
156. 1988, Pub. L. No. 100-690, 102 Stat. 4404 (1988); 1989, Pub. L. No. 101-73, 103 Stat. 502 (1989); 1990, Pub. L. No. 101-647, 104 Stat. 4831, 4910, 4925 (1990); and 1994, Pub. L. No. 103-322, 108 Stat. 2097–99 (1994).
157. Economic Espionage Act of 1996, Pub. L. No. 104-294, tit. II, § 201, 110 Stat. 3488, 3491–96 (1996).
158. 18 U.S.C. § 1030(a)(1) (2002).
159. *Id.* § 1030(a)(2).
160. *Id.* § 1030(a)(3).
161. *Id.* § 1030(a)(4).
162. *Id.* § 1030(a)(5)(A).
163. *Id.* § 1030(a)(5)(B).
164. *Id.* § 1030(a)(5)(C).
165. *Id.* § 1030(a)(6).

9.   extortion by threatening to damage a protected computer.[166]

In the period following "9/11," portions of § 1030 were amended and expanded by provisions of the antiterrorism legislation entitled "Uniting and Strengthening America by Providing Appropriate Tools Required to Intercept and Obstruct Terrorism Act of 2001," also referred to as the USA PATRIOT Act of 2001.[167] The PATRIOT Act significantly modifies the CFAA's anticipated scope of international jurisdiction through the expansion of the definition of the term "protected computer" to include "a computer outside of the United States that is used in a manner that affects interstate or foreign commerce or communication of the United States."[168] By expanding the definition of the domestic crime to include computers located in foreign countries, the United States has broadened the scope of authorized investigations subject to recognition by foreign countries.[169]

Additionally, other traditional federal criminal laws may be used to prosecute computer related crimes and satisfy the domestic legislative requirements of the CoE Convention. The most important are: copyright infringement,[170] conspiracy,[171] wire fraud,[172] illegal transportation of stolen property,[173] the Electronic Communications Privacy Act,[174] illegal interception devices and equipment,[175] the Internet False Identification Act,[176] unlawful access to stored communications,[177] and the Child Pornography Prevention Act.[178] Congress also recently enacted the Cybersecurity Enhancement Act of 2002.[179] These statutes are discussed in more detail in other areas of the text.

---

166. *Id.* § 1030(a)(7).

167. Pub. L. No. 107-56, § 814 (d)(1), 115 Stat. 272 (2001).

168. *Id.* (*revised section* 18 U.S.C. § 1030(e)(2)(B) (Supp. II 2003)).

169. U.S. Department of Justice, Field Guidance on New Authorities (Redacted) Enacted in 2001 Anti-terrorism Legislation 27 (2001), *available at* http://www.epic.org/privacy/terrorism/DOJ_guidance.pdf (last visited Nov. 9, 2004).

170. 17 U.S.C. § 506 (1997).

171. 18 U.S.C. § 371 (1994).

172. 18 U.S.C. § 1343 (2002).

173. 18 U.S.C. § 2314 (1994).

174. 18 U.S.C. §§ 2510-21 & 2701-10 (2002).

175. 18 U.S.C. § 2512 (2002).

176. Pub. L. No 106-578, 140 Stat. 3076 (2000)) *amending* the False Identification Crime Control Act of 1982, 18 U.S.C. § 1028 (2003).

177. 18 U.S.C. §§ 2701-10 (2002).

178. 18 U.S.C. § 2252A (eff. April 30, 2003).

179. Pub. L. No. 107-296, § 225, 116 Stat. 2135, 2156 (2002).

VIII. Continuing Policy Review by the United Nations

Countries which do not have adequate criminal laws governing cybercrime have become "havens" for cybercriminals. "Inadequate procedural tools in just one country can also shield criminals from [international and transborder] investigative efforts."[180] Recent efforts of the United Nations demonstrate a marked response to this problem by organizing regional conferences worldwide to develop action plans, particularly in less developed "e-nations" where no legal infrastructure exists to address cybercrime. These efforts bear review as part of the continuing process of developing international cooperation in this field.

The United Nations Economic and Social Commission for Asia and the Pacific (UNESCAP) adopted a Draft Action Plan on Cybercrime and Information Security for the Asia Pacific Region [the "UNESCAP Plan"].[181] The UNESCAP Plan recognizes that few countries in the Asia Pacific region have appropriate legal and regulatory frameworks to meet the challenge of cybercrime. In fact, there is inadequate data in the region to allow for an accurate estimate of incidences of cybercrime.[182] However, "[i]n the Asia-Pacific region the incidences of malicious attacks on the confidentiality, integrity and availability of computer data and systems, computer-related offenses such as forgery and fraud, content-related offenses such as those related to child pornography and intellectual property rights (IPRs) violations, are significant."[183]

The UNESCAP Plan envisions the establishment, within a five year period, of a regional response including the enactment of legislation criminalizing computer related offense conduct and giving priority to international cooperation with more developed nations. The UNESCAP Plan

---

180. Comments of the United States Government on the European Commission Communication on Combating Computer Crime 5, *available at* http://www.usdoj.gov/criminal/cybercrime/intl/USComments_CyberCom_final.pdf (last visited Oct. 20, 2004).

181. United Nations Economic and Social Commission for Asia and the Pacific, Draft Action Plan on Cybercrime and Information Security for the Asia Pacific Region (2002) (adopted at the Asia Pacific Conference on Cybercrime and Information Security), *available at* http://www.unescap.org/icstd/documents/actionplans/cybercrime%20action%20plan.doc (last visited Oct. 20, 2004).

182. *Id.* at 1.

183. *Id.*

design avoids duplication by building on existing cooperation frameworks, including the CoE Convention and other UN General Assembly Resolutions, as specified, and the International Convention Against Transnational Organized Crime.[184]

In the fall, 2003, the United Nations General Assembly Resolution 57/239,[185] "Creation of a Global Culture of Cybersecuirty," based on the OECD Guidelines for the Security of Information Systems and Networks, was adopted. The Resolution calls upon all nations to engage in cybersecurity risk assessment and to seek a global security agreement between member nations by 2005. The document is seen by the United States as a "common sense roadmap" for future action.[186]

Resolution 57/239 was followed by United Nations General Assembly Resolution 58-199.[187] Specifically, this Resolution draws attention to cyber-vulnerabilities and threats to the infrastructures that support cyber and physical security. The Resolution proposes eleven elements for protecting critical information structures and calls upon member nations to take formal action at the 2005 World Summit on Information Society to be held in Tunis in November, 2005.

IX. The Threat of Organized Crime

Dr. Ulrich Sieber, Director of the Max Planck Institute for Foreign and International Criminal Law, observes that "most types of cybercrime can be dangerous, especially if they are committed by organized crime groups or terrorists."[188] Dr. Sieber, along with thirty-two of the Council of Europe member states and others, contributed startling information about the rise

---

184. *Id.* at 3, para. 4.

185. G.A. Res. 57/239, U.N. GAOR, 57th Sess. (2003), *available at* http://ods-dds-ny.un.org/doc/UNDOC/GEN/N02/555/22/PDF/N0255522.pdf?OpenElement (last visited Oct. 20, 2004).

186. Bloomfield, *supra* note 2.

187. G.A. Res. 58/199, U.N. GAOR, 58th Sess. (2004), *available at* http://ods-dds-ny.un.org/doc/UNDOC/GEN/N03/506/52/PDF/N0350652.pdf?OpenElement (last visited Oct. 20, 2004).

188. Interview with Dr. Ulrich Sieber, Director of the Max Planck Institute for Foreign and International Criminal Law, Council of Europe Cybercrime Conference, Freiburg, Germany (Oct. 9, 2004), *available at* http://www.coe.int/t/e/com/files/interviews/20040910_interv_sieber.asp (last visited Oct. 20, 2004).

of organized crime as participants in international cybercrime. In 2004, the CoE compiled this information in the "Summary of the Organized Crime Situation Report 2004, Focus on the Threat of Cybercrime" ["Situation Report"].[189] The Situation Report reveals a trend of increasing use of the Internet by organized crime to perpetrate fraud schemes, engage in the theft of credit cards, and engage in cyber-extortion crimes. "As economic crime is already a primary activity of organized crime, [information and communication technologies] will further facilitate offenses such as credit card theft, 'pump and dump' schemes and other kinds of fraud, money laundering, counterfeiting, but also modern forms of traditional crimes such as electronic bank robberies or cybercrime."[190]

The Situation Report also identifies the proliferation of child pornography on the Internet as "an important activity of organized criminals."[191] Several major cases uncovered in different European countries since 2001 revealed that offenders were not merely members of pedophile networks exchanging images and videos of victims, but were also criminals organizing child pornography for profit.[192]

The Internet attracts criminal organizations for several reasons, according to the Situation Report: increased anonymity reducing the risk of capture and prosecution, global outreach increases the pool of potential victims, and less personal contact requires less trust and enforcement of discipline usually required in criminal organizations.[193] A recent evidence seizure demonstrates the economic value to criminal organizations as well. In April, 2004, eleven countries participated in a coordinated search that uncovered contraband in the form of software, CDs and DVDs with a value of 50 million dollars.[194]

The CoE also recognizes that terrorists do use the Internet for propaganda purposes, recruiting, fund raising and to assist in planning terrorist activities.[195] However, the CoE is unwilling to conclude that cyberterrorism

---

189. Council of Europe, *Summary of the Organized Crime Situation Report 2004, Focus on the Threat of Cybercrime* (2004), *available at* http://www.coe.int/T/E/Legal_affairs/Legal_co-operation/Combating_economic_crime/organized crime/Documents/OrgCrimeRep2004Summ.pdf, Strasbourg (last visited Oct. 20, 2004).
190. *Id.* at 8.
191. *Id.* at 9.
192. *Id.*
193. *Id.*
194. *Id.*
195. *Id.* at 10.

represents a true link in the network of cybercriminals engaged in organized crime activities.[196] The United States has taken a materially different view of the matter, enacting Section 813 of the PATRIOT Act. Section 813 adds the terrorism offenses listed in 18 U.S.C. § 2332(b)(5)(B) (Supp. II 2003) to the list of predicate offenses that can be charged under the Racketeering Corrupt Practices Act.[197] Accordingly, the United States has, by law, linked terrorist organizations into the prosecution of organized crime.

X. The Problem of Enforcement between Differing Legal Systems

There is obvious tension when a foreign national is prosecuted in an American court or when an American corporate entity or U.S. citizen must answer to foreign authorities. The Internet implicates many constitutional freedoms including the First and Fourth Amendments, affecting the freedom of speech and the right to be free from unreasonable searches and seizures, respectively. How the application of American jurisprudence will play out in the arena of domestic and foreign cybercrime prosecution remains to be seen. Arguably, American courts are willing to be expansive in the scope of their jurisdiction where a foreign national has engaged in wrongful conduct, even to the point of denying constitutional protections. On the other hand, foreign courts are held to the highest standards of American constitutional jurisprudence where American interests are at stake. Judicial fairness will be required if global cooperation in the investigation and prosecution of cybercrime cases is to succeed.

The courts have traditionally applied domestic legislation to cybercrime offenses originating through the use of a computer in a foreign country by a foreign national. For example, the court rejected a motion to dismiss an indictment charging several offenses, including the CFFA and the Hobbs Act,[198] where the defendant nonresident alien was physically present in Russia and using a computer there at all times relevant to the offense conduct. Because the intended and actual detrimental effects of the defendant's conduct occurred within the United States, the court held that the extraterri-

---

196. *Id.*
197. 18 U.S.C. § 1961(1) (2003).
198. 18 U.S.C. § 1951 (1994).

torial application of the domestic criminal statutes was permissible.[199] Moreover, courts have held that the Fourth Amendment does not apply to law enforcement agents' extraterritorial access to computers in foreign countries (Russia) and their copying of data contained in the computers. Simply, the Fourth Amendment is not applicable to a search and seizure of a nonresident alien's property outside of the territory of the United States.[200]

In the First Amendment arena, a U.S. court refused to honor a French court order entered against a U.S. corporate Internet provider to limit the corporation's right to publish materials on its website, which material was illegal in France and could be viewed by French citizens. The U.S. court concluded that the scope of the French court order infringed on the Internet provider's First Amendment Rights and therefore, it would not be enforced by the courts and further discovery in the case was denied.[201] In fact, U.S. courts recognize that Americans sued in foreign courts, arising out of Internet violations, may be subject to legal systems that "may not measure up to our constitutional mark or may even do violence to public policies and principles ... not only those valued under the First Amendment, but under other vital protections of our jurisprudence."[202]

XI. Conclusion

A world consensus is that global deterrence of international cybercrime and cybersecurity can only be achieved through the development of international law and jurisprudence. The CoE Convention is the only, albeit imperfect, treaty formulated to facilitate global definitions of cybercrime and to establish the contours of enforcement within the confines of differing legal systems and cultural beliefs. The future effectiveness of the treaty will depend in large measure upon the number of nations that choose to participate. As with most pieces of complicated legislation, future refinements can be expected after treaty implementation takes place.

---

199. United State v. Ivanov, 175 F. Supp. 2d 367 (D. Conn. 2001).

200. United Sates v. Gorshkov, 2001 WL 1024026 (W.D. Wash. 2001).

201. Yahoo! v. LaLigue Contre Le Racisme et L'Antisemitisme, 169 F. Supp. 2d 1181 (N.D. Cal. 2001), *rev'd on other grounds*, 379 F.3d 1120 (9th Cir. 2004) (holding that the district court lacked personal jurisdiction over the defendant French association).

202. Dow Jones v. Harrods, Limited, 237 F. Supp. 2d 394, 411 (S.D.N.Y. 2002), *aff'd* 346 F.3d 357 (2d Cir. 2003).

INDEX